The Evangelical and Oxford Movements

edited by

ELISABETH JAY
Senior Lecturer in English
Westminster College
Oxford

CAMBRIDGE UNIVERSITY PRESS

Cambridge
London New York New Rochelle
Melbourne Sydney

ALBRIGHT COLLEGE LIBRARY

Published by the Press Syndicate of the University of Cambridge
The Pitt Building, Trumpington Street, Cambridge CB2 1RP
32 East 57th Street, New York, NY 10022, USA
296 Beaconsfield Parade, Middle Park, Melbourne 3206, Australia

© Cambridge University Press 1983

First published 1983

Printed in Great Britain at the Pitman Press, Bath

Library of Congress catalogue card number: 82–9605

British Library Cataloguing in Publication Data

The Evangelical and Oxford Movements.–(Cambridge
English prose texts)
1. Evangelicalism—Church of England
2. Oxford Movement—Church of England
3. Theology, Anglican
I. Jay, Elisabeth
230′.3 BX5125

ISBN 0 521 24403 X hard covers
ISBN 0 521 28669 7 paperback

P.P.

283.09
E92

189811

For my parents

Contents

Acknowledgements

The task of annotation inevitably leads one into the by-ways and recesses of another man's brain. I should like to express my gratitude to all those who have made this process more enjoyable for me by contributing from their own store of recondite information.

I am also grateful to Westminster College for giving me a sabbatical term in which to complete the work. My thanks are finally due to my husband and daughter for their tactful blend of encouragement and forbearance.

Editorial note

Where appropriate the extracts have been taken from the first edition of the particular work. Authorial footnotes, when retained, have been included in the endnotes; editorial footnotes are indicated by letter and endnotes by number. In bibliographical references the place of publication is London, unless otherwise stated.

Introductory Essay

Mid nineteenth-century England thought of itself as a religious society. The intellectual atmosphere of the period cannot be fully appreciated without recognizing this. Religion and the form of one's religious allegiance were matter for public debate. One third of all books published were religious in content. Religion was an important force in politics, shaping attitudes to secular and ecclesiastical reform. The 1851 Religious Census with its revelation of a two-tiered society in which the lower tier was working class and godless, untouched by the church- or chapel-attending Christianity of the higher echelons, shocked precisely because it attacked the prevailing assumptions. Mid eighteenth-century England, however, had been very different. 'There is no religion in England', wrote Montesquieu in 1730, 'If anyone mentions religion people begin to laugh.' This volume seeks to examine the contribution made by the Evangelical and Oxford Movements in effecting this change of heart.

Changes of heart are not effected by abstract theories. Behind the decision to illustrate these movements from the writings of their leading figures lies the belief that individual men gave the imprint of their own style of life and thought to the ideologies they helped to formulate. Each of the authors included was a prolific writer and so I have tried to operate consistent principles in making my selection. The extracts aim to provide some idea of the main areas of debate taking place within each movement, and to suggest the distinctive flavour of the individual's participation. For this reason I have excluded the wholly idiosyncratic or the numerous pieces solely devoted to the refutation of a previous contribution to the voluminous polemical warfare of the period. I have not sought to exclude the polemical element entirely because this is in itself one characteristic of an age which believed itself involved in spiritual warfare against the infidel without and the traitor within. Since social and political factors played an important part in influencing the changing direction of religious debate, I have chosen in the main to confine my examples to a distinctive period between the mid 1820s and the year 1850. The Evangelical Movement, of course, began in the eighteenth century and influential works such as Henry Venn's *Compleat Duty of Man* (1763) and William Wilberforce's *Practical View of the Prevailing Religious System of Professed Christians* (1797) continued to be read well into the nineteenth century. To offer these alongside Tractarian writings would merely confirm the false sense of historical perspective which has so often suggested that, after the advent of the Oxford Movement in 1833, Evangelicalism remained a watertight, or even atrophied, body of opinion, exerting a popular influence but intellectually devoid of interest. Concentration upon a particular period will, I hope, convey two movements *on the move*, and reacting to one another. Neither would have developed as it did without the stimulus or irritant of the other to define its position more narrowly.

It is the purpose of this introductory essay to place the period and writers chosen within the broader context of their movements' history and to comment in general terms upon the literary styles employed by men, so influential in their own day, whose renown has faded as their ideas have become discredited, or lost their distinctiveness in the process of gaining widespread acceptance within twentieth-century religious life.

To return, then, to eighteenth-century England. In the Established Church aristocratic patronage rather than spirituality obtained livings. Absenteeism was the rule rather than the exception when livings were held in plurality and stipends varied so enormously. Dissent, freed from the persecution of post-Commonwealth days by the 1689 Act of Toleration, still found itself socially despised and educationally deprived. Provincial Dissent lost its proselytizing fervour and contented itself with the separatist life of a minority culture, whilst the intellectual urban leadership, free to develop Dissenting Academies, turned their minds to theological debate rather than the spiritual needs of their flock. By 1730 the Deist influence was reaching its peak. Fostered by the spirit of Newtonian science in examining Nature, God's Book of Deeds, and by a desire to achieve urbane consensus after so much bitter doctrinal dispute, the Deists produced a God whose existence could be rationally deduced from the evidences of His Creation, which were equally available to all men. Civilized man had no need of supernatural Revelation but had merely to look at the orderly design of the universe around him for the proof of a benevolent Creator and to look within for recognition of divinely implanted norms of conduct which the rational man would follow.

Orthodox Anglicans, who defended Revelation as given to us through the Scriptures as well as through Nature, reflected the spirit of the age in the arguments they employed. The title of Bishop Butler's *Analogy of Religion Natural and Revealed to the Constitution and Course of Nature* (1736) declares his assumption that the God of Revelation can be defended in the same way as the God of Nature: that is, by arguing that the miracles and prophecies of Scripture present to our limited minds difficulties and mysteries analogous to those found in Nature. In the realm of morality, Butler's sermons do not engage with the Deist assumption that religion is ultimately a matter of ethics, but with the Deists' optimistic view of man's capacity to calculate what is really in his rational self-interest.

Even in the teaching of High Churchmen (those who continued to stress the importance of the Visible Church, the ministry and the Sacraments) man's endeavour, moral piety rather than a sense of sin and a need for God's grace, received the major emphasis. In the attempt to live up to the standards set in books like William Law's *Serious Call to a Devout and Holy Life* (1729) some earnest men encountered despair. One such was John Wesley. On 24 May 1738 'about a quarter before nine' he experienced conversion from the anguish of failure and self-disillusion to belief in and reliance upon the love of a personal Saviour who had died to free him from the law of sin and death. The drama of this particular conversion and its importance for the subsequent history of Methodism should not blind us to the fact that his was one of a number of often less sudden but essentially similar conversions experienced between 1735 and 1760 wholly independently by a number of Anglicans from Yorkshire to Cornwall.

The nickname 'Evangelical' was acquired by these men because of the zeal they showed in spreading the Evangel or Gospel: lukewarmness was disgusting to God and infidelity a disease of the heart rather than of the understanding, asserted Wilberforce in his *Practical View*. The hub of Evangelical theology was a conviction of total depravity. Sin was not, as those with an optimistic view of humanity were claiming, a matter of voluntary transgression, but, since the Fall, endemic to man's nature, marring every part, and preventing even the Christian from obeying God's law. The only way in which to escape eternal punishment for disobedience was to lay hold of the promises made in the Gospel. Since these promises were incomprehensible, in any but a notional way, to the natural man, the direct inspiration of the Holy Spirit was necessary to effect the 'great change' when a man acknowledged his own helplessness and relied wholly upon Christ's sacrifice upon the Cross to pay his debt. Conversion, whether long-drawn-out or sudden, was an intense and central experience, leading to Assurance, the certain consciousness of personal salvation. Good works might be the evidence of a man's desire to be like Christ, but they played no part in a scheme of salvation that proclaimed him 'justified' (made righteous before God) only by faith in the sufficiency of Christ's sacrifice.

In the course of the attempts made by isolated Evangelical clergymen to preach this message differences emerged. First, where did one's parish stop? John Wesley declared that he looked 'upon all the world as my parish'. The implication of this remark was that the duty of preaching the Gospel was paramount and overrode the constraints, such as parish boundaries, sanctioned by Church discipline. In the early years some Evangelical clerics actively sympathized with the need for itinerant preaching to bring light to 'dark' parishes, but, whatever Wesley's own avowal of loyalty to the Anglican Church, the administrative methods he employed (licensing preaching houses under the Act of Toleration, ordaining ministers, establishing 'circuits' for an itinerant ministry) resulted in the separation of the Methodists from those Evangelicals within the Anglican Church. By 1800 'Evangelical' had become a party label within the Established Church, but in the world of Dissent, although new sects had emerged from the Evangelical Revival, the old sects too (e.g. Baptists and Independents) had been touched by the appeal to renew the apostolic fervour of the Primitive Church.

Secondly those involved in the Evangelical Revival agreed that the Bible, as God's divine Revelation of Himself, contained all that was necessary for salvation. Whilst 'enthusiasm' (reliance upon the direct inspiration of the Holy Spirit) might be kept at bay by testing the communications of the Holy Spirit against the Scriptures, the Scriptures did not themselves provide a coherent theological system. Controversy arose between Calvinists and Arminians, who differed primarily upon the question of predestination and freewill: the Arminians claiming that Calvinist belief in the predestination of man to election or reprobation limited the value of Christ's sacrifice and man's moral responsibility, whilst Calvinists felt that the Arminian offer of grace freely extended to all made too little of the way in which all men merit damnation and can contribute nothing of their own to God's eternal plan.

The first extract in this volume provides a more detailed review of the differences as seen by Charles Simeon, who, in the course of over fifty years' ministry in Cambridge, attained greater influence over successive generations of ordinands than even Newman was destined to do at Oxford. Like the majority of Anglican Evangelicals by the turn of the century he was a moderate Calvinist. These men claimed to be Anglicans first and foremost, drawing their doctrine not from Calvin's *Institutes* but from the Scriptures as interpreted by the Reforming divines of the sixteenth century in the Prayer Book, Articles and Homilies. Wherever possible their preaching avoided the debate of doctrinal niceties and emphasized the practical piety which was the evidence of man's conversion. In this way they avoided the excesses such as Antinomianism (the belief that predetermination to election or damnation makes it possible to disregard all moral laws) to which the rigidities of high Calvinist logic sometimes led. Simeon's sermon notes (Extract 3) show how Evangelicalism contributed to the Victorian idealization of the home by presenting family life as an immediate test of spiritual commitment, where a Christian should use every opportunity to turn his relatives from 'nominal' to 'serious' (in earnest) Christianity. A wider interpretation of the 'family' to whom it was a duty to manifest Christ's love combined with a desire for each individual to attain a personal experience of God, motivated much nineteenth-century philanthropy and reforming zeal. The societies formed for the dissemination of the Word, for the reformation of manners, for the relief of the poor and oppressed, in turn provided a cohesive force for Evangelicalism. Indeed in many societies Anglicans and Dissenters pooled their resources. The theological emphasis upon the primacy of the individual experience, reinforced by a new awareness of fields of social endeavour, in which the laity might sometimes be better equipped to operate than the clergy, meant that laymen achieved prominence in religious affairs.

If it had been easy to bar individual Evangelical clergymen from livings it was not so easy to resist the social authority of a converted governing-class élite such as the Clapham Sect – a politically active, socially reforming group, which included, *inter alios*, William Wilberforce, Zachary Macaulay, James Stephen and Henry Thornton, who, with their families, lived for a time as a community around Clapham Common. The foothold gained by Evangelicalism within the two major universities, and particularly in Cambridge, was important because it ensured a succession of Evangelical clergy to spread 'vital' religion throughout the land. Rough estimates suggest that between 1810 and 1830 the percentage of Evangelical clergy had grown from one in twenty to one in eight.

By the late 1820s Evangelicalism was approaching a time of crisis. The clarity and brevity of Evangelical theology had been a strength in reaching the hearts and consciences of well-educated and ignorant alike. These 'few, simple truths' proved less stimulating for those brought up within, rather than converted to, Evangelicalism. Clarity could easily deteriorate into dreary thinness and miss the mystery of religion's symbolic force. Moreover the dangers of a religion which regarded the Bible as its supreme source and paid scant regard to doctrinal interpretation as offered in the traditional development of Church dogma were increasingly visible. The imaginative and the literally-minded alike could find scope by concentrating upon the prophetical books of the Bible. For those who chose to look abroad, as the young Edward Bouverie Pusey was doing, the current religious debate in Germany proved instructive. German Pietism, which had sought to re-invigorate the life of the Church through Bible-reading, prayer and practical Christianity, had encouraged the reading of the Bible as God's dictated Word, thus providing easy prey for Rationalist critics.

Growing numerical strength amongst clergy and laity also brought its own problems. The previous generation of acknowledged leaders, like Simeon and Wilberforce, were now old men; a new leadership of comparable weight seemed slow to emerge and was soon to be sapped by the Oxford Movement. A broader social composition gave rise to differences between cultured, urban, upper and middle classes and more conservative provincial flocks. Evangelicals were divided in their stand upon such matters as Roman Catholic Emancipation (1829). The increase in Evangelical periodicals and newspapers reflected these divergent interests. This very multiplicity makes the task of selecting representative writers the more difficult. The leading Tractarians can more clearly be seen lending the imprint of their characters to the burgeoning Oxford Movement than can prominent Evangelicals contributing yet another strain to the ever-changing accumulation of views that characterized the longer history of Evangelicalism.

The heady atmosphere of the Great Reform Bill era prompted a desire to sift all institutions. In religion, no less than in politics, men became polarized into liberal and anti-liberal, left and right wing, experimental and orthodox. The secession of a small number of Evangelical clergy between 1820 and 1835, some of whom proved hesitant in attaching themselves definitively to any new order or old sect, suggested unease about the spiritual welfare and apostolic purity of Evangelicalism in either its Anglican or Dissenting manifestations. Indeed Evangelicalism's very success, it was felt, had rendered it popular, prosperous, and therefore, worldly.

As so often in nineteenth-century politics, Ireland was to prove the smouldering fuse igniting religious and political controversy on the mainland. The Irish Church Bill of 1833 proposed the suppression of a number of bishoprics in a country where the richly endowed State Church was supported by funds levied from a community the majority of whom were Roman Catholics. Convinced that disestablishment of the Church in England would be the next step of a reforming Parliament, Nonconformists were swift to marshal their forces under a disestablishment banner and in Anglican circles the cry of 'the Church in danger' was raised. Anglican Evangelicals were thrown into disarray. They were embarrassed by the militancy of Dissenters with whom they had long worked in co-operation. Despite their recognition of the benefits offered by a constitutional framework and a liturgy which preserved a pure and decorous form of Protestantism, they had believed in the supremacy of the Church Invisible over the Church Visible – the one body of true believers over a body to which nominal Christians might belong. Indeed, might not any reform be imposed by anti-Evangelical bishops?

Meanwhile, as the Bill neared completion, High Churchmen were preparing their defences. In late July 1833 six clergy attended a conference at Hadleigh, Suffolk, to discuss tactics. Two participants, Richard Hurrell Froude and William Palmer, fellows of Oriel and Worcester respectively, returned to Oxford and talked with two more fellows of Oriel, John Henry Newman and John Keble, once Froude's tutor.

The shy Evangelical Newman who had entered Oriel in 1822 had been brought out of his shell by the diverse company he encountered there and by 1830, partly under Froude's influence, become a High Churchman. As college tutor (1826–30) and Vicar of St Mary's, Oxford (1828–43), Newman's intense sense of pastoral responsibility, his ascetic example, and his compelling sermons and conversation had begun to win him a growing band of friends and disciples. His own record of friendships made at this period suggests a curious combination of emotional attachment and an almost ruthless capacity to distil the philosophical contributions they had offered to his subtle, dynamic mind. A commitment to following truth wherever it led him and an ability to assimilate and discard fresh ideas, in a manner utterly alien to the conservative Keble or Isaac Williams, was to leave former friends with a sense of betrayal and future foes with apparent grounds for the accusation of dishonesty.

Keble had been a resident fellow between 1811 and 1823, gaining entrance to academically prestigious Oriel by virtue of a rare double first in classics and mathematics. In 1823 he departed to act as his elderly father's curate and eventually in 1836 accepted the living of a quiet country parish near Winchester. He retained his links with Oxford, partly as a tranquil source of guidance for restless, troubled minds like Froude's and Newman's and partly as Professor of Poetry (1832–41) – a distinction achieved after his volume of devotional poetry *The Christian Year* (1827) had become a best-seller. On 14 July 1833 Keble's view of the current crisis had been made clear in an assize sermon denouncing the Government's intention as National Apostasy.

As discussion proceeded, division emerged between the conservative High Church approach, favouring associations and petitions to defend the Established Church and the more radical approach of Froude, Newman and Keble, who regarded political disestablishment as important only in so far as it focused discussion upon the claim of the Church to a spiritual authority greater than that accorded to Dissenting teaching. Anxious to alert other clergy to the Church's plight Newman anonymously produced three short, stirring tracts, dated 9 September, which were then privately circulated to potential sympathizers. Soon Keble and Froude became contributors and by the end of the year twenty had been circulated.

In December 1833 Pusey contributed *Tract No. 18*, which he initialled to distinguish it from the corporate view of other anonymous contributors. Pusey's social position as a member of the landed aristocracy, combined with his reputation for piety and scholarship (he was made Oxford's Regius Professor of Hebrew in 1828) were to lend greater *gravitas* to the *Tracts* as he identified himself more closely: by mid 1835 the *Tracts* were no longer broadsides but reflected in length and content the scholarly evidence that the Tractarians had been accumulating for their cause. Yet Pusey's personality was unsuited for leadership. Humility, springing from a deep sense of sin and unworthiness, was the keynote of his teaching. A certain morbidity of temperament, which made Byron sympathetic reading during adolescence, was confirmed by the events of his later life: he interpreted his wife's death in 1839 and his daughter's in 1844, as punishment for his 'secret faults' and contrived to live, within Christ Church, a life of penitential withdrawal from social intercourse. Contemporaries and later disciples all spoke of his immense private influence, but the comparative failure of so many of the projects he worked for (*The Library of the Fathers*, the series of devotional books adapted for Anglo-Catholic worship, the establishment of Anglican sisterhoods) suggests a man who found it difficult to work closely with others. He was to remain a revered rather than a persuasive or commanding figure in the life of the Anglican Church.

It is ironic then, that Tractarians came to be pilloried under the name of Puseyites, but the other two nicknames that the movement attracted, 'Tractarianism' and the 'Oxford Movement' are also in some degree misleading. The *Tracts* need to be set in the context of the other sermons, writings, and indeed lives of their contributors. Whilst it is undoubtedly true that Oxford men, from the university historically more inclined to display High Church sympathies, were prominent in the movement and that *in* Oxford Newman produced preaching of such compulsive power that the Heads of Houses were forced to change the undergraduate dinner hour in an effort to diminish his congregation, the movement was never intended to be confined to the intellectual world. Newman's brother-in-law. Thomas Mozley, claimed that from the start Newman was so inundated with correspondence from country clergy that he had little time to contemplate the overall direction he was taking. Two of its leaders, John Keble and Isaac Williams, were Oxford fellows with country livings. Isaac Williams, friend and valued confidant of Froude, Keble, Newman and Pusey in turn, served first as Newman's curate at Oxford before working with a group of like-minded priests gathered around him by John Keble's brother, Thomas. In this way he was able to provide a continuing source of inspiration to those who strove to put Tractarian principles into practice in country parishes long after the initial fireworks at Oxford seemed extinguished.

The founders of the Oxford Movement perceived two arenas for spiritual warfare: Rationalism, or liberalism as it was more commonly called in the 1830s, and popular Evangelicalism. To be more precise they recognized certain inadequacies in the Evangelical response to Rationalism. Newman's personal history made him profoundly aware of the problem, for he had entered the Oriel Common Room, which 'stank of logic', as an Evangelical. Keble, Williams, Pusey and Froude, brought up in High Church households, had less experience of Evangelicalism but all shrank instinctively from the spirit of liberalism which recognized no appeal to the authority of tradition. They agreed with Evangelicals that religion appealed first to the heart. Newman's consistent teaching as Evangelical, Tractarian and Catholic, was to defend the primacy of faith in religion. 'Man', he says, 'is *not* a reasoning animal; he is a seeing, feeling, contemplating, acting animal.' Reliance upon the reason finally leads man to admire his own powers rather than to recognize God's powers for changing man's nature. Against this habit of self-contemplation Evangelical faith provided no safeguard, because, although it drew upon emotions, ultimately it rested its case upon the individual judgement. If a man has only to be assured that Christ has saved him he will be tempted to dwell upon his own sensations, disregard the evidence of his actions, and disparage the Church's teaching. Evangelicals would claim that their consciousness of God's Spirit was checked by reference to God's Word, but Scripture, as we have seen, was subject to many different interpretations. Moreover, Evangelical emphasis upon the Atonement (the work of Christ, culminating at Calvary, in reconciling the broken relation between God and man) seemed to have resulted in a devaluation of moral and devotional teaching and to have led to a neglect of the objective but unseen efficacy of the Sacraments. How then could a man be sure that he had 'right feeling', to use a favourite Tractarian phrase? By submission to the authority of the Church which supplied the means of prayer, repentance and sacramental grace to lead the heart aright.

Tractarians cared just as little as Evangelicals for the 'High and Dry' desire to preserve the formal constitution and privileges secured by alliance with the State, so what did they mean when they talked of the Anglican Church? What distinguished the Visible Church from Dissenting sects, the Tractarians claimed in 1833, was its divinely appointed order, instituted by Christ and His Apostles as a means by which God is revealed and imparts His grace to men through the Sacraments of Baptism and Eucharist: these were to be administered by those who received their commission in direct line from the Apostles. The way for the contemporary Church to ensure that it was fulfilling its commission to maintain purity of doctrine was to refer to the practice of the Ancient Church which provided an inspired oral tradition, partaking with the Bible of the nature of divine Revelation. The writings and decrees of all subsequent authorities, whether Roman Catholic or sixteenth-century Anglican Reformers, must be tested by their conformity to the undivided Catholic Church of Antiquity. Schisms which had taken place in the Universal Church were to be deplored – an attitude which animated Pusey's persistent attempts at re-unification of the Churches. Although the Reformers had framed their formularies (Anglican doctrine as set out in the Prayer Book, Homilies and Articles) in a Protestant spirit, to be a true part of the Universal Church the Church of England must be shown to be the Catholic Church in England. The Tractarians, therefore, wished to establish an Anglo-Catholic Church, to give life to a *via media* between the extremes of Protestantism and Rome. The spirit of the Reformers and subsequent practice might have favoured a Protestant interpretation of the Thirty-Nine Articles, to which clergymen had to subcribe, but the Tractarians set out to prove the possibility of interpreting these in a Catholic manner. It was the detailed working out of this proposition by Newman in that unconciliatory document *Tract No. XC* (1841) which was to bring the series to an end in a storm of controversy. Those who, like Newman, grew to believe that the Anglican formularies were incompatible with Catholic belief and practice, whilst Roman dogma was not, seceded.

It is, I think, no accident that three of the leading Tractarians, Newman, Keble and Williams, were poets, for they sought always to convey the spirit behind the literal word. The Church was for them no mere man-made system but a living Body, greater than its immediate adherents. When they read the Bible they spoke of 'a doctrine *lying hid* in language': they studied the imagery and typology through which God had revealed Himself. Similarly when they spoke of Nature, God was not to be abstracted from it by later more sophisticated generations, for He spoke through material Nature, using it as an instrument to convey something of His mysterious presence.

As the extracts chosen from Keble and Williams make clear this 'sacramental principle' was closely related to the 'doctrine of reserve in communicating religious knowledge'. God has chosen to reveal Himself by glimpses, not in a 'few, simple truths' to be loudly proclaimed and easily discernible by all. He is objectively present in His Creation, and thus pagans may have attained a dim apprehension of Him, but a reverently undertaken course of preparation, directed by the initiated, is necessary for the full perception of the hidden truth.

Tractarian 'Sacramentalism' had far-reaching implications precisely because it was fundamental to the debate between competing theories of Revelation which had dominated the theological scene over the last hundred years or more. It is this debate which informs the radically different approaches to education displayed in Newman's 'Tamworth Reading Room' (Extract 12) and the lecture by the Evangelical spokesman on education, Francis Close, *Divine and Human Knowledge* (Extract 4). The high estimate in which Tractarians held the Sacraments ordained by the Church attacked another central proposition of Evangelical theology. As the opening pages of Pusey's sermon (Extract 13) make clear, for Tractarians the Sacraments of Baptism and Eucharist were no mere outward observances but channels of divine grace, whilst for Evangelicals it was the change, experienced inwardly, when a man personally laid hold on Justification by Faith, that was paramount. Baptism and Communion, Evangelicals maintained, might be emblems of divine grace but they did not necessarily effect regeneration and could not be *felt* to do so. Although Evangelicals might disagree about their precise understanding of these rites, they became very clear that they must ensure their right to disagree *within* the Anglican Church, resisting always the move towards a more Catholic dogma. The celebrated Gorham Judgement of 1850 secured an apparent triumph for Evangelicals when the Judicial Committee of the Privy Council delcared that an Anglican cleric need not assert that regeneration always occurred in Baptism.

With Newman's virtual retirement from Oxford in 1842 the Oxford Movement was deprived of its acknowledged leader. The three years which were to intervene before his secession in 1845 weakened it yet further by focusing public attention on the individual drama and dividing Tractarians over the desirability of continuing to pursue a *via media*. Those who had been mainly attracted by Tractarianism's offer of authority and firm leadership in an age of turmoil felt betrayed when the personality by which they had been really held in thrall disappeared and they departed in search of other prophets or embarked upon the sea of doubt.

What then had Tractarianism achieved? Initially it had given an impetus to doctrinal examination and discussion, disturbing the Anglican equilibrium which had largely subsisted on a tacit agreement to differ upon vexed questions, but its lasting impact was stronger on devotional life than on dogmatic theology. Freed from the notion of a simple divide between regeneracy and unregeneracy it was possible to concentrate upon sanctification (the continuous process of the Holy Ghost in making the believer holy), through prayer, worship, confession, periods of retreat and the new life of monastic foundations. In wider terms, by their response to liberal and utilitarian elevation of the intellect and contempt for precedent, the Oxford Movement had partaken of and fostered certain elements of the Romantic sensibility. Tractarians openly opposed the

Byronic cult of the individual, but they expressed their debt to Wordsworth and Coleridge, particularly in their recognition of the power of metaphor over literalism, in their assumptions about the nature and growth of the mind, and in their vision of the Church as a living organism rather than as a man-made system. The neo-medievalism flourishing in early Victorian England, could not fairly be laid at the Tractarians' doorstep. However, their distrust of the Reformers and their selective reverence for the past, when forced into the narrower channels of socio-political and economic anti-liberalism, manifested themselves in the Tory radicalism of the Young England movement. The criticism of religious liberalism offered by the Oxford Movement was to form a strand in the opposition offered on a wider front against secular liberalism and cultural philistinism by Matthew Arnold. Pater's aesthetics were to be fed by the same Oxford source. Pater's pupil, Gerard Manley Hopkins, was to be converted to Roman Catholicism partly as the result of the terrible spectacle of Dr Pusey, his spiritual adviser, tenaciously, but ultimately unavailingly, continuing the fight against Broad Church liberalism as personified by Jowett, Master of Hopkins's college, Balliol.

But Arnold, Pater and Hopkins were speaking of Tractarianism as seen from the vantage point of the 1860s. Pusey, the movement's surviving Oxford figurehead, deplored the excesses committed by Tractarianism's Ritualist successors. Pusey's generation had taught that ceremonies and ornaments sanctioned by God's Church were no mere matter of human taste but assumed a sacramental character in preaching silently to man's aesthetic sensibilities. Impervious to distinctions based upon a theory with which they had no sympathy Evangelicals like Francis Close saw only Romanizing tendencies in attention paid to externals. (See Extract 5.)

In Evangelical circles the comparatively urbane manner of Charles Simeon increasingly gave way to crude anti-Popery campaigning during the quarter of a century these extracts cover. The writings of two men who had passed through Simeon's hands at Cambridge chart this process. Francis Close, Vicar of Cheltenham and later Dean of Carlisle, swiftly became the bellicose guardian of Protestant Anglican Evangelicalism: he once publicly remarked that he would not trust the author of *Tract No. XC* with his purse. More disturbing is the change in tone which occurs between the two extracts by William Goode, universally acknowledged to be an able and learned theologian. In 1842 he wisely recommended Evangelicals not to be deflected into party warfare but to meet the Tractarian challenge with the weapons of scholarly research and spiritual witness. By 1850 his voice is indistinguishable from the popular Protestantism, or anti-Roman prejudice which had rallied to the Evangelical cause. This defensive alliance fought its battles not by practical or spiritual piety but with legalistic aggression. Diocesan bishops, unwilling to re-enact the protracted and unseemly legal wrangling which had characterized the Gorham Case, were for the most part reluctant to take action against Anglo-Catholic preaching or practice. Dissatisfaction with such pusillanimity led to a parliamentary campaign, spearheaded by the Evangelical leader Lord Shaftesbury, aiming to diminish the power of the bishops in the ecclesiastical courts by permitting the laity to initiate prosecution. The 'Low Church' Church Association, founded in 1865 to uphold Anglican doctrine against Romish incursions earned for itself the nickname of 'the persecution society' by its funding of repeated prosecutions of Ritualist practitioners. As Evangelicals turned to pursue the foe through the secular courts they forgot that legislative machinery was a double-edged weapon which would wed them to an Erastianism (a belief in the right of the State to legislate on the religious matters of the Established Church) at odds with their old support for the Church Invisible and curtail the limits in which that private judgement they had once held paramount could be exercised. It was to be another twenty years or so before a new generation of leaders recognized the secularization of Evangelical concerns which this policy had produced, abandoned the political arena, with a consequent loss of popular Protestant support, and immersed themselves in purely spiritual matters again. The years spent safeguarding Anglican Protestantism's heritage, when Evangelicals were inclined to close their minds to innovation or development in doctrine and practice, do much to explain why many cultured Victorians saw them as a negative force, rigidly antagonistic to intellectual inquiry and starving the imagination of those Romantic sensibilities which Tractarianism had tapped.

Since Dissenting Evangelical theology bore many resemblances to its Anglican counterpart I have confined myself here to pinpointing a divisive element. *The British Churches in Relation to the British People* (1849) by the editor of the *Nonconformist*, Edward Miall, gave a clarion call to all Dissenters who believed that their Anglican brethren, in their concern for the privileges of the Established Church, had lost sight of the Church Invisible and their duty to spread the Gospel to all. The work also makes clear that Dissent was not unaffected by the spirit of self-criticism and dogmatism blowing through the Established Church. In an attempt to free themselves from the taint of radicalism and heresy some sects had favoured a retreat to orthodoxy and an inward-looking separatism. Miall urges afresh a sense of Christian commitment and particularly a positive use of the business ethic, allegedly fostered by Nonconformity, in God's service. It is in this sense of accountability for every activity of one's life that Evangelicalism's most pervasive contribution to the Victorian habit of mind can be seen. Those whom Evangelicalism had once touched rarely lost their conviction that life demanded an ever present moral awareness. That common inheritance is visible equally in the strenuous ethical teachings of Leslie Stephen or T. H. Green and in the moral demands made upon art by Ruskin or George Eliot. The flowering of the novel of social realism in the second half of the century owes something to the influence of Evangelical strictures upon the use of the imagination. Evangelicals had stressed that the escapist element in fiction dissipated love for one's fellow creatures upon imaginary figures and diverted the mind from the consolations of the Gospel, and so responsible writers became the more anxious to demonstrate that the use of the imagination might be spiritually profitable in extending a reader's knowledge of and directing his sympathies to his fellow creatures.

It was in the practical application of Evangelical principles that this movement's real strength also lay. Whilst its leading organs concerned themselves with the defence of Protestantism, Anglican and Dissenting ministers and laity continued to examine their souls, preach the Word and bring relief to the poor. The education provided in their various schools might be narrow in intention but the ability to read opened broader horizons. Such endeavours created a feeling of Christian community, if only in the limited sense of demonstrating that England's more fortunate classes did care about the lives of the poor.

Ultimately the religious ideas at the centre of this volume had the effect of interesting many English people in the debate between competing dogmatisms and the liberal, sceptical enquiring spirit. Some were attracted by the offer of certainty, some moved back and forth between the different dogmas on offer, and some were repulsed by the acrimonious, factious spirit of religious controversy. The dialectical spirit of inquiry was fostered among those who refused to accept that any *one* view could be right to the exclusion of all others. Both the intelligent, sophisticated Newman and the popularizing Close had spent so long in persuading their hearers of the essential alienation between faith and reason, morality and secular education, that their disciples were ill-equipped to deal with advances in Biblical criticism or with scientific rationalism.

The writings in this volume do not, of course, reflect the most widely read religious material of the time. This was to be found in the plethora of religious periodicals, biographies and tracts which formed the staple diet of Sunday reading. Evangelical tracts could sometimes achieve a circulation figure of over a million when aimed at a readership more used to the crude sensationalism of the cheap press. As Thomas Mozley astutely remarked of the Tractarians, 'the only one who could write a tract, possibly because the greatest reader of tracts, was Newman himself'. His fellow collaborators wrote not tracts but treatises, 'learned, wise, and good, but not calculated to take hearts by storm'.

It is important to remember the intended audience when reading the following extracts. Evangelicalism prided itself on making a simple creed intelligible to any who would listen and this populist approach contrasts strongly with the arduous searching after truth engaged in by some of the Tractarians who assumed a similar intellectual and spiritual engagement in their readers. Many of the *Tracts* were addressed specifically to the clergy. Those by Keble and Williams printed here were originally prepared as papers for a theological society set up by Pusey. Pusey's own sermon aims not at conversion but at offering guidance to those already committed to the religious life. The conviction that they were apostolically commissioned to speak for the Church, the doctrine of reserve and, no doubt, academic habit, lent an authoritatively learned tone to much Tractarian writing. Mozley offers us an entertaining picture of 'a young clergyman cast in a remote and secluded agricultural parish' preaching the new doctrine 'especially to the few educated neighbours who could understand him, and who soon settled the question by reducing their intercourse to occasional and unavoidable civilities'.

William Goode's *Divine Rule of Faith* arose from his awareness of the sparsity of theological literature in most clerical homes. Lack of such resources made the Evangelical imperative to speak out clearly on every issue no less pressing. At best the white heat with which they dashed out essays and pamphlets sharpened the ideas and lent a consciseness often absent from self-indulgently lengthy sermons or the excessively documented reflections of the Tractarians. At worst it led to relying upon stale Evangelical jargon as a denunciatory weapon. The temptations of demagoguery are always present to a man who believes God speaks through him, rather than through the

Church, and is accustomed not to a language of reverence and mysticism, but to announcing stern truths in plain tones to a large and sympathetic following.

All these writers would have found any discussion of their work which confined itself to aesthetics utterly repugnant. Two of their number, however, Simeon and Newman, are notable for their deliberation upon the manner in which their message might best be conveyed (Newman's most considered comments can be found in the essay devoted to literature in *The Idea of a University* (1852–9); Simeon published an essay on style as a preface to copious pattern sermons). They share only one characteristic: a preference for a 'conversational' rather than an 'ornate' or 'architectural' style. The inadequacy of such a tag as 'conversational' becomes readily apparent when it is made to describe Simeon's well-ordered, but abrupt series of remarks and the fluency and flexibility of Newman's 'thinking out into language'. Undoubtedly personality had some bearing on this – Newman's aversion to abruptness or pomposity of manner advertised itself even in his gliding walk – but their respective 'conversational' styles also emerge from different traditions.

As a set text on the Oxford Greats syllabus Bishop Butler's *Analogy* exerted an influence on matters of style as well as thought. His writing demonstrated how the informality of the essayist Addison's style, 'familiar but not coarse, and elegant but not ostentatious' (Samuel Johnson, *Life of Addison*) might be adapted to the demands of philosophical debate. Such a style, capable of presenting the twists and qualifications of an argument without being impeded by ornate flourishes or undue concern with balance and antithesis, offered a readily available model to Newman, Keble and Williams as a suitable register for reasoned exposition to men of similar educational background. In this respect the idiosyncratic archaism of Pusey's style is as much a further reminder of the brevity of his sojourn in the Oriel Common Room as of his continuous and direct contact with the language of the Fathers and Biblical and liturgical translators. Tractarian teaching also required that the rhythms of logical exposition should accommodate the language of religious feeling. Except in so far as Wordsworth's strictures reinforced the tendency to use an unadorned language of ordinary men, Romanticism did not affect Tractarian prose rhythms so much as it supplied the Oxford Movement with a vocabulary in which to seek to express the sublimity of their vision. Their God is characteristically described as 'awful' and 'mysterious' and needs to be approached with 'reverence and wonder'.

Despite alleged 'enthusiasm' and distrust of 'outward forms' Evangelical style developed in the hands of men educated in Augustan decorum. When John Wesley or Henry Venn found themselves preaching to men of less education than themselves they continued to rely upon classical restraint rather than emotional ejaculation, but consciously simplified their style. 'Clearness is necessary for you and me', Wesley told Methodist preachers, 'because we are to instruct people of the lowest understanding. . . . We should constantly use the most common, little easy words (so they are pure and proper) which our language affords.' Venn employs an altogether more complex and mellifluous sentence structure when addressing his fellow clergy than he does in his popular manual, *The Compleat Duty of Man*, where simple injunctions and advice emerge in a more hortatory manner. Hannah More, the *belle-lettriste* of Anglican Evangelicalism, developed three quite distinct styles for writings addressed to the upper, middle and lower classes of society. As the appeal of Evangelicalism widened to embrace all classes and the need for a prose in which to discuss the practical ethical implications of Christianity, rather than to indulge in theological speculation, remained constant, clarity in conveying statement and instruction determined the dominant style. The clipped assurance of Simeon's 'conversational' prose looks back to John Wesley's calm, trenchant preaching style and forward to the emphatic manner with which the essayist and historian Thomas Babington Macaulay, an Evangelical *manqué*, expressed his opinions as though they were obvious truths. Simeon's Evangelical successors lost his compelling forcefulness when they blurred the edges of his staccato sentences by rhetorical iteration rather than adding substance by refinement of the doctrine.

Although Evangelical or Tractarian traits or traditions can be discerned, perhaps more striking, given a time span of about a quarter of a century, is the diversity of style displayed by men who shared a common cause. The imprecision of the label 'Early Victorian prose' becomes clear when it has to describe the comparative modernity of Newman's prose, instantly recognizable to many of his readers despite a cloak of anonymity, and the impersonal formality and reverence of a religious register aimed at by Pusey's archaizing style.

Finally these authors all share in certain literary characteristics which seem remote to a twentieth-century readership. First, in arguing a religious position, they clearly regard as entirely proper a display of emotional commitment which post-Freudian readers have been taught to regard with suspicion. Secondly, whatever their disagreements upon the adequacy of Scripture as the sole guide to the Christian life, we can observe not only an ease of arcane Biblical reference natural to writers on theological matters, but also the Biblical rhythms and metaphors which formed the common property of nineteenth-century writers and readers. Thirdly, all but three of the extracts were, at some stage of their composition, intended to be read aloud. In their appreciation of the art of rhetoric they can help us find our way back from an age which favours instant verbal comment, the chat show in preference to the informed monologue, to a world where the formal written and spoken word were less discrete and an audience had been created for the reception of lengthy, didactically inclined, imaginative literature.

Charles Simeon

(1759–1836)

1. 'Notes on Calvinism and Arminianism', A. W. Brown, *Recollections of the Conversation Parties of the Rev. Charles Simeon* (1863), pp. 267–71, 273–8, 279–88

'As to Simeon, if you knew what his authority and influence were, and how they extended from Cambridge to the most remote corners of England, you would allow that his real sway in the Church was far greater than that of any primate', wrote the historian Macaulay (G. O. Trevelyan, *The Life and Letters of Lord Macaulay* (2 vols., 1932), vol. 1, p. 64n.). This influence was obtained partly by providing and supervising Evangelical funds to enable 'poor pious' men to qualify for the ministry and partly by the informal theological training, unavailable on any official basis, offered to successive generations of Cambridge undergraduates wishing to take Holy Orders. His Sunday evening sermon classes were supplemented in 1813 by conversation parties on Friday evenings at 6 p.m. Abner William Brown, who attended these occasions between 1827 and 1830, took notes which he published in 1863, hoping that they would convey 'the raciness of his remarks, the pithiness of his short replies' missing from the memoirs or Simeon's published work. These notes certainly reveal the confident chattiness of Simeon's manner at these weekly gatherings of anything up to eighty people. The regular respectful attention of the young doubtless encouraged the arrogance and affectation of which his critics accused him. Simeon was aware of this trait, as a birthday entry in his diary shows: 'Sept. 24. 1822 . . . I spent this day, as I have for these forty-three last years, as a day of humiliation; having increasing need of such seasons every year I live' (W. Carus, *Memoirs of the Life of Charles Simeon* (1847), p. 572).

Yet the style is the result not only of Simeon's personality but the nature of his convictions. Evangelicalism emphasized individual judgement as a paramount obligation and its witness was always experiential. The belief that a man might at any stage fall from grace made him an ever-vigilant and outspoken critic of even the most prominent stars in the Evangelical galaxy. Since Evangelicals recognize no source of Revelation beyond the Word as interpreted by the Spirit, Simeon seems sometimes to be praising his own sanity and shrewdness and, at other times, to be glorying in the apparent irreconcilabilities of Biblical teaching in the tones of a complacent ostrich. The notion that God cannot be reduced to a system or a series of rational propositions would have found favour with the Tractarians, but Simeon's words lack the sense of paradox and mystery they create in depicting God revealing Himself through His Church and Creation. Moreover competing dogmatisms are dismissed in a style which is itself dogmatic. Brown's notes, written up scrupulously each evening, catch precisely the tone and mannerisms present in the full text of Simeon's sermons. The sparsity of conjunctions or qualifying clauses denotes a prose of statement rather than exploration or consecutive reasoning. The energy, simplicity and certainty behind Simeon's message emerge through strings of rhetorical questions which are built up only as a platform on which Simeon can proceed to hammer out staccato assertions. The freedom and directness with which he approaches all doctrinal matters and his willingness to use his personal experience as a yardstick all help to explain Simeon's attractions as a teacher, whilst also making more readily comprehensible Tractarian distrust of such an Evangelical style.

The first extract, in which he reviews the lively and often bitter debate between Arminianism and Calvinism which had preoccupied many eighteenth-century Evangelicals, serves to explain and define terms which are apt to make Evangelical literature seem jargon-ridden to us.

Calvinists and Arminians

Both of them are right in all they affirm, and wrong in all they deny. Dr Copplestone, Provost of Oriel College, Oxford, was struck with this remark of mine, and assented to it. Indeed, my preface, twenty-five years ago, takes substantially the same ground as his new book.[1] There is much more of the right kind of orthodoxy at Oxford, as a general rule, than there is here. The Oxford divines frequently err in the nature of regeneration, but are not nearly so far from evangelical truth as is generally the case here.

Calvinists affirm the doctrine of free election apart from any excellence in man; of utter helplessness in our nature; of salvation entirely by faith, and that not of ourselves. This is all right and scriptural. On the other hand, the Arminians affirm that we shall be saved according as we do good or evil; that man is a free agent; that he is wholly responsible for his actions; that he must work out his own salvation. This also is all right and scriptural. But as soon as either party makes use of their own half of these doctrines to disprove those of their opponents, they are wrong. What though these doctrines are irreconcilable by us: does God any where require us to reconcile them? And are these the only difficulties connected with human nature which we cannot explain? Can we explain how mind acts upon matter? yet who denies that it does do so? How do we move a finger by a simple act of volition? If we cannot explain such things as these, why seek to explain the mysteries of redemption, or to describe the nature and character of the impenetrable, incomprehensible God? When you affirm to a child or peasant that the stone which they throw must always move in a parabola, and they deny it, because they cannot understand it, do you not think them obstinate and foolish? What better are you who deny Divine mysteries because you cannot comprehend them? What we know not now we shall know hereafter. Look at this watch: here is a wheel turning to the right, there is another turning against it to the left, and yet they do not stop each other, but propel each other. Nay, further, the radius of each wheel is a quarter of an inch, whilst the two centres are *fixed* at less than half-an-inch apart from each other. Surely they must come to a dead lock. No: examine closely, and you will see that each circumference is notched with cogs, which exactly fit each other in the opposite wheel, and that they would not and could not work unless for the seeming impossibility produced by the centres being too near each other. This will explain Scripture truths. We see not the cogs now, but we shall hereafter. Take another illustration. That ball lies in the middle of the table. I wish to propel it straight forward, but at the same time to act by two opposite powers on the right hand and the left, either of which singly would propel the ball away from the straight line. I combine both, and they propel it in the way I wish. Thus, in Scripture, there are Calvinistic principles to act on man's hopes, and Arminian principles to act on his fears; both are needful, and combine to produce the right effect. Man has hopes and man has fears, and God has given us a revelation exactly suited to all the wants of our nature, and exactly adapted to *all* our capacities. He has mercifully adapted His revelation to our dispositions, nay, even to our vices. For the desponding and broken-hearted sinner, here is a salvation not depending on his own merits, or his own feeble efforts. For the sluggish, or confident, or easily quieted conscience, here is a salvation which we must work out, a danger of becoming a castaway even after preaching the Gospel to others, a danger that one who thinketh he standeth may nevertheless fall. Give an Arminian cup to the former class, and it is poison; give a Calvinist cup to the latter, and it is poison.

Calvinism is a system. God has not revealed His truth in a system; the Bible has no system as such. Lay aside system and fly to the Bible; receive its words with simple submission, and without an eye to any system. Be Bible Christians, and not system Christians. Scott adopted Calvinism *as a system*, and was therefore obliged to put a forced construction on many passages.[2] Never allow yourselves to *pit* one passage against another. Thus, Rom. ix. 15, 'I will have mercy on whom I will have mercy,' with the subsequent statement that God had raised up Pharaoh in order that the evil of his heart might show itself, seems opposed to 2 Peter iii. 9: 'God willeth not that any should perish.' But opposites may possibly be true, especially in Scripture, where we know so little of the mysteries to which passages point. A strong Calvinist looks on statements like that of Paul's possibly becoming a castaway (1 Cor. ix. 27) as a dog looks on a hedge-hog: he knows not what to do with it. But we must be cautious of slighting any passage of Scripture. We cannot understand all now; but hereafter the veil shall be removed, and then we shall understand the whole. The earth is kept in its orbit by the joint but directly opposite action of centripetal and centrifugal forces. This we know. But the corresponding explanation as to scriptural principles which are opposite remains for a future world to open to us.

Nor need we resort to the idea of reprobation, which is not in Scripture. Suppose God gave us permission to go amongst the lost and rebel angels and select five for pardon. Is He reprobating the rest, and should we be doing any injustice to the remainder whom we did not choose? And are we, in merits, better than the rebel angels? What if God left us *all* to perish: would He be unjust? and is He unjust in electing whom He willeth, of His sovereignty alone?

Election, but not reprobation[a]

The whole course of events in Scripture history and otherwise shows election. God chose Abraham, Isaac, Jacob. Why not Ishmael? why not Esau? Why choose fallen man, and not the fallen angels, for salvation? Why cause us here present to be born in a Christian instead of a benighted heathen land? These things result either from God's free choice, or from chance, or from something in us. The last two it cannot be. What is there in us more than in the souls born in heathen lands? If you admit God's choice in one degree, how can you limit it from going further? If He chose us to the means of grace, why not choose us altogether? If you admit anything like election in God's dealings with man, you cannot stop short of the absolute sovereignty of election.

Suppose I said to twenty friends, I will give you so and so, if you will ask me. Those who despise the offer, and do not ask, will lose the benefit, and yet the asking is not the meritorious cause of their obtaining it. God saith, I will give you strength and wisdom to ask me, if you will but ask. Is not each one wholly culpable if he neglects or refuses to ask?

If God sent a message of mercy to the place of torment, and said, I will save twenty of those now undergoing punishment, is He unjust to the others, by His offer of mercy to those twenty? Suppose He went further, and said, I will save all who cry to me for mercy and believe in

[a] The state of being rejected by God and ordained to eternal misery.

189811
ALBRIGHT COLLEGE LIBRARY

Christ, and I will give strength to all who desire to cry. Can those who do not cry complain? Their inability to cry was their own fault. . . .

I never had any distress on these subjects since I was an undergraduate, and about half a year after I began to think of serious things; and that was in consequence of a remark of Hervey's.[3] I could not separate election from reprobation; and yet I knew election must be true, for I was forced to admit that, of myself, I should no more have returned to God than a cannon ball would return to its cannon, and I felt reprobation could not be true. A friend, who was not himself serious, recommended me to read Sharp's sermons, (he was Archbishop of York, 1691,) and they set one all right again. Matthew Henry's remarks, too, on the subject are good.[4]

Predestination and freewill

The Calvinist wishes for some texts to be expunged from Scripture; the Arminian wishes the same as to others. They may say otherwise, but they secretly do so. I wish for all the Bible to remain as it is; there is room enough in any text for me. I have felt thus for now fifty years.

I believe in predestination as fully as possible. It is entirely of God's free grace that any soul is saved. I know it is so of my own soul. I never should have done anything towards going to Christ if left to myself. Yet there is in all this nothing of reprobation; I do not find it in the Scriptures.

Yet I as explicitly believe also in freewill, and so does every candid man in his heart. Will any man look at a bad action of his own, and say, 'I was compelled to do this: it was impossible for me to have refrained?' Or let any man look at a good act which he may have done, and say, 'I was compelled to do this, and could not possibly have avoided it.' All the good we do is of God; all the evil is of ourselves.

The elect are saved by the agency of faith and obedience; they are saved 'through sanctification of the Spirit.' – (1 Peter i. 2; 2 Thess. ii. 13.) Faith and works are not separable. St. Paul and St. James do not contradict one another. If I were to say to a friend. 'What a poor mortal is man!' and he was to reply, 'What an immortal is man!' we should not be contradicting each other; one spoke of the body, the other of the soul. Thus St. Paul speaks of faith as a principle and as the instrument of salvation. St. James speaks of works as an evidence by which only we can know of the existence of faith. It is remarkable that while St. Paul quotes Abraham's sacrifice as proving his faith, St. James quotes the same sacrifice as proving that he was justified by works; they both mean the same thing. Yet Abraham's faith is not a work; it was only *accounted* for righteousness.

Salvation is not of faith solely, nor is it of repentance solely. The scapegoat shows us the real union of the two. It is the confessing our sins, together with the transferring them to Jesus, that bringeth salvation. Salvation is by a penitential faith – by a believing repentance. – (Lev. xvi. 8–26.)

Melancthon was a Predestinarian as strong as Calvin. He saw the subject more clearly in his after life, and even Calvin's later works are quite different on the subject from his earlier ones.[5] When earnest men came fresh to the new field of Scripture, after escaping the horrible sins and errors of Popery, what wonder that the truths they found should make a strong impression, and that the deductions which seemed to rise from those truths should be viewed by them as equally clear with the naked truths themselves? This was the case with the early Reformers. They were men working too much on the large scale to weigh points in balances suited for gold. Their hands were not habituated to weigh by grains.[6] Scott's continuation of Milner is a valuable book, and he has rendered good service to the Church of God by putting things in their true light. It is more full than Milner, for it necessarily brings us more in contact with individual character than the previous history. The author has his father's head, but a much nicer hand.[7] At the present day I think Calvinism and Arminianism, as parties, are vanishing from the Church. And so too will Millenarianism.

God predestinated individuals to eternal life. Every human being has a free will, and, if lost finally, has only himself to blame. Both these things are true, and we have no need to reconcile them. Dean Milner's little book,[8] in which he attempts to do so, had better never have been published. How preposterous would it have been of Columbus, when he first discovered the New World from his ships, to have immediately set about describing the extent and character of the unknown land! And we, who are just setting foot on the vast world of Scripture, and will never be equal in this life to attain the knowledge of it, how foolish of us to attempt it! how foolish of us to say, because we think so and so, that therefore it is so and so!

The sovereignty, goodness, and severity of God

(Rom. ix. 13.) – 'Jacob have I loved, and Esau have I hated.' This had reference either to temporal or to eternal matters.

Election of the redeemed is made by God's sovereignty, quite irrespective of any good in them: if there turn out good in them, it is the consequence, not the cause, of their election. For the nature of man is wholly corrupt, and any good in it is put there by God. So far I agree with the Calvinists. Jacob was chosen by God, and saved by free and sovereign grace. But rejection or reprobation is not irrespective of evil in those who are rejected, because in that case God would *will the death of a sinner*, and would take pleasure in his death, and not that he should turn to God and live. No man will be rejected who does not reject himself, and refuse God's grace; and I put it to any man living, whether he has never resisted wilfully the voice of God's striving with him by his conscience. Esau was hated because he deserved to be rejected, and refused to be saved. But I will never agree with the Calvinists, that both election and rejection are irrespective of man's character; nor with the Arminians, that they are both dependent on it.

A state of grace and a state of election are so far the same, that grace given is a consequence of election; though, doubtless, there is a kind of grace given even to the lost; for there is a striving of God in every man's heart.

'Foreknew,' 'Foreknowledge,' (Rom. viii. 29; 1 Pet. i. 2), mean the knowledge of God, which in the Divine mind is contemporary with eternity. The expression does not mean, as Leighton[9] supposes, recognize; that is a Calvinistic strain put on the expression. All Calvinists and Arminians pull texts aside to suit their respective systems, instead of getting their own ideas drawn into the texts. Half of Scripture is Arminian, half Calvinistic, and each party strains or else slurs over the other half of Scripture.

God's anger towards His children has nothing in it retributive, because the smallest retribution for any of our sins is everlasting fire. But it is a father chastening us: some sins He punishes with more, some with less, indignation; but all with love and for our good. When a man has indulged in a sin, God lets him feel that sin all his life, in order to show him how unreasonable and foolish it was in him to serve another God, and to forsake his own happiness. The sinner is made to taste of his own sins, that he may know their natural fruits. Thus the slothful man, or the impure man, even after conversion, probably suffers all his life from the effects or the temptations of sloth and impurity, and is made at every turn to feel that sin once indulged in is bitterness in its very nature. Do not bring the doctrines of predestination and election expressly forward in your sermon – that is not their use. Yet let not any sermon which you preach be without their pervading meaning. The lump of sugar sweetens the cup of tea; it ought not itself to be perceived, yet every drop of the tea tastes of it. It is imperceptibly diffused and gives a character to the whole.[10] So let these doctrines be in your sermons. . . .

Final perseverance[a]

Saints shall be preserved to the end, not because they cannot fall, for they may; but because God will uphold them. When Benhadad sent to Elisha to know whether he should recover of his sickness, the prophet answered, 'Say, Thou mayest certainly recover; howbeit the Lord hath showed me that he shalt surely die.' – (2 Kings viii. 10.) There was nothing fatal in his disease, yet he foresaw that Hazael should, under pretence of healing, really murder him. God had decreed the death of Benhadad. So there is nothing in the saint that makes his salvation certain, yet God hath decreed that he shall not perish. He is preserved by God, but not by anything which God hath put into him.

God makes use of the folly as well as of the good designs of men. He often allows a servant of His to fall into errors, which even common prudence would have avoided, in order to humble him and make him hang upon God.

Erskine's book on the 'Evidences' is good, but I do not like his second book, and his third is too metaphysical.[11] Malan also is wrong in making assurance to be of the essence of faith.[12] The assurance of faith, and that of hope, are quite distinct. They are different in their objects, grounds, and effects.

Faith hath for its object what Christ has done; hope what the saints shall receive. Faith has for its grounds the declarations of God and the promises of what Jesus is, and will do, and is exalted for; hope has for its grounds the seeing ourselves to be of that description to which the promise of happiness is given. Faith has for its effects an unchanging reliance and belief in Jesus; hope has for its effects a greater or less degree of joy, according as we see ourselves

[a] The Calvinist tenet which states that those who are elected to eternal life will never permanently lapse from grace or be finally lost.

more or less like the character to whom glory is promised, viz., believers and holy. That I, A. B., am in a state of salvation, is not revealed by God, therefore it is not an object of faith. If I, A. B., am sure that I am saved, and that I never can fall, holy fear is taken away, and I may go to sleep.

Arminians and Calvinists are both right in their principles, both wrong in their inferences. Luther, Melancthon, and others, went too far in many of their principles. Emerging from Popery, they fell into the opposite extreme; they would not have thought as they did had they lived now. One of the great blessings of a Cambridge education is, that here we lose our rigidity: as stones on the sea-shore lose their angles by rough friction, so do we. Love, and collision with others, soon rub off our asperity of doctrine.

We must remember that faith is not effective as a work, – it is not a work. Abraham believed God, and it was only accounted to him for righteousness; it was not a work which earned anything.

I do not like the Calvinistic distinctive expression, '*True believers*;' it is not a scriptural distinction, but one invented to suit their own system of final perseverance. Scripture abounds with instances of persons who are said to have believed in Jesus, and who yet fell away. Many believed in Jesus, yet did He not commit Himself to them, for He knew what was in man. – (John ii. 23–25.) Simon Magus believed.[13] I can easily conceive of a man having faith and yet falling away, if he neglect the principle of faith, and also neglect to come constantly for new supplies of grace. A kite has no buoyancy of its own, and yet it is kept up in the air; how? by the wind, the string, and the hand. If the wind drops, if the string be cut, if the hand changes its mind, the kite falls. But so long as these three remain, the kite is safe; yet without for one moment losing its natural liability and certainty of falling. This illustration shows what I should say of the soul: the wind is the grace of the Holy Spirit; the hand is the mind of God, which cannot change; the string is faith, – God's appointed connexion between the soul and Himself.

'Sin shall not have dominion over you: for ye are not under the law, but under grace.' (*Rom.* vi. 14)

The law, or the covenant of works, requires everything, but gives no power to fulfil. But grace, or the covenant of grace, gives everything, and requires nothing for justification, or in fact nothing beyond what is needful to attest the fact that the individual is under the covenant of grace, and is a child of God. Of course, then, he who is not under the covenant of works is not under the dominion of sin, for he is not subject to its consequences, nor to its bondage. He is freed from sin; he cannot 'commit sin,' or is not a worker of sin (*οὐ ποιεῖ ἁμαρτίαν*). – (1 John iii. 9.) There are the remains of the influence of sin in our hearts; there are, as it were, two wills within us. That which we do we allow not; that which we would not, we do; but we long to be delivered from it, and we love not sin, and run not along with it. The righteous falleth seven times, yet always riseth again. – (Prov. xxiv. 16.) But he that is under the dominion of sin is different; he never hates sin. He may go as far as to say, 'I approve the good, but follow the bad;' yet he goes after the bad with all his heart, and habitually. He may in all this be going against his convictions, but then these convictions are not like a distinct will within him.

Imputed righteousness[a]

That the doctrine is true is beyond doubt. We are only justified by the righteousness of Christ imputed to us. But such views as Hervey's are too refined – go too far, and are wrong. Not that any one has ever yet gone to the full scriptural limits of the subject. But when Hervey makes a distinction between the active and passive obedience of Christ, making one the occasion of our pardon, and the other of our glorification, he goes beyond Scripture. We are justified by the 'obedience unto death' of our Lord Jesus Christ. – (Phil. ii. 8.)

The truth of the doctrine may be seen from the manner in which St. Paul quotes a text from David to prove it. – (Rom. iv. 6, compared with Psalm xxxii. i. 2.) David describeth the blessedness of the man unto whom God imputeth righteousness without works, saying, 'Blessed are they whose iniquities are forgiven, and whose sins are covered,' and there he stops. But observe, St. Paul has put that into the text which David did not do, namely, making it show the imputation of righteousness, whereas David's words only show the non-imputation of sin. And St. Paul has left out of the text that which David had put in, namely, the sanctification produced: 'And in whose spirit there is no guile.' Thus has St. Paul detached faith as a justifying principle from the sanctifying effects of that faith, and shown that it is not by making us holy that faith saves us, but by

[a] The Calvinist belief that Christ's righteousness is substituted for man's, leaving man's sinfulness unaffected.

connecting us with the blood and the righteousness of Christ. You will hear many say that faith saves us as an operative principle, by sanctifying us. No! Estimate faith as an operative principle, and you will find it far inferior to love; but its saving efficacy springs from its being a justifying principle, and not from its being a sanctifying one, though it is inseparably both. Paul has here shown also the extent and nature of imputed righteousness; that it is co-extensive and corresponding with imputed sin. He who had no sin was made sin for us; we who had no righteousness are made righteous in His stead. – (2 Cor. v. 21.) It is an exchange. He was clothed with our sin, we with His 'obedience unto death.'

St. Paul quotes that text (Psalm xxxii. 1, 2) from the Septuagint[a] (plural instead of singular, &c.), but the Septuagint has the clause respecting sanctification, which Paul leaves out. He wrote by the inspiration of the Spirit of God; he also made his interpretation and alterations by that unerring Guide. It could not be accidental, for the subject is too important; and the interpretation given in St. Paul's preface, and the omission of one part of David's passage, were far too weighty changes in a matter of heaven and hell to have been accidental. His preface and quotation were to prove the doctrine of imputed righteousness; nor would he have rested his proof on a single text unless it had been a doctrine well established by Scripture. He omitted the latter part of the text, lest it should mislead by confounding the effects of faith with the principle of it. He was explaining the justifying nature of faith, and the omitted clause had nothing to do with the justifying nature of faith, and, therefore, he did not digress from his subject by inserting it. But it is a wonderful proof, and far before any direct affirmation. He quotes a passage as proving what, on *the face of it*, it does not prove, and leaves out a part which might lead an antagonist to say that the passage only refers to persons in whom is no guile. He did it by the Holy Spirit.

Hervey and others make this doctrine of engrossing importance, yet, clearly as it is proved and implied in Scripture, it is, nevertheless, not there made all in all. It has its place. It is natural in man to swell a favourite doctrine into transcendant importance, and make it occupy every thing. Whitby has in this spoken well against Hervey, but has himself gone too far the other way,[14] and good Mr. Fletcher has gone, almost wickedly, too far.[15] Some one has called it imputed nonsense. It is liable to abuse, because it may lead to our thinking

[a] The Greek version of the Old Testament.

that, since the viler we are, the greater monuments of grace; so it is glorifying God to make ourselves vile; a doctrine at which St. Paul shudders. Our works cannot be the ground of our salvation, of our pardon, or our reward, but they will be the measure of our reward. We shall not receive because of our deeds done here, but we shall receive according to them. And imputed righteousness is a comforting doctrine; for, if we knew that we were to be saved by our works, we should never be sure whether we had done enough to secure us; but it is not so, if we trust altogether to Christ's righteousness.

The practice of mankind as illustrating deep doctrines

The godly ought to be very cautious of giving the ungodly an opportunity of blaming them deservedly. Abraham denied his wife, and a heathen gave him a just rebuke: a heathen rebuking Abraham!

Jacob and Rebecca sinned grievously in their fraud to obtain the blessing from Isaac. Isaac did not, as he should have done, advert to God's declaration, that Jacob was to be the chief. Rebecca did; but she was afraid of leaving it in God's hands, and so committed grievous sin. Had her faith been effective, she would have waited, and not made haste. 'He that believeth shall not make haste.' – (Isaiah xxviii. 16.) Hence they all suffered. Scripture does not, perhaps, expressly refer Jacob's sorrows to his sin; but doubtless they were the effects of it. Perhaps God's controversy with Jacob mentioned by Hosea (xii. 2, 4, 12) may have reference to his personal sin; for his personal conduct is spoken of immediately after.

Prov. xiv. 14. – 'The backslider in heart shall be filled with his own ways,' – a passage referring rather to the sin than to the temporal consequences. The man who yields to drunkenness shall feel that he is given up by God to the power of that sin. The man who yields to any sin shall be left by God's righteous judgement, so far, in the power of it. We often see, also, that backsliding draws on us temporal judgements, connected with that backsliding, which God, however, will over-rule to our spiritual good. But we do not read, for instance, of Demas having suffered any temporal loss by his going to Thessalonica. – (2 Tim. iv. 10.)

Calvinists say that one cannot fall away finally: St. Paul says they can, (Heb. vi. 4, 5, 6,) and seems to show how far men can go in religion, and yet fall away. The love of many does truly wax cold, and when temptation or tribulation arises, they fall away. They leave their first love. It is possible for a man to know externally everything of religion as an abstract truth, and yet not be a child of God. The very devils believe all, but not for salvation to themselves. Irreligious men may know the facts, the particulars, the notions; but they do not know the real qualities of Divine things. They may reason about the colour of honey; but, unless they have tasted it, they are in the dark about its peculiar excellence, its characterizing quality. They may love religion in others, but not in themselves. I know a town, near this, where a Pastor in one parish preached the Gospel so well, that the adjoining parish desired and prayed for him to come to them. It chanced that, in fact, he was appointed to their parish, and then they hated him thoroughly. 'A man's foes are they of his own household;' 'a prophet has no honour in his own country.' – (Matt. x. 36; John iv. 44.) So long as the light is at a little distance, men admire its beauty; but, when it comes close, and makes manifest their own foulness, they are enraged at it. So, when a godly man is at a little distance, the neighbours admire him; but, when brought into contact with him, they are in some way reproved, if he be faithful; and then they are angry, and hate the light. – (John iii. 19, 20.)

The natural man receiveth not the things of the Spirit of God, because they are spiritually discerned. – (1 Cor. ii. 14.) I do not like to call this spiritual discernment a new sense, because it really is not so; and if it were, it would be an apology for men's darkness. But it is *something like* a new sense. When we look at the sky by night, with the naked eye, we cannot see above two thousand stars; but, if we use good telescopes, we may discern eighty millions. These millions were always before us, and full in our view, yet we saw them not, could not see them, for want of the right medium. Now, the Holy Spirit gives us the medium by which we may see things that were always there, but which we never could see without it. Or, again, one man sees an object dimly, or, perhaps, not at all, because of the convexity of his eye; another, because of its concavity: a proper medium enables each to throw upon the retina a correct representation of the object. Thus, the Holy Spirit applies the proper medium to our sin-blinded eyes, and enables us to see realities before unknown to us, and still unknown to the world, and not even conceived of by it.

It is possible to hold the truth in much error; who is there that is not in error on some points? yet, if he hold the real truth, his erroneous sentiments, provided they do not nullify some essential and fundamental truth, will not prevent his salvation. The Apostle points out (1 Cor. iii. 15) that if the foundation be good, and yet any man build on it wood, hay, stubble, which will not stand the test of fire, he shall still be saved, yet so as by fire, although his edifice may be burned. Real Christianity is like a narrow isthmus between two oceans; and one of these oceans is Antinomianism. We must and do know that for us to say, 'We are not bound by the law,' is very erroneous; but though not the truth, it is yet *very near* the truth. For the law, as a covenant, is of no force to us, yet as a rule it is. And, further, as a condemning or a rewarding rule, it is not binding on us; but as a rule of acting and living, it is binding on us.

The difference between a merely well-informed divine, and any real believer, is like that between an able navigator, before the discovery of the mariner's compass, and an ordinary pilot of the present day. When the sun and stars shone, the ancient able navigator knew his way, and could keep tolerably clear of danger; but, when the sky was over-clouded, he knew not how to steer. Just so the mere divine. But the real Christian, like the modern pilot, carries his compass in his bosom; and if he trusts to it, he will not go wrong.

2. 'Notes on Irvingism, Millenarianism, and Assurance', A. W. Brown, *Recollections of the Conversation Parties of the Rev. Charles Simeon* (1863), pp. 315–16, 317–21

A sense of transition or hiatus was abroad in England in the 1820s, as political change and reform was discussed. An apocalyptic mood characterized this period of late Romanticism in literature and art. The religious world saw an increased interest in eschatological studies and, arising from this, hot debate about the nature of the impending millenium. Two major schools of thought emerged: post-millenialists believed that the recent founding of numerous missionary societies was one sign that the millenial period, which Christ's arrival of earth would conclude, had already begun. The pre-millenialists, to whom Simeon particularly alludes, dismayed by the realization that some twenty years had passed without wholesale conversions, began to pull out of the missionary societies and rely upon Christ's imminent arrival to usher in the period of a thousand years, Himself effecting the conversion of the heathen world, starting with the restoration of the Jews to the Promised Land. Even Simeon had been swept along by the first school's enthusiasm, campaigning earnestly on behalf of the London Society for Promoting Christianity amongst the Jews and was increasingly alarmed by the spiritual dangers of the 'waiting game' played by the second school.

In 1822 the Scottish preacher, Edward Irving (1792–1834), friend of Carlyle and Coleridge, was given his first parish in London, where he swiftly attracted society audiences with his highly dramatic sermons. His interest in the mysterious and non-rational found a natural channel in millenarian studies. Brown's editorial headnote indicates that subsequently 'Irvingism' became a sect in itself. Tried and convicted of heresy in 1832, Irving was dismissed from his cure by the Scottish Church. He was disregarded by the seceding 'Irvingites' in their new Holy Catholic Apostolic Church, since he did not possess the 'gift of tongues' he had done much to encourage.

Irvingism and Millenarian views

In Irving's 'Orations,'[16] page 410, is a passage frightfully blasphemous, representing us as being worsted by Satan, and redemption as being merely a further chance given to us, degrading Christ into a mere second to the fight, and declaring that Jehovah gives us this chance, because we had not a good fair chance at first.

To preach the second advent to the Jews, is to preach to them what they have all along desired, what was held out to them when they left Egypt, and what is no stumbling-block at all. To preach it to the Greeks, the men of this world, is to preach to them what is incomparably less foolish in their eyes than the preaching of the Cross, and the incarnation and its effects. To preach it at all, – do we see, by a change wrought in the life and temper, that it is the power of God unto salvation to any? See whether preaching it be the style of Paul's preaching, and its effects those of the apostolic preaching, as described in 1 Cor. i. 23, 24.

Suppose I granted Millenarians all they chose, what the better are they? I would rather be in heaven with my Saviour: I shall be as happy as they. I do not object to their thinking as they please, provided they do not thrust their opinions down people's throats, and disturb the simple Christian. Go to a man at the hour of death, one thoroughly awakened; offer him Christ crucified, and then offer him all the joys of earthly though glorified existence; which will be to him the most substantial stay, the greatest relief and comfort?

I do not say they are not holy men; but I say that none of them have grown in religion since they entered upon these views; nay, that just in proportion as they have followed these Millenarian views, they have been losing the lowly, subdued humility and tenderness of spirit which they had before. I do not know an instance the other way. . . .

In the very days of the Apostles, it was needful to caution their hearers against being carried away with every wind of doctrine, and hence we gather that divers and strange doctrines were broached. Who would have expected in the Apostles' days to find some saying 'that the resurrection was past already,' and that 'Christ was not come in the flesh,' but only in appearance? There always have been, always will be, wild delusions, and when one has died away, Satan has another ready. – (2 Tim. ii. 18; 1 John iv. 3.)

Those who maintain and those who oppose the doctrine of the personal reign of Christ appear to be both too prejudiced in respect of their own views. No doubt both are partially right, yet I cannot approve of the wisdom of those who moot the question as it is now done, for they put a constraint on the whole Scriptures. Probably, Christ will in some way appear; there will be evident manifestations, as there were to the Old and New Testament saints, or as there were at Mount Tabor. I do not see why it should not be so; but I cannot adopt the idea of an actual residence here for a thousand years, cannot understand it. As to the first resurrection, (Rev. xx. 5,) I do not understand it literally, although there may, perhaps, be some such manifestation and resurrection of the saints as at the day of Christ's crucifixion; but I believe that there will be such a growth of piety, that it shall be as if the days of the Apostles were returned again.

Our translators were admirable Hebraists, better, perhaps, than any of the present day. It is wonderful how careful and scrupulous they were in not making their translation explain a point which the original leaves in indistinctness. They have left things as they found them in the original, and very few alterations could be made which would be for the better, viewing all points of their bearing.

The present mode of interpreting prophecy, and the dogmatizing spirit in which too often it is done, are truly lamentable, and greatly against the genuine spirit of Christianity. It is disseminating a bad spirit in the Church. Even holy and sweet Mr —— is too much carried away with the spirit which it breeds. Irving's new book is a lamentable one. His text, *The Book of Ebn Ben Ezra the Jew*, has some good things in it, but the comment is painfully against the spirit of Christianity, and the preface is wild, egotistical, and full of self-conceit, I think.[17]

The doctrine of assurance[a]

This doctrine, in its extremes, as held by Erskine, is fearful. Twist or hide the truth as you will, it is this – that all men are pardoned, and

[a] A personal and absolute conviction of salvation, entirely independent of the daily evidence supplied by a Christian life.

were so 1800 years ago; that if any man believes that he was then pardoned, he will go to heaven, whether he repents, whether he comes to Christ, whether he be renewed in heart, or not. But if any man do not believe this, he is damned, whether he repents, or goes to Christ, or is renewed, or not. Now, this doctrine, if fully received, is a fatal heresy, and will cost a man his soul. That the holders of such doctrines deny the imputation of Christ's righteousness, is of small moment; for a man may be dark on that point, and yet having saving faith. But their views on the humanity of our Lord are fearful and horrible indeed.

'The Memoirs of Isabella Campbell' is a frightful book: no young female friend of mine should read it. She was, I doubt not, an excellent young woman, but she committed suicide. There is about her character, as pourtrayed in the book, a prominence of religion, rather than a religious change of heart and life. There is enthusiasm and extravagance; but there is wanting the lowly and childlike spirit of real religion; the unobtrusive, self-loathing nothingness of one who thinks that nothing he does is aught but evil.[18]

I agree with much that there is in these doctrines. I care not for people thinking as they please; but it is the unwarrantable prominence given to certain doctrines that I object to. Both the dogmas of these schools were great favourites with the old Puritans. Men cannot and will not all think alike on immaterial points. Our dear friend Mr P., who has just filled my place with so much acceptance, has a hobby,[a] but I love him; he is a blessed man, though perhaps he thinks too strongly, and possibly a little erroneously, on these points; yet what of that? he has done much good. After I have got into my old way in my pulpit for a month, any little derangement of my peoples' mind will settle down again.

Among other false doctrines, Romanism is forcing itself forward. Let every man master the arguments, and touch on the subject in his sermon occasionally with a passing remark of weight; but eschew controversy in the pulpit. Hartwell Horne's, for a little book, and Jewell for a larger, are the best works on the subject.[19]

So far as I can I prevent persons from coming here to injure our young Cambridge friends with wild notions of prophecy, or assurance, or other doubtful matters. I say, 'Let well alone. You may take the bloom off a peach easily, but you can never put it on again.'

[a] An undue devotion to a personal obsession.

2. 'Irvingism, Millenarianism, and Assurance'

Malan's doctrine of assurance is distressing and frightful. Baxter ('Saint's Rest,' chap. 8, sec. 7) shows that some in his day held the same views.[20] If the doctrine be true, I may say to the holiest of men, You are as ignorant as a beast of the things of God: you are yet in the gall of bitterness. Yet Malan has some kind of modification. He will ask any one, 'Are you saved?' And if they answer, 'I hope so,' he will tell them they are not in a state of grace. Yet he does not go so far as to assert that it is in all cases impossible for a man to be saved who does not feel assurance.

Walker's (of Truro) sermons are the best in the English language.[a] Marshall's sermons are good for the simple-minded, who have no bias to Antinomianism; but they are dangerous in a general way, although he, good man, was no Antinomian. He makes Christ our sanctification as well as our justification.[21] Romaine's sermons,[22] and Hervey's sermons, are both of them dangerous, for they say that there is no faith without assurance, and they deny all evidences of our being in a state of grace.

That kind of preaching is dangerous and erroneous. Faith is affiance[b] – reliance upon the merits of Christ. Faith is always our duty; unbelief never. But we may doubt *our* interest in Christ's atonement, and, in some cases, ought; as when we are overtaken in guilt. There are mentioned in Scripture Faith, Assurance of Faith, and Full Assurance of Faith, – three grades. The woman of Canaan had the full assurance of faith, and her faith had the Saviour for its object. St. Paul supposed the possibility of even himself becoming a castaway. Not to believe in Christ, is sin; but we are nowhere told that it is sin for us not to believe that we believe, or for us to doubt our own belief in Christ.

And there are also three other grades – Hope, Assurance of Hope, and Full Assurance of Hope. The woman of Canaan,[c] who had full assurance of faith, had no grounds for the full assurance of hope, for heaven is the object of hope. If a man commit murder, he ought not to disbelieve in Christ, for that were sin. But he ought to doubt that he belongs to Christ, doubt his being in a state of acceptance with God. Assurance would in him be presumption, because he had been guilty of allowed sin. To confound assurance and faith is to remove Christ (the only object of true faith) out of His place. Assurance of hope cannot be of the essence of faith.

[a] Samuel Walker (1714–61), one of the first generation of Anglican Evangelicals.

[b] The word preferred by moderate Calvinists so as to avoid the extreme implications of Assurance.

[c] Matthew 15:22–8.

Charles Simeon (1759–1836)

3. 'Abraham's Care of His Family', *Horae Homileticae, or Discourses, in the form of skeletons, upon the Whole Scriptures* (5 vols., 1819), vol. 1, pp. 128–33

Formally Simeon's work, like that of many of his Evangelical contemporaries, was occasional, not to say fragmentary, in nature. His one major work is, in one sense, no exception. The five-volume *Horae Homileticae*, subsequently reaching twenty-one volumes, offered to the hesitant, unconfident, or merely hard-pressed preacher pattern sermons to be fleshed out as the occasion demanded. The title chosen was not inappropriate since the first five volume reputedly cost Simeon some 7,000 hours' work. These immensely popular models (the work eventually raised £5,000 which Simeon devoted to charity) not only served as 'patent crutches' for many clergy well into the second half of the century, but also provided a form in which other aspiring clerical writers could offer their goods to the extensive sermon-buying public. 'Abraham's Care of His Family', indicates the importance Simeon attached to clarity in exposition and the passionate conviction which animated his preaching. It is not difficult to imagine the monotonous or even vacuous catalogues into which Simeon's less dynamic disciples were led by copying his favourite pedagogic device of reinforcing a point by repetitive variation. Simeon's overall sense of structure and the urgency of his message ultimately prevent his being seduced by prose rhythms of the 'This is the house that Jack built' nature. The blueprint this sermon offers for the conduct of Evangelical family life helps to explain many Victorian accounts of patriarchal tyranny whilst offering an insight into the motives behind Evangelical reverence for the family.

Gen. xviii. 19. *I know him, that he will command his children and his household after him, and they shall keep the way of the Lord.*

Wonderful is the condescension of Almighty God. His attention to his own peculiar people surpasses almost the bounds of credibility. Who would think that He 'whose ways are in the great deep' should yet so far humble himself as to 'do nothing without first revealing his secret unto his servants the prophets!'[a] He had in his righteous judgement determined to take signal vengeance on Sodom and Gomorrah for their horrible iniquities. But he had a favoured servant who was particularly interested in the fate of those cities; and he knew not how to proceed in the work of destruction until he had apprised him of his intention, and given him an opportunity of interceding for them: 'The Lord said, Shall I hide from Abraham that thing which I do?' No; I will not: 'for I know him,' how faithful he is in the discharge of all his duties to me: and since he so delights to honour me, I also will delight to honour him.

[a] Amos 3:7.

3. *'Abraham's Care of His Family'*

The duties, for the performance of which Abraham was so highly commended, were of a domestic nature: 'I know him, that he will command his children and his household after him, that they keep the way of the Lord.' He eminently excelled in the observance of what may be called, family religion. And this being of such incalculable importance to the maintenance of piety in the world, I will propose him as an example to you; and with that view will shew,

I. The use we should make of influence –

Influence, of whatever kind it be, should be diligently improved; –

1. To enforce the commands of God –

[Nothing should be of importance in our eyes in comparison of the honour of God. To uphold it should be our chief aim. The power given us, of whatever kind it be, is bestowed for this end. It is, in fact, God's own power, delegated to us; and, so far as we possess it, we are responsible to him for the use of it. Magistrates are invested with it by him, and are therefore called 'his Ministers' and Vice-gerents upon earth.[a] Masters in like manner bear his authority, and are his Representatives in the exercise of it.[b] To encourage virtue, to repress vice, to enforce the observance of 'justice and judgement,' and to make men 'keep the way of the Lord,' *this*, I say, is the true end of authority, whether it be official or personal, civil or religious. In particular, every thing that dishonours God, no less than that which is injurious to society, must be opposed with determined vigour. The violation of the Sabbath, and all kind of profaneness, must be discountenanced to the utmost: and all the maxims and habits of the world, as far as they are contrary to the commands of God, must be held up to decided reprehension. The Gospel too, which above all things most exalts the honour of God, must be patronized, inculcated, enforced. The utmost possible exertion should be made to diffuse the knowledge of a crucified Saviour, 'in whom all the fulness of the Godhead dwells,' and 'in whose face all the glory of the Godhead shines.' In a word, the legitimate use of power is, so to exercise it 'that God in all things may be glorified through Christ Jesus.'[c]]

2. To promote the best interests of men –

[Were this world our only state of existence, it would be sufficient so to use our authority as most to subserve the present happiness of mankind. But men are immortal beings; and their chief concern in this life is to prepare for a better. In this work then we should aid them to the utmost of our power. To this should all our instructions and exhortations tend. We should, as far as we are able, make known to them 'the way of the Lord,' and especially the way in which they may find acceptance with Him in the last day. With this view we should enable, and indeed require, them to attend upon the ordinances of religion. We should inquire from time to time into their proficiency in divine knowledge, and their progress in the heavenly road. This is not the duty of Ministers only, but of all, according to their ability, and to the measure of influence which they possess. Parents should pay this attention to their children; and Masters to their servants, and apprentices. They should not be content to see those whom God has committed to their care prospering in a wordly view, but

[a] Romans 13:1–6. [b] Colossians 3:24. [c] I Peter 4:11.

should be anxious for the good of their souls, praying for them, and praying with them, and using every effort for their eternal welfare. St. Paul speaks of his 'power as given to him for edification:'[a] and the same may be said of all influence whatever: it is a talent committed to us for the benefit of others: and we are not to hide it in a napkin, but to improve it for the good of all around us. Of course, the nearer any are to us, the stronger claim they have upon us for our exertions in their behalf: and hence our domestic duties are of primary obligation. But we are not to say in reference to any man, 'Am I my brother's keeper?' but to do him good in every way that we can, and to the utmost extent of our ability. As our blessed Lord did all imaginable good to the bodies of men, yet did not neglect their souls, so in relation to these more important duties we must say, 'These ought we to do, and not to leave the other undone.']

That we may be stirred up to exert our influence in this way, let us consider,

II. The benefit of using it aright –
This is great,

1. To those who exercise it –

[So Abraham found it: he was approved of his God, and had the most astonishing testimonies of Divine approbation given to him. 'I know him,' says God; 'and he shall know that I know him. Go, ye my angels, and make known to him my purposes respecting Sodom and Gomorrah. He has a zeal for my honour, and a love for his fellow-creatures: go, give him an opportunity of exercising both. He has Relations too in Sodom: go and deliver them. This holy man shall never want a testimony of my love: I will fulfil to him in their utmost extent all the promises of my covenant.'[b]

And shall any other person 'give unto the Lord, and not be recompensed again?'[c] The ungodly have indeed said, 'What profit is there that we should serve him?'[d] but he never gave occasion for such an impious charge. Say, ye who have endeavoured to live for His glory, has he not favoured you with his visits, and 'lifted up upon you the light of his countenance?' Has he not shed abroad his love in your hearts, and 'by the witness of his Spirit enabled you to cry, Abba, Father?' Yes, his promise to you is this; 'Because he hath set his love upon me, therefore will I deliver him: I will set him on high, because he hath known my name. He shall call upon me, and I will answer him. I will be with him in trouble: I will deliver him, and honour him. With long life will I satisfy him, and shew him my salvation.'[e] This, I say, is his promise to his faithful servants; and the whole of it shall be fulfilled to you in its season. Faithful is He that hath called you; who also will do it.[f]]

2. To those over whom it is exercised –

[It is said, 'Train up a child in the way he shall go, and when he is old he will not depart from it.'[g] This is not to be understood as an *universal* truth: for it is in many instances contradicted by experience: but it is a *general* truth: and there is ample ground to hope for its accomplishment. At all events some benefit must accrue to those who are brought up in the fear of God. Innumerable evils, which under a different education would have been committed, are prevented; and good habits are, for a time at least, induced. And though afterwards the force of temptation may

[a] II Corinthians 10:8. [b] verse 20. [c] Romans 11:35. [d] Malachi 3:14.
[e] Psalms 91:14–16. [f] I Thessalonians 5:24. [g] Proverbs 22:6.

prevail to draw them aside from the good way, yet in a season of trouble they may be brought to reflection, and the seed long buried in the earth may spring up, and bring forth fruit to their eternal welfare. The prodigal son is no uncommon character. The advantages of a father's house may be forgotten for a season; but in a day of adversity may be remembered, and be realized to an extent greater perhaps in proportion as they were before neglected and despised.]

That this subject may be more deeply impressed on our minds, let us pursue it,

1. In a way of inquiry –

[Are we, brethren, 'walking in the steps of our father Abraham?' Can God say respecting each of us, 'I know him:' 'I know *his principle*: he regards all that he possesses, his wisdom, his power, his wealth, his influence altogether, as a talent committed to him by me, to be improved for the good of others, and the glory of my name. I know *his inclination*: he has a zeal for my honour, and longs to be an instrument of exalting and magnifying my name: he has also a love to his fellow-creatures, and desires to benefit them in every possible way to the utmost of his power. I know *his practice* too: he calls his family together from day to day, to unite in worshipping and serving me. He catechizes his children; he instructs his servants; he labours steadily and affectionately to guide them all into the way of peace. His heart is set upon these things: he enters into them as one who feels his responsibility, and has no wish but to approve himself to me, and to give up a good account of his stewardship at last.'

Say, brethren, whether the heart-searching God can testify these things respecting you? Must he not rather, respecting many of you say, 'I know him,' that he cares no more for the souls committed to him than he does for his flocks and herds, or for the cattle which are employed in his service. If only they are well, and subserve his interests, and do his work, it is all he is concerned about. Even his very children are not regarded by him as immortal beings: if they do but get forward in their respective callings, and prosper in relation to the present world, he is satisfied, and leaves all the rest to 'time and chance.' Alas! alas! what an account will such persons have to give at the judgement-seat of Christ! When the Lord Jesus shall say to them, 'Is this the way in which you dealt with the souls committed to you, the souls which I purchased with my own blood?'. Beloved brethren, if ye are so unlike to Abraham in this world, do you think that you can be numbered amongst his children in the world to come? O judge yourselves, that ye may not be judged of the Lord in that great and fearful day.]

2. In a way of reproof –

[Surely this subject administers a severe reproof not only to *those who never employ their influence at all for God*, but *those* also *who exert it only in a tame and timid ineffectual way*.

Think, ye who have children, servants, apprentices, have ye no responsibility on their account? Has not God constituted you watchmen to give them warning of their subtle enemy, and to shew them how they are to escape from his assaults? And, if they perish through your neglect, shall not their blood be required at your hands? Did God entrust them to you for your comfort and advancement only, and not at all for their benefit? And the many Sabbaths which he has given you to be improved for them, shall not a fearful account be given of them also? Is it pleasing to Him, think you, that you suffer the ordinances of divine worship to be neglected by them, and the Sabbaths to be wasted in idle vanities, instead of being employed by them and you for their welfare?

But perhaps you will say, 'I do occasionally give them good advice.' What is that? Abraham did not satisfy himself with giving good advice to his children and his household, but 'commanded them:' he maintained authority in his family, and exercised that authority for God. And thus should you do also. Eli could say to his sons, 'Nay, my sons, this is no good report that I hear of you: ye make the Lord's people to transgress.' He even went further, and reminded them of the day of judgement: 'If one man sin against another, the judge shall judge him: but if a man sin against the Lord, who shall intreat for him?' But was this all that his situation called for ? No: he should have 'commanded them,' and have thrust them out from the priestly office, if they did not obey his injunctions: and because he neglected to do this, God sent him a message that 'made the ears of all that heard it to tingle.' And some awful message shall you also have, if you neglect to employ for God the authority you have received from God: for 'them that honour him he will honour; and those who despise him shall be lightly esteemed.'[a]]

3. In a way of encouragement –

[True it is, that though you may command, you cannot insure obedience to your commands; and notwithstanding your utmost care, there may be much amiss among those who are under your control. In Abraham's family there was a mocking Ishmael, in Isaac's a profane Esau, and in Jacob's many a sinful character. But still, if you fail in many instances, and succeed in only one, will not one soul repay you for all your trouble? The testimony of your own conscience too, confirmed by the witness of God's Spirit, is this no recompence? Will not this amply repay every effort you can make, even though you should never succeed in one single instance? Reflect too on the testimony which God himself will give you in the last day: 'I know him:' I know how he persevered under the most discouraging circumstances: I know the battles he fought for me: I know the contempt he endured for me: but he was determined to persevere: and 'he was faithful unto death: and therefore I award to him a crown of life.' Say, brethren, is there not enough in such a prospect as this to carry you forward, though your difficulties were ten thousand times greater than they are? Say not, 'I am not able to conduct family worship, and to instruct my family.' If this be the case, as doubtless in many instances it is, are there not helps sufficient to be obtained from books of instruction and from forms of prayer?[23] Do your best; and beg of God to bless your endeavours: and you shall not labour in vain nor run in vain: for 'out of the mouth of babes and sucklings God will ordain strength, and perfect praise.']

[a] I Samuel 2:22–30.

Francis Close

(1797–1882)

4. *Divine and Human Knowledge* (1841), pp. 7–49

Close's involvement in the politics of religion, both at national and parochial level, where his exertions earned him the title of 'Parish Pope' and Cheltenham the dubious reputation of being run on the lines of Calvin's Geneva, left little time for scholarship. Author of over seventy publications he was essentially a popularizer. In formulating his rapid responses to contemporary issues, he relied happily on other men's thought and used the cudgel of assertion rather than the rapier of subtlety and wit. Simeon's influence is everywhere detectable in Close's dogmatic expository style, yet the overall effect is less assured, more strident in tone, as if Close could not afford to leave simple truths to speak for themselves. Significantly Close's favourite conjunction is 'and' and his characteristic device for punctuation the dash, for each work contains only a thin central core of ideas submitted to extensive amplification. Habitually he pairs nouns and phrases or exclamatory adjectives to lend apparent weight to affirmations or denunciations which repeat rather than justify his arguments.

Published in the same year as Newman's 'Tamworth Reading Room' and concerned similarly with the absolute division between knowledge and faith, Close's lecture, *Divine and Human Knowledge*, presents a fascinating Evangelical companion piece. Whilst Newman is concerned, not to devalue learning, but to challenge the complacently false optimism of the liberal spirit of the age, Close seems at first sight to display that contempt for education which acquired for Evangelicalism the bad name it enjoyed with so many cultured Victorians. Yet Close, who became chief Evangelical spokesman on education, was far from decrying education. His campaigning transformed Cheltenham from a town which, when he arrived in 1824, boasted a decayed charity and grammar school and one National School. By 1850 there were six infant schools; two National Schools; a commercial school for tradesmen's sons; a revived grammar school and a comparable school for girls; Cheltenham College, where he sent his own sons; and Cheltenham Training College, producing efficiently and Evangelically trained teachers. He was an earnest advocate of compulsory education for all, but, because in this passage he is fighting two erroneous ideas about education simultaneously, caution and distrust seem the dominant tone. This text formed the inaugural lecture for the Cheltenham Church of England Working Men's Association founded to counter the Chartist influence of the new Mechanics Institutes. Like Newman he is reacting against the assumptions of the age of the 'Steam Intellect'. The advent of the steam press might have enabled 'useful knowledge' to be printed cheaply and in bulk but both Newman and Close deny that increased educational opportunity will necessarily result in a Utopian society. As the lecture proceeds, however, the adversary changes. When Close refers to those who see philosophy and literature as the 'handmaids of religion' he is aiming a blow at Tractarian thought. Whilst agreed on the inefficacy of natural religion,

Francis Close (1797–1882)

Close and the Tractarians part company on the usefulness of pagan literature and learning. A sacramental view of the universe led Tractarians to see, in Keble's words, that before 'Truth itself was fully revealed, simple untrained races were being taught by some dim outlines and types', whilst Close's Calvinist view of Revelation was confined to the Scriptures as given by the Holy Spirit. Excluded from this source, pagans and heathens were unable to make use of such evidence of God as remained in a fallen universe.

Lecture I

It gives me much pleasure to find myself for the first time among you in the character of Lecturer to the Cheltenham Church of England Working Men's Association; which has for its object the improvement of your minds in religious and useful knowledge. With such an object in view, the deeply interesting subject which I have chosen for my consideration cannot be innappropriate – '*Divine and Human Knowledge*.' But I must observe that the terms of my theme by no means adequately express all that I intended to convey. I would speak not merely of *knowledge*, but of the power, *the mental perception*, by which knowledge is received. And as there are two kinds, or great branches of knowledge, viz; *divine and human* – so are there two kinds of mental powers by which they must be acquired. It will be the great object of my present lectures to mark the peculiar characteristics by which these two principles or powers are to be distinguished – the confusion of these appears to me to be the fruitful source of all error in our philosophical and educational pursuits in the present day.

These two powers are in their very nature totally distinct. First, the powers of the human mind, or *intellect*; and second, the faculty by which the renewed man comprehends spiritual truths, and which may be termed, *the spiritual perception*; and is the gift of God's grace to the soul. In reflecting upon these two subjects, their dimensions have grown upon me so much, that I find it impossible to discuss them in one lecture. I must, therefore, defer the consideration of '*Spiritual Perception*,' to a future occasion; confining myself at present, to what must be a brief and imperfect enquiry into *the power of man's mind, unassisted by revelation*.

What are the natural powers of the *human intellect*? Have they, in themselves, any *moral qualities*, and of *what* kind? What will be the *result* of an enlargement and development of these powers, unaided by moral, religious, or divine influence? And, as arising out of this question, another – whether education, taken in the vulgar sense of word (for the mere acquisition of secular knowledge), tends directly to moral virtue and religion. I shall contend that it does not – I shall endeavour to strip *mere human philosophy* of some of its gaudy habiliments, and exhibit the moral deformity of its natural character.

Consider, then, the philosophy of the human mind! Its intellectual capacities! How vast, how illimitable do they seem! Mysterious, unsearchable! When we gaze upon the material frame in which that mighty spirit dwells – the human body – we pronounce it wonderful: but here we are assisted by the inferior senses. The skilful surgeon can dissect the body, classify its members, and trace in all its complicated construction the Creator's wisdom; but who can dissect the human soul? Who can analyze its parts? Who can define or limit its powers of ratiocination – reflection – memory – combination – deduction – fancy? How rapid are its operations! Many *bodies* in the physical world – as light and electricity – move with prodigious rapidity; but their movements may be measured and calculated – but who can follow intellect in its flight, or set bounds to its ramblings? This moment my thought may rise to the highest heaven, and in less than a second it may descend into the depths of hell! I do not wonder that men, unacquainted with the higher powers of *spiritual perception*, and untaught by revelation, bow down and worship this intellectual deity – *the human mind*!

Yet viewed again, in the light of true philosophy, and examined by the Holy Scriptures, this vaunted power is infinitely reduced in its dimensions. Wonderful as these powers seem, there is a limit, and a *very* finite limit, with which they are circumscribed. The human mind in an intellectual machine, formed by the Great Spirit for certain purposes; and these only can it accomplish. Mind actually creates nothing. As a cotton machine receives the raw material, and produces the colour and patterns intended by the manufacturer – so the mind *receives all its ideas from without* – it has incalculable powers of combination and separation, and the results we call *invention;* but if nothing were imparted to it, that is, *if no knowledge were communicated to it, the mind would be vacant and idiotic*! Could a child be wholly excluded from all channels of outward perception, it would be an idiot. This experiment, indeed, it would be next to impossible to try, because He who formed man's mind, has created such an infinite diversity of means of acquiring knowledge, that the hand of man could not wholly exclude them.

I believe this theory of the mind to be that received by the best metaphysicians.[1] And if it be correct, we might here at once take our stand, and argue that if, even in secular knowledge, all the furniture of the human mind must come from without – and its powers are rather *digestive* than *inventive* – then it follows, of necessity, that this must be pre-eminently the case as to spiritual things – *as to the knowledge of God*! My ideas on this point are perspicuously stated in the following quotation from a learned annotator.

From a consideration of the powers and faculties of the human understanding, it is demonstrable that it cannot attain to knowledge of any kind without some external communication. It cannot perceive, unless the impression be made on the organs of perception; it cannot form ideas without perceptions; it cannot judge without a comparison of ideas; it cannot form a proposition without this exercise of its judgment; it cannot reason, argue, or syllogize, without this previous formation of propositions to be examined and compared. Such is the procedure of the human understanding in the work of ratiocination; whence it clearly follows that it can, in the first instance, do nothing of itself; this is, it cannot begin its operations till it be supplied with materials to work upon, which materials must come from without; and that the mind, unfurnished with these, is incapable of attaining even to the lowest degree of knowledge. Without revelation, therefore, it is certain that man never could have discovered the mind or will of God, or have obtained any knowledge of spiritual things.[2]

But we come now to a further and most important enquiry: has the mind, the intellect of man, in itself any moral qualities, and of what nature are they? We hear and read much in praise of intellectual pursuits, as if they must necessarily be innocent and virtuous in their tendency: and the pure intelligence, and refined spirit of man, is spoken of as if it were an angel from heaven. Reason is deified; as if man would listen to *that*, he would no longer yield to his passions and be led away from virtue. But we are prepared to contend that *that* very reason, and all his intellectual faculties, are in themselves tainted and corrupted by the fall: not only so – that it is the nobler powers of man that enslave his baser ones, and that he is the victim of his passions, only because he is an *intellectual sinner*; that his *mind is fallen*, and his senses and passions are therefore under the guidance of a corrupt principle within; that it is the corrupted, degraded intellect of man which is the very fountain of all the miseries of the human race, – and that to speak of the purity of man's intellect in his present fallen state, is to speak against that only book, to which I, as a Christian, or as a minister of God, will consent to bow even on a metaphysical subject: believing, as I do, that in that book the truest principles of philosophy are to be found, excelling far all the books of ancient or modern philosophers.

To the scriptures of God then I appeal on this *moral, metaphysical point; what is the moral state of man's mind*? The earliest record on this point is found in Genesis vi. 5. 'And God saw that the wickedness of man was great in the earth:' – and in what did it consist? '*Every imagination of the thoughts of his heart was only evil continually*.' The language of the original is very comprehensive, and our translators in the margin say it includes all 'the purposes and desires.' The judgement, will, and all the combination of the thinking and reasoning faculties were exclusively and continually evil. Of the few survivors of the flood, of whom the whole world was overspread, this same testimony is given by God himself: – 'The imagination of man's heart is evil from his youth.' Long afterwards, St. Paul confirmed the same truth; for he says – 'that *the understanding* of men is *darkened*, and that they are alienated from the life of God through the ignorance that is in them, because of the *blindness of their hearts*.' – (Ephes. iv. 18.) The fall of man was an *intellectual fall*; effected by that master-spirit of evil, Satan – a being of intellectual power far surpassing ours. Man became as to his passions, *animal*, and as to his *mind, satanic*: his intellect lost the moral image of God, and received the impress of the power of darkness: and the result necessarily is, that though he reasons well on all secular subjects, on religious ones he draws only false conclusions. And hence it is that some men of gigantic intellect have been guilty of the most absurd puerilities on sacred subjects. The first display of the fallen reason of man was made in Paradise itself; he had attained forbidden knowledge – and the possession of it drove him away from God; and when dragged from his hiding place and convicted – his defence was a sophistry, impugning the goodness of God. 'The woman which thou gavest me – she gave me of the tree, and I did eat' – insinuating that God was the occasion of the fall, and the author of evil! And to similar conclusions the unassisted intellect of man has ever since disposed him. Reason in fallen man is a corrupt judge; all the powers of the mind of man are in themselves sinful; mighty they may be, and of vast dimensions, but mighty only from evil and averse from good.

The same scriptures teach us, not only, that the intellect of man is immoral, but that it is at enmity with God, and often in its most highly cultivated state has proved the most formidable barrier to the reception and diffusion of truth. Philosophy and human wisdom are continually found in array against the servants of God. Who opposed Moses in Egypt, Daniel in Babylon, or Paul at Athens? Was it the ignorant rabble, or the wise men, and astrologers, and magi? All the powers of the philosophic world in three ages, and in their respective ascendency, ranged themselves against God's truth. Perhaps of all the faithful antagonists who encountered them, St.

Paul is the most unexceptionable witness: as well because he was himself a man of no mean capacity of intellect, nor despicable education, and because he came in contact with the schools of the learned in every part of the civilized world; and that at a period when those schools had reached the zenith of their excellence. Yet in none of the recorded addresses of St. Paul, at Athens, and at the different seats of learning, nor in his epistles, do we find one word of approval of the ancient philosophy: we never find him complimenting the intelligence or mental accomplishments of those times – he never tells us 'that a good education is the best pioneer of religion:' – He found it otherwise; the most literate were the most opposed to him – and philosophy formed a barrier to his progress only equalled by the bigotry of the Rabbies – and viewing both these powers of evil he placed them in the same scale, among the enemies of God. 'The Jews required a sign' – they are ignorant, superstitious, bigotted; 'and the Greeks seek after wisdom' – they are proud, philosophic, infidel; but to the one and the other 'we preach Christ crucified, to the Jews, a stumbling block, and to the Greeks foolishness, but to those that are saved, Christ the power of God and the wisdom of God.' Thus ignorance and wisdom, stand in the same position – either of them, or both, are equally God's enemies if unsanctified by grace! And why? – because of *the moral deformity of the mind itself*! If that mind be essential enmity to God – if its rational and reflective powers have received an evil bias by the fall – then it follows of necessity that no degree of cultivation will alter their moral quality, although it may increase their power of mischief. Education, or the mere imparting of secular knowledge, cannot therefore produce moral results beneficial to man.

Dr. Channing, an American, a philosopher, and a Unitarian, may be received as a witness to this point by some who may despise my testimony: and he says –

> The exaltation of talent, as it is called above virtue and religion, is the curse of the age. Education is now chiefly a stimulus to learning; and thus men acquire *power, without the principles which alone can make it a good*. Talent is worshipped – but if divorced from rectitude, it will prove more of a *demon* than of a *God*.[3]

I fear these observations are applicable, not only to some modern schools of philosophy, but even to some well meaning religionists; there seems a coquetting in some quarters between philosophy and religion; a disposition to confound things which differ; and to attribute to mere literature a moralizing and improving quality which it by no means really possesses. The intellectual person may be as far from God as the sensual – and the two are very frequently identical; the highest attainments in science, philosophy, and literature, have been found in persons infidel in principle and profligate in practice.

The late Rev. J. G. Dowling, of the neighbouring city of Gloucester, though a divine, was generally admitted to have been a person of singular attainments in general literature and science. His early and sudden death cast a general gloom over the neighbourhood. Yet he, in a lecture delivered on a similar occasion to the present, expressed sentiments very similar to those I am endeavouring to establish.

'To expect,' said he, 'that secular knowledge of any sort is ever likely to produce any beneficial effect upon the moral condition of society in general, is mere fanaticism. All history shews, that hitherto the increased diffusion of literature has, in fact, operated rather injuriously upon morals. It is religion only that can elevate and improve them.'[4]

He was a man of extensive reading; and hear his deliberate opinion of the general character of modern literature; and *this fact*, if it be true, *bears strongly upon the immorality of man's mind itself*. – (p. 27.)

A very large portion of the existing literature of all nations is decidedly noxious. To say nothing of one extensive class, I mean sophistical and licentious books, the great mass of literature is of an exceedingly equivocal nature. A very few only of the most popular authors can be admitted, by the largest charity, to have been men of wisdom and virtue. Most works of imagination which have obtained celebrity, derive their value from the power they possess of raising the passions, and producing an excitement which is very far from salutary to the moral being. There are very few books of which a great part is not positive falsehood and ignorance.

Had this been the testimony of any but a distinguished scholar, I should not have adduced it; neither should I have cited it, did I not believe it to be most strictly and accurately true.

Such, then, is the estimate I take of the moral delinquency of man's intellectual powers, and of the noxious tendency of *merely secular*, philosophical, pursuits.

And here I shall be met by some objections to this theory, which must be noticed. It may be asked, for instance, how I reconcile this theory with the generally admitted fact, that even in this day, we have recourse to the writings of the ancient philosophers, poets, and historians, for some of our sublimest ideas in morals and science – men immersed in the darkness of heathenism? I should be happy to join issue on this exact point, and take the truth or falsehood of what I must call the scriptural theory, upon it. It may be easily proved – and at greater length than I can possibly attempt now – *first*, that whatever was most noble in morals, and certainly every gleam of truth in religion, which is found among the ancients, was stolen from our sacred altars; and secondly, that all the chief and greatest of the ancient writers, were themselves the dupes of a silly superstition, and the victims of the most degrading vices.

Upon the former point I will only observe, that it is well known that the ancient Greek writers down to a certain date, were *polytheists*, and had no conception of one Supreme Being; after that date the unity of the Deity begins dimly to be discovered by them; and, at the same time, more just and sublime views on morals. Now, it is matter of historic evidence, that at *that* exact time the sages of Greece visited Babylon, in search of the fountains of wisdom. By comparative chronology we discover that they must have visited that capital of science, while Daniel presided amidst its scavans;[a] they beheld the holy fire of revelation, and stealing a torch, lighted up the fires of Grecian literature: insomuch that, in some of the Greek plays, there are elaborate figures borrowed from Jeremiah and Ezekiel! I must not stop to do more than record this indisputable fact, whence it appears that all subsequent excellence in the later writers may be traced to a divine source.[5]

But after all, miserable are the gleanings of truth or virtue in the writings of the ancient heathen, and they overflow with pollution in morals and folly in religion. In an admirable volume, pubished some years ago by an estimable Christian philosopher, Dr. Olynthus Gregory, of Woolwich, there is a letter devoted to this subject, where the evidence against the ancients is brought to a small, but convincing compass.[6]

It is painful to cite some of the passages; but in an age when men will deify the powers of the human mind, and raise carnal science to a level with revelation, truth must be spoken. The most distinguished of these philosophers disbelieved all the great verities of religion, and credited the most absurd mythology. I need not observe that the ancient deities were mere personifications of all the vices, and some of them of a description too abominable to be named. 'The belief of a future state was totally set at nought by the majority both of Greeks and Romans.' – (p. 23.) Socrates remarked that the opinion of the soul being *blown away and perishing with the body*, was that most generally received.[7] Polybius[b] esteems future rewards and punishments as only *useful fictions*. Caesar, Cato, Pliny, judged them, '*senseless fictions of mortals, who are ambitious of a never-ending existence*.'[8] Of love to God or man, the ancients were wholly ignorant. This has been disputed. Yet what is the bene-

[a] Probably a misprint of scavants: learned men.

[b] Greek didactic historian (*c.* 204–122 BC).

volence of Plato, but the refinement of malice. 'By no means,' says he, 'punish your enemy for having injured you, *for so you defeat your own purpose of revenge*. Leave him to the whole, uncontrolled, uncounteracted influence of his moral depravity, *because that is the greatest evil which can be endured*.' Legislators, poets, and philosophers, were all equally involved in the same errors. Take Lycurgus himself,[a] one whom history terms 'rather a god than a man,' many of his laws were fraught with cruelty and vice. He encouraged the whipping of boys to death at the altar of Diana Orthia![b] he enacted that deformed infants should be cast into a cavern, to perish gradually! healthy boys were to be trained up to *dexterous thieving*! the Spartans had, also, *common baths*, in which persons of both sexes were *compelled* to bathe together! and Lycurgus, himself, decreed that the youth of both sexes should dance together in a state of nudity at solemn festivals! *Such were philosophic legislation and morals, without revelation!!*

The Greek and Latin poets are notoriously immoral – and deeply must a Christian father regret that his sons cannot receive a literate education without being necessarily plunged in some degree in the mire of heathen pollution! Would that some Christian scholar would lend his powers to the publication of editions of classical authors, from which such dreadful evils were expunged![9]

The practices of the ancient philosophers accorded with their principles. Socrates, Plato, Zenophon, Aeschines, Cebes, &c. were chargeable with unnatural lusts and vices, which they reckoned among things of an indifferent nature.[c] They generally allowed of fornication, as having nothing in it sinful, or contrary to reason. 'Many of them pleaded for suicide – most of them thought lying lawful, when profitable.' – (p. 32.) 'A wise man might, upon a fit occasion, commit theft, adultery, and sacrilege; for that none of those things are base in their own nature,' and the opinions against them were only *'for restraining fools!'*

Socrates died dedicating 'a cock to Aesculapius' – taught the doctrine of the transmigration of souls; but only for philosophers, who had the privilege 'of becoming animals of a social kind, such as bees and ants!' *Sublime destiny of the philosophic tribe*! Socrates also recommended *divination* – for infidelity and superstition are twins – and Turtullian[d] remarks that he was condemned at Athens, among

[a] Possibly legendary Spartan legislator of ninth century BC.
[b] Artemis, the moon goddess, worshipped at Sparta.
[c] Plato, Zenophon, Aeschines and Cebes were disciples of Socrates whose teaching informed their dialogues.
[d] Early Latin Father, author of a defence of Christianity.

other things, for unnatural offences and *corrupting of youth*, and was addicted to incontinence and fornication. *Plato*, his great disciple, appears to have rivalled the modern Owen,[10] and to have rendered vice gregarious. 'He prescribes a community of wives in his commonwealth,' (not the '*new moral world*,' but the *old*!) 'and lays down laws for the express purpose of destroying all parental and filial affection – affirms that all things respecting women, marriage, &c. should be entirely common among friends – decrees infanticide – allows of drunkenness at the feast of Bachus.' Who would not say, '*Plato, thou reasonest well*!' *Aristotle*, the profound logician and critic, affirms 'that the stars are true eternal deities' – exactly the creed of the modern *New Zealand savage*!! He denies that any providence extends to things below the moon – approves of infanticide – encourages revenge – and teaches that death is annihilation! The time would fail, and the task is loathsome, to cite the great literati of Rome, who followed too closely in the steps of the Greeks. Cicero, Pliny, Plutarch, Cato of Utica, and Seneca, all plead for, or practised, suicide, drunkenness, fornication, and childish superstitions.

And is this all that intellect, in its best estate, could do for the children of men? Alas, for philosophy! it may be said that these were faults, not of men, but of *times*! But who make times, but the people who flourish in them? The absence of revelation only proves all I wish to prove, viz: that the *mind, genius, imagination*, and *reason of man*, are *atheistical* and *immoral*; and that whenever revelation is lost, these are the fruits of unsanctified science, literature, and philosophy. Rousseau's testimony[11] to the character of *such infidel philosophy* in his day, is, to say the least, curious:

> I have consulted our philosophers, I have perused their books, I have examined their several opinions; I have found them all proud, positive, and dogmatizing, even in their pretended scepticism; knowing every thing, proving nothing, and ridiculing one another; and this is the only point in which they concur, and in which they are right. Daring when they attack, they defend themselves without vigour. If you consider their arguments, they have none but for destruction; if you count their numbers, each one is reduced to himself; they never write but to dispute; to listen to them was not the way to relieve myself from my doubts. I conceived that the *insufficiency of the human understanding was the first cause of this prodigious diversity of sentiment, and that pride was the second*. If our philosophers were able to discover truth, which of them would interest himself about it? Each of them knows that his system is not better established than the others; but he *supports it because it is his own*. There is not one amongst them who, coming to distinguish truth from falsehood, would not prefer his own *error* to the *truth* that *is discovered* by another. *Where is the philosopher, who, for his own glory, would not willingly deceive the whole human race*? Where is he, who, in the secret of his own heart, proposes any other *object than his own distinction*.[12]

4. *Divine and Human Knowledge*

Another objector may say – while you thus mow down all evidences in favour of mere philosophy and literature, as tending to morals and religion; you appear to forget how much good service they do to revelation when it is possessed, what powerful tributaries at least, they are – or as they are often termed '*the handmaids of religion.*' True – but handmaids are sometimes apt to forget their place, and to thrust out their mistress, or at least to sit beside her! infidel philosophers, historians, and literati, even when waging war against religion, have often become the reluctant witnesses of truth. Many, merely scientific persons in the pursuit of simple philosophy, and without any pious intention, have also yielded a rich harvest to the evidences of the truth of revealed religion; *but no thanks to them – they meant not so* – it was farthest from their thoughts – and it was not until some Christian, imbued with that *spiritual perception* of which I shall speak in my next lecture, seized their facts and pressed them into the service of religion, that they were convertible to this purpose! And after all, it should be remembered that all the service, which human science can do for religion, has reference to external evidences only: facts and arguments may be suggested which may carry the doubts of the sceptic, as it were, by storm – he may be convinced of the truth of revelation against his will; but he is not a true believer – 'his faith only stands by the wisdom of man, and not by the power of God.' The heart, the affection, the life, may be uninfluenced – he is not a Christian.

For this reason it is that (if I may be allowed to digress) I confess I am a little jealous of the mode in which secular, is blended with religious learning in some of our Christian schools, especially in *Sunday Schools*. It is in its measure important that the children's minds should be informed respecting the geography of the Holy Land – for locality often gives interest to incident: the manners and customs of ancient Eastern countries often throw light on scriptural allusions; but it is very necessary to keep up clearly in the minds of the children what is *divine* and what is *human knowledge*; to mark that which has the impress of God, and to distinguish it from that which is merely of man. In our day schools, I would rather that *secular knowledge* were imparted *religiously*, than that *religious knowledge* should be conveyed in *a secular manner*; the inferior may be sanctified by the superior, but the superior is weakened by the inferior: there must be direct, holy, devout, personal, spiritual, instruction in our schools, above, and beyond, and distinct from secular – even from the secularities of scripture itself – as its geography, its history, and its evidences. This is indeed in close affiance with the chief object of my present and subsequent lecture, viz: to distinguish between mere intellect, and spiritual understanding, between the knowledge which is of man, and that which is of God. The former I have now considered and examined; as to all purposes of morals and religion (*which is the only point I am canvassing*) I have proved that it is imbecile, or worse than imbecile. When I have considered the nature and extent of spiritual perception, I shall find science and literature in their proper places, at the feet of revelation – not its precursors, but its followers – not its masters, but its servants; and when occupying their proper station, useful, praiseworthy, and contributing to the glory of Him who is alike the God of *creation*, of *providence*, and of *grace*. May that gracious God guide us into all truth!

5. *Church Architecture spiritually considered from the Earliest Ages to the Present Time* (1844), pp. 12–19, 22–3, 68–80, 103–12

This book was the opening shot in Close's war with the Cambridge Camden Society and its organ the *Ecclesiologist*. Founded in 1839 by Cambridge undergraduates, led by J. M. Neale, under the aegis of a senior High Church member of the university, the society concerned itself with the building and restoration of churches in such a way that the Rubrics and Canons of the Anglican Church might be best observed and the Sacraments decently administered. A pamphlet written in criticism of Close's book received a swift reply and the debate culminated in his sermon for Gunpowder Plot Day, *The Restoration of Churches is the Restoration of Popery: Proved and Illustrated from the Authenticated Publications of the 'Cambridge Camden Society'* (1844). Although this sermon is thought to have effected the collapse of the Camden Society as then constituted, resulting in the resignation of the university's Chancellor and Vice-Chancellor and two of the sixteen bishops who had joined, I have chosen Close's opening sally because it sets out his position in bolder tones, with less concern for refuting the minutiae of the *Ecclesiologist*'s claims.

The sermon does, however, make unequivocally clear the root of Close's complaint: 'in a word, that the "*Ecclesiologist*" of Cambridge is identical in doctrine with the Oxford *Tract for the Times*' (p. 4). 'It is not a question of brick and stone – of taste or of science – the points at issue are purely doctrinal – it is whether Romanism or Protestantism shall prevail' (p. 14). Actually Close was wrong in his first assertion. Whereas the Tractarians looked to the Caroline divines and the Fathers for their theological inspiration in renewing men's hearts, the Camdenians looked to medievalism, to ritual, to symbolism in structure and decoration of churches to teach men how to worship. The leading Tractarians were involved in the building of new churches but Newman's Gothicizing brother-in-law, Thomas Mozley, claimed that Newman 'never went into architecture, though very sensible of grand effects, and ready to appreciate every work, of whatever style, good in its way', whilst Keble was a 'latitudinarian, if not a utilitarian, in architecture' (*Reminiscences* (2 vols., 1882), vol. I, pp. 216–18), and Pusey looked back in sorrow at the way 'ritual has been forced upon the people, unexplained and without their consent' (H. P. Liddon, *Life of Edward Bouverie Pusey* (4 vols., 1893–7), vol. IV, p. 212). This last remark makes the distinction well. Newman, Keble and Williams all preached and wrote about the symbolical meaning and significance of churches because they saw these as a means of 'true Gospel preaching', but they remained suspicious of forcing innovations in external matters if this might detract from the primary importance of doctrine and piety. 'To begin with outward things', Pusey wrote, 'seems like gathering flowers, and putting them in the earth to grow' (*ibid.*, vol. III, p. 369).

Churches were, for Close, at best functional (he built three whilst at Cheltenham to accommodate the increasing Evangelical population), commemorative of men's sin, rather than the expression of a sacramental view of the universe. The ethical judgements which characterize Close's attitude to the arts are characteristic of the age, but, in his case, overlaid by the Calvinist belief that all arts partake of the corruption implied by the Fall and by ferocious suspicion of the revival of Gothicism as being associated with Roman Catholicism. The young Ruskin's Evangelical upbringing was to make him feel the need to include passages of vehement denunciation of Rome whilst his aesthetic sensibilities were deployed in praising the Italian Gothic.

Although Close has won an immediate victory, in the long term the Camden Society's championship of the Gothic Revival and their tyrannical scrutiny of architects' work were to ensure that most Gothic churches were restored in accordance with their instructions and indeed that their design, with the chancel regaining its former prominence, became the model for new Anglican churches well into the twentieth century.

As the experienced architect is disturbed by any violation of good taste, or by any departure from the rules of art, in the building on which he gazes, so should the pious and enlightened Christian be at least equally offended if he discovers in buildings consecrated to the simple worship of the LORD JESUS CHRIST, decorations and emblems more worthy of the ponderous ceremonial of the Jewish, or the idolatrous corruptions of the Papal system.

And inasmuch as it appears essential, more particularly at the present time, that we should form a sober and scriptural judgement in this matter, alike remote from the barbarism of the tabernacle, and from the pompous superstition of the Vatican – a *scriptural* investigation of the subject cannot be uninteresting or uninstructive.

Ecclesiastical architecture existed long before the Christian era – and it would appear to be in accordance with sound reason, and philosophy, as well as with the principles of revealed religion, to look back over the early history of man as recorded in the Book of God, and to examine the various modes in which through succeeding ages he has been approached: – the formless spontaneous devotions of our sinless parents in Paradise – the rude altars of the patriarchs – the costly and elaborate ceremonial of the Israelites – the extreme simplicity of primitive, apostolic, Christian worship – the decorative style of the medieval ages – the return to primitive simplicity at the blessed Reformation – and the final, glorious, perfect worship of the Redeemed in heaven: – all these various transitions in the method of approach to the Great GOD by his accepted worshippers ought to be well pondered, before we form our judgement as to the propriety or impropriety of prevalent opinions on this subject.

This then shall be the object we now propose to ourselves: – searching for truth amidst its deep fountains, in the everlasting hills of God's formation, the holy Scriptures – we shall not greatly err – and perhaps by GOD's blessing upon our meditations we may not only arrive at sound conclusions on controverted points – but may find spiritual edification in contemplating the wisdom of GOD as displayed in the beautiful adaptation of successive systems of worship to the genius of the dispensation to which they belong.

But before we attempt to follow the progress of ecclesiastical architecture from Abel's rude altar to the temple of Solomon, and thence to the modern ages of the world – an enquiry suggests itself relative to the mode of man's approach to his Maker, as well in his state of primitive innocency, as in that of his restored perfection in the final glory. In these we justly expect to discover the most acceptable manner of worship – THAT which is most pleasing to ALMIGHTY GOD, offered as the willing homage of an innocent creature, or as the grateful sacrifice of those who once were guilty and impure, but now are redeemed, restored, and glorified. We thus gaze on man at his beginning, and at his end – as he first came forth from the hands of his Maker, and as he is again brought near to him in his final blessedness.

A wonderful coincidence is here observable: neither in Paradise, nor in CHRIST's glorious kingdom, is there any temple! No altar – nor propitiatory – nor sacred place is there! 'I SAW NO TEMPLE THEREIN,' exclaims the inspired evangelical Prophet, as he beheld the New Jerusalem – coming down out of Heaven, fitted for the new Heaven and the new earth which had already been created for its reception![a] A Jerusalem – but stripped of the old Jerusalem's chief glory – A JERUSALEM WITHOUT A TEMPLE! What can this denote but that in that final triumphant state no form of worship will be found – none of those various methods of approach now so needful for man in his present state of separation from his GOD – no temple because the GOD of the temple is there – no reflectors of the image of GOD, because GOD himself is there – as it is added, 'for the LORD GOD

[a] Revelations 21:22.

ALMIGHTY, and the Lamb are the temple of it!' His people see him as he is – eye to eye and face to face; – 'that which is perfect is come,' so 'that which is in part is done away.'[a] The building is complete, therefore the unsightly scaffolding is removed! The journey is over, therefore the provisions of the way are needed no more. Churches, temples, ordinances, sacraments, are the means by which GOD reveals himself to his people now – but there will be no temple there!

And as in man's final glory, so in man's primitive innocence – there was no temple in Paradise! The holy pair, unconscious of sin, needed neither altar, nor propitiatory, nor oratory, nor sacred place of worship, for all was sacred and holy! When at the dawn of day these holy, happy beings rose from their soft slumbers, and walked forth to meet their GOD and to present their welcome orisons, they beheld indeed a glorious temple! What though no stately building raised by man's device was there – no lofty spire, nor groined roof, nor intersecting arches, nor tessellated pavement – nor proud altar – nor fragrant incense – nor gorgeous decorations – yet did they worship in GOD's holy temple! And when the soft mist arose, as a thin veil, before the breath of the morning, (for neither rain, nor storm, nor tempest yet were known) revealing the beauties of that creation of GOD, what a glorious temple burst upon their view! Beneath their feet the verdant carpet of nature sprinkled with her choicest flowers – above them, the high vault of heaven lighted up with the ascending sun – the trees and shrubs sparkling in its glories – the murmuring of the streams which 'watered the garden' – the warbling of the happy tenants of the air – and the gentle lowing of cattle as yet untutored in suffering – this, and more than we can decribe or conceive, was the temple, and the only one, in which our first parents worshipped![13] GOD himself dwelt in his pure creation – he met his innocent creatures and they rejoiced! Neither man in his sinless state, nor man in glory needs the feeble help of temple services! – an affecting, a humbling conclusion is unavoidable – ALL TEMPLES, ALTARS, CHURCHES, AND RELIGIOUS CEREMONIES, ARE THE BADGES AND PROOFS OF THE FALLEN, GUILTY STATE OF MAN! . . .

Let then every student of ecclesiastical architecture, as he pursues his favourite subject, remember that the foundation of every religious structure in the world is laid deep in the corruptions of the human race – and that but for the sin and wickedness of man He had lost his occupation! He dwells among the tombs, he stumbles

[a] I Corinthians 13:10.

over the gravestones – while he searches out his favourite style – let him not forget, in the elaborated details of an earthly structure, to record in his heart ITS ORIGIN and ITS OBJECT![14] . . . [A lengthy section examining Biblical references to temples and temple architecture follows here in the complete text.]

Here then we might at once turn to the modern attempts to revive the decorative style of Church Architecture; and testing it by the general principles now established, and by the practice of the apostles and their converts in the first century, we might at once decide the question – whether it is consistent with the simplicity and spirituality of Christian worship to lavish vast sums of money on the decoration of the outward structure and the mere ceremonies of worship? But inasmuch as the present disposition extravagantly to adorn our Churches is not an INVENTION but an IMITATION – and as the perfection of modern effort consists in copying that which is considered ANTIQUITY – it will be more satisfactory to glance at the rise and progress of that style of Architecture which is to be restored; and if we should trace its source to some of the most benighted and corrupt periods of the Church, and find it identified with, and contributing towards, the superstitions which were then prevalent, our fears will at once be awakened, and a holy jealousy will be excited in our minds, lest with the restoration of the varied emblems of superstition and idolatry – the corruptions with which they were allied should gradually be introduced along with them.

Ascending, then, to the earliest days of the Christian Church, of which there are but scanty records in uninspired history, we find a singular conformity with all we have traced in the canon of scripture. It is a disputed point whether any churches, or distinct places of worship, existed at all during the SECOND CENTURY. Friends and foes admitted in these early days that 'the Christians had neither ALTARS, nor TEMPLES, nor IMAGES; but affirmed that God could be worshipped in every place, and that his best temple upon earth is the heart of man.' Lardner[15] says, (vol. ii. p. 212) 'Moreover it is now generally allowed that in the first and second centuries, Christians had not any regular or spacious buildings to meet in.' And again, (vol. iv. p. 526) 'It may be suspected that the early Christian Churches were only private houses, or buildings very like them, consisting of several rooms, separated from each other by walls and partitions.' The earliest authorities given upon this point occur at the commencement of the THIRD CENTURY: when it appears, that places of Christian worship began to be erected and to be multiplied. But it is most important to observe that, until the close of this century, NONE of those peculiarities of construction were known, which are now considered ANTIENT, PRIMITIVE, and almost necessary to the very character of any building to be termed A CHURCH.

As yet churches were not built in THE FORM OF A CROSS – the distinctions of CHANCEL and NAVE – and the separation and portioning off one part of the congregation from another – were unknown![16] The original and most antient form was oblong – and is said to have been intended to imitate a SHIP – alluding at once to the Ark of Noah – and to the tempest-tossed character of the people of God. Hence the subsequent term NAVE – from *ναυς*, A SHIP – not from *ναος*, A TEMPLE. The latter term was rejected with indignation by the early Christians, as well as its kindred word *βωμος*, ALTAR[17] – as savouring either of Judaism, or of heathenism. Well would it have been for the Church if the same jealousy had been continued in succeeding ages; and well were it for us, if the same spirit could be awakened now! Until the Fourth Century there is no trace of the CONSECRATION of churches[18] – and the extravagant notions about holy places had not yet become prevalent. Neither is there any notice of the ASPECT of churches – the virtue attached to building them due east and west – had not yet been discovered;[19] nor yet the superstitious and unfounded notion that one part is more holy than another. In fact it may safely be affirmed that not one of the peculiarities of the churches of the subsequent ages had been introduced at the close of the third century – and therefore it follows that the whole system of structure and internal arrangement now so strenuously advocated, and which so many persons are devoting themselves to introduce, are copies of a later and more corrupt age, and are neither PRIMITIVE, APOSTOLIC, nor SCRIPTURAL!

With the opening of the fourth century a change, at first gradual, but subsequently rapid and widely diffused, took place in regard to Church Architecture. Then it was that the opinion became prevalent that churches should be divided into three parts, distinguishing the CLERGY, the FAITHFUL, and the CATECHUMENS[a] – a servile imitation of the division of the Jewish temple – the holy of holies – the sanctuary – and the court! It would far exceed the limits of this Essay to follow the infinity of details of structure which followed from this commencement. But it would be easy to trace to this one false step all the divisions, and subdivisions, the chapels, sanctuaries, shrines, and redundant superstitions which subsequently disfigured the buildings in which professed Christians worshipped. The principle

[a] New converts receiving instruction before Baptism.

once admitted, that Christian presbyters were sacrificing or interceding priests – and of necessity holier than the people to whom they administered – the consequences became unavoidable – and they are inscribed in visible characters on every antient ecclesiastical building still remaining in the world. In fact the ceremonies of Christian worship in the fourth century lost alike their simplicity and spirituality; Levitical[a] and mythological observances were interwoven with Christian services, and the ecclesiastical structures were built with a view to accommodate the superstitions of the times.

THEN CHURCH ARCHITECTURE AROSE AND FLOURISHED! Then ecclesiastical buildings were multiplied, in which scenes were enacted alike disgraceful to Christianity, morality, and reason. In fact, the huge piles which were raised towards the middle and close of this century might more justly be considered as vast mausoleums – in which truth, scripture, light, salvation, and common sense were entombed together – than churches of the saints, in which 'the GOD of the spirits of all flesh' was to be worshipped, through the SON of his love. Superstition, and the extravagant decoration of churches, progressed together – now was the age of lying wonders, false miracles, holy places, altar, shrines, of MONACHISM[b] and CELIBACY – with all the monstrous evils which naturally followed in their train. The testimonies of the early fathers of this age, and even of preceding ages, establish the existence of the evils which they laboured in vain to suppress. They expected 'to gather grapes of thorns, and figs of thistles' – and they wondered that they were disappointed! The holiest and best of the fathers, along with much precious truth, cherished the very principles whose baneful, though legitimate, fruits they sincerely lamented!

The Church Architecture of that and the following centuries evidenced the spiritual state of Christendom, and contributed its share towards establishing the almost universal reign of spiritual darkness which followed. The mania for extravagant decoration of Christian temples, as they were now called, reached its height, when, at the opening of the sixth century, JUSTINIAN I encouraged the infatuated and false devotions of the people, who loaded the priests and their shrines with costly decorations, which they were taught to believe would contribute to the salvation of their souls. This emperor it was who raised that vast and pompous temple, the church of St. Sophia, at Constantinople – of which its imperial

[a] According to the Judaic law and thus, by extension, ritualistic. [b] The monastic system.

architect is said to have exclaimed, in the pride of his heart, 'I HAVE SURPASSED THEE, O SOLOMON!'

Spiritual pride and superstition seem to have exhausted themselves in this age – and whether from the subsequent disturbances of Europe, or from some other cause, the mania for ecclesiastical architecture, in a measure, subsided after this period; until, in the tenth century, the opinion, universally prevalent, that the end of the world was approaching, prevented entirely the erection of new churches, and even, in some cases, suspended the repairs which were necessary to maintain the existing edifices. In the ELEVENTH CENTURY architectural taste revived, and the art was cultivated with great assiduity until, in the THIRTEENTH CENTURY, CHURCH ARCHITECTURE REACHED THE HEIGHT OF ITS PERFECTION![20]

What the spiritual condition of Christendom was, during this same period, it were superfluous to record. But whether it be coincidence or causality, the fact must be admitted that whenever extravagant attention was paid to Church Architecture, then the most debasing superstition prevailed, and the most notorious corruptions were dominant. Superstition and church decoration were coeval from the beginning: departure from simplicity in doctrine and worship, was accompanied with an equal departure from the simplicity of primitive architecture: each contributed to promote the other – until, in this thirteenth century, spiritual darkness, the most profound, dwelt and reigned in the gloomy aisles of structures, architecturally speaking, of surpassing beauty.

The greater part of all the splendid ecclesiastical buildings, whether religious houses or churches, which arose after the eleventh century were erected by funds drawn from the resources of the deepest superstition! The splendid cathedral of Notre Dame, at Paris – St. Peter's at Rome itself – and many other churches of the same date, were built with money RAISED BY THE SALE OF INDULGENCIES! All the finest specimens of Gothic architecture, which now form the models of imitation to our modern artists, are monuments of the most debasing ignorance, and the most notorious imposture. The pointed arch – and the fretted roof – and the gloomy crypt – and the secret stairs – and stone altars – and elevated chancels, credence tables, and painted windows; the reredos, the trypticks, the reliquary, &c. &c. are the emblems of a gloomy, false, idolatrous, and persecuting worship, from which we were mercifully delivered at the blessed Reformation!

Yet it is to these – and none but these – that the modern students of Church Architecture would bring us back. There is no relic of the medieval, or dark ages, which is not now commended – and efforts are making to introduce them even into our parish churches. . . .

It is hardly possible to conceive any thing more opposed to the modern mania for the restoration of architectural relics than the entire testimony of the Fathers of the Reformation; and surely they must be at least as competent judges of the tendency of these antient decorations of churches as we are! He, indeed, must be infatuated by a superstitious love of antiquity, or must be ignorant of all the natural tendencies of man as illustrated in his religious history from the beginning, who can persuade himself that all these relics of the deepest superstition can be restored, and the eyes of the people become familiarized with them, without producing the most baneful effects upon the character of the national religion. It is easy to be conceived that many young enthusiasts in the restoration of our churches to the pattern of by-gone ages, are far from intending to introduce the superstitious usages with which these things were connected. Just as artists and professional persons are reported to study paintings of a most objectionable character without any corruption of their morals, while they forget the effect which will be produced on ordinary minds by their exhibition – so these students of antient architecture, disconnecting the objects of their artistical admiration from the errors in doctrine and discipline in which they originated, do not know, or do not consider, what irreparable mischief they may occasion to the public mind!

Yet to the furtherance of such objects – the restoration of churches to their original superstitious models, are we now urged to contribute vast sums of money, while the teeming thousands of our population have neither school house, nor church, nor pastor, nor teacher! At the risk of being charged with acting upon 'the principle of Judas Iscariot,'[21] it may be affirmed, that under such circumstances, this is money grievously wasted. At all times, and under any circumstances – the restoration of such emblems of an idolatrous superstition ought to be opposed by a Protestant clergy and laity – but in the present times most especially – when not only is every farthing valuable that can be raised for encreasing church accommodation for the people – but when there are not wanting those who are ready to avail themselves of the EMBLEMS of superstition to revive the USAGES of superstition.

Were the present disposition to lavish money on decorative church architecture a mere matter of taste, or of cultivated pursuit, it might be less reprehensible – but when this art is magnified into such undue importance – when it swallows up funds which would avail to build many a church for the poor man – and when, above all, it is made subservient to the introduction of superstitious practices – surely it is time for all who love the truth to rally around it, and to resist, by all lawful measures, the revival of antiquated heresies by means of WOOD AND STONE, AND TAPESTRY, AND HANGINGS, AND PICTURES, AND IMAGES!

It is one of our worst signs that some faithful watchmen do not see the danger which threatens them – they regard these pursuits as trivial and childish – as mere matters of fancy; and do not perceive that it is impossible to restore the IMAGES OF SINS without fostering the introduction of the SINS THEMSELVES! They vainly imagine that we may have crosses, pictures, and images in our churches without either worshipping them, or promoting the worship of them – they may discover their error when too late!

In vain do we look for any similarity between these popish, or medieval restorations, and the simple unadorned worship of the times of the apostles, or of the century which succeeded them – there is no authority for this extravagant decoration of buildings in the New Testament – none in the truly primitive church – and it is opposed to the spiritual character of the dispensation under which we live. In exact proportion as attention has been paid to such things in any age of Christianity – and places, vessels, and ceremonies have been esteemed holy – in that proportion has the church lost sight of the true sanctity of the heart, and removal of the spirit by divine grace. And earnestly is it hoped that ere long the dangerous tendencies of these pursuits will become apparent to all right minded persons; and that the true Prostestantism, which is the hidden energy of our church, may awake from her slumbers, and shaking off at once the follies of her deluded sons, may exhibit herself in her genuine resemblance to pure, primitive, scriptural Christianity, before it was corrupted by the Judaeo-pagan superstitions of the fourth century, or disfigured by the more modern additions of Popery.

But it may be asked in conclusion – would you then desecrate the houses of God in the land – strip them of all their ornaments – or assemble the people in barns, or in the open air, to worship God? Far fom it! Although it is denied, in accordance with the cloud of witnesses of the Protestant Reformation, that any forms of any church can impart the same kind of CONSECRATION and CHARACTER of holiness to a Christian building as that which was imparted to the one only temple in which JEHOVAH Himself dwelt – while it is denied that the consecration of churches can be argued from the New

Testament, or can be established by reference to a dispensation which, IN THIS RESPECT, bore no analogy to that established by CHRIST – yet would all pious Christians humbly and thankfully acquiesce in that ordinance of man, through the church, which has set apart a house in which the rites of our blessed religion may be performed, the holy GOD may be worshipped, CHRIST may be preached, and the souls of men converted and edified! That such a building should be severed from all secular uses, and devoted to holy services, is accordant with all the best feelings alike of the natural and spiritual man! – But that one part of that building is more holy than another – that one should be elevated above another – that one should be for the priests, and another for the people – one for those initiated in the mysteries, and another part for the uninitiated, is utterly repudiated as UNSCRIPTURAL – UNSANCTIONED BY PRIMITIVE USAGE – AND CALCULATED TO INTRODUCE FALSE NOTIONS AND SUPERSTITIOUS PRACTICES.

And as to the decorations and ornaments of churches; if any rule could be laid down it would be this; – that a Christian church should not only in all its details harmonize with the simple and spiritual genius of Christianity – but that there should be an adaptation to its position in its own locality. There is the same propriety attainable in this – the 'quid decens, and quid non'[a] – as in the character of a Christian's dress. Our garments were originally given us to hide our shame, and we have made them the food of pride, and the means of displaying our conceit and folly – so it is with our churches. We have proved that they are memorials of our sin and separation from GOD, while they bring us near to him – and we by senseless, extravagant decoration make them minister to our pride and arrogance! – But as in the one case, so in the other – the perfection of a Christian's apparel is such an adaptation to his situation in life, that no one should remark either its affected simplicity, or its studied costliness – so should it be with church decorations. Let the modest village church yet raise its humble spire among the cottages by which it is surrounded – and amidst the palaces of the great, let the noble church, with its suitable architectural beauties, and becoming ceremonial, appear worthy to stand among the abodes of wealth or rank, by which it is chiefly furnished with guests.[22] – 'Let all things be done decently and in order!'[b]

[a] What is, and what is not seemly. [b] I Corinthians 14:40.

William Goode

(1801–1868)

6. Preface to *The Divine Rule of Faith and Practice* (2 vols., 1842), vol. 1, pp. vii–ix, xii–xiii, xxi–xli

Goode was an Evangelical by inheritance (his father had been curate and successor to the Calvinist Romaine) and by conviction. When, as editor of the *Christian Observer* and spearhead for the Evangelical defence, Goode was preferred at the height of the Gorham Case this was seen as a partisan declaration by the Primate, Archbishop Sumner.

Already in *The Divine Rule of Faith and Practice* Goode was claiming Protestantism as the central Anglican tradition. The Preface was written in the aftermath of *Tract No. XC* (1841). In *Tract No. XC* Newman had examined fourteen of the Church of England's Thirty-Nine Articles to see how far they might be subscribed to in a 'catholic' spirit. Treating them, not as a religious but as a legal document, he discounted the duty to read the Articles in the spirit of their framers, the Protestant Reformers, preferring to bring them in harmony with the more catholic spirit of the Book of Common Prayer and ultimately with the faith of the Ancient Church. When Newman used the phrase 'Catholic church' in 1841 he intended by it the ancient and undivided church, not the Roman Catholic Church. To a critic like Goode the distinction, as Newman made it, was mere sophistry. If the Anglican Church claimed to base itself upon the 'one catholic and apostolick church' where was the source of Newman's complaint? Since Newman's dislike of the Reformers and their Protestant faith was abundantly clear, he must, in fact, though not in so many words, critics reasoned, be arrogating for the unreformed Popish Church true 'catholicism', that is, using 'catholic' in the narrower sense of 'Roman Catholic'.

Whilst the condemnation of *Tract No. XC* by the Heads of Houses on 12 March 1841 might weaken Tractarianism's position in Oxford, the movement's influence seemed to be increasing in the rest of the country and it is to the reasons for this success that Goode next turns. Tractarianism is diagnosed as one version of man's search for authority in an age of uncertainty. The title of Goode's book addresses the precise source and nature of this authority, scrutinizing Tractarian teaching on tradition as found in such works as Keble's *Primitive Tradition recognised in Holy Scripture* (1836) or Newman's *Lectures on the Prophetical Office of the Church* (1837).

Given contemporary standards of polemic and the sense of the holy war in which he feels himself engaged, Goode's Preface is a model of restraint and meticulous scholarship. His task of denouncing Tractarian casuistry is complicated by a prayerful desire to search earnestly for God's purpose in allowing such a controversy to arise and so his prose incorporates the clichés of Protestant invective (e.g. 'the fopperies of monkery itself', 'the deadly leaven of Popery'), caustic irony and the compassionately expressed formulaic interpolations of a litany. The Preface begins with an interesting use of functional irony as Goode lulls his readers' expectations or prejudices with an apparently neutral description of this important new movement. The way in which the impartial language of the first paragraph slides into the insinuations of concealment and betrayal in the second re-enacts for the reader the way in which the Tractarian mask of reserve has cloaked dangerous conspiracy beneath it.

Unfortunately, however, Goode's style as a whole lacks the flexibility and compelling energy such variations demand. Unlike Close's or Simeon's work, written with the speaking voice in mind, Goode's prose emanates from the study. Carefully contrived and balanced parallel or antithetical phrases and clauses, reminiscent of high Augustan prose, often collapse under the weight of qualifying clauses. For the sake of emphasis Goode characteristically resorts to awkward syntactical transpositions rather than brevity (e.g. beginning a sentence with a clause dependent for its understanding on the main clause, or transposing the negative marker and eliding the auxiliary verb as in 'I deny not' or 'It becomes not'). The singularity of his style was ultimately self-defeating. One cannot but admire the determination to enable his hard-pressed and often ignorant brethren to form their own judgement on these great matters, but there is no doubt that the bulk of his potential readers would have preferred a more popular manner, even at the expense of losing the subtlety of Goode's scholarship. 'If the trumpet give an uncertain sound, who shall prepare himself to the battle?' (I Corinthians 14:8) was a quotation favoured equally by Tractarian and Evangelical as an epigraph to their pamphlets.

Preface

The movement that has lately taken place in our Church under the auspices of the Authors of the Tracts for the Times, whatever may be the view taken of it, must be admitted to be one of a very important kind. Whether for good or evil, the degree of developement it has already attained, amply shows that its success must be attended with a great and thorough change in the principles and practices of our Church in various most important points.

That such would be the case, was for a long time studiously concealed from public view. So much caution, indeed, was exercised in the earlier part of their career by the Tractators, that to none but those who were somewhat acquainted with the controversial writings of divines on the points touched upon, so as to see the full force and tendency of the terms used, was it apparent whither they were going; though to such, I may add, it was abundantly evident. And the first intimation of it to the public mind was in the very seasonable publication of Mr Froude's Remains, a work which clearly and most opportunely revealed the real spirit and views of the (to use Mr Foude's *own* term) 'conspirators' against the present order of things in our Church.[1] As time has advanced, and the number of their adherents increased, the reserve formerly practised has been gradually thrown aside. Perhaps, indeed, their own views have become more fixed and definite than when they commenced their labours. And we are far from laying to their charge any other concealment than such as they judged to be wise and prudent for the inculcation of new and unpalatable truths; though we may be pardoned for observing, that a more open course appears to us to be (to use a mild term) much freer from objections.

It is now, then, openly avowed,[a] that the Articles, though 'it is notorious that they were drawn up by Protestants, and *intended for the establishment of Protestantism*,' are not to be interpreted according to 'the known opinions of their framers,' but in what the Tractators are pleased to call a 'Catholic' sense, which interpretation we are informed 'was intended to be admissible, though not that which their authors took themselves,' in order to 'comprehend those who did not go so far in Protestantism as themselves;' though the Articles are said, in the very title prefixed to them, to have been drawn up 'for the avoiding of diversities of opinions, and for the establishing of consent touching true religion;' and were put forth in compliance with the request of the lower House of Convocation,[b] 'that certain articles containing the principal grounds of the Christian religion be set forth, as well to *determine the truth of things this day in controversy*, as also to show *what errors are chiefly to be eschewed*.' And the 'Declaration' prefixed to the Articles, requiring them to be interpreted in the 'literal and grammatical sense,' 'sanctions' such a mode of interpretation. That is, the 'literal and grammatical sense' comprehends that 'uncatholic' and Protestant doctrine against which the Tractators protest, and *also* that *opposite* 'catholic' doctrine which they embrace. And this 'catholic' doctrine is such as is *consistent with the decrees of the Council of Trent*.[c] And the Declaration, forbidding any person to 'affix any *new* sense to any article,' 'was promulgated,' we are told, 'at a time when the leading men of our Church were especially noted for catholic views.' But surely, if the 'literal and grammatical sense' of the Articles comprehends so much as the Tractators suppose, and men had all along subcribed the Articles with propriety, though varying in their sentiments from the Protestantism of Bishop Jewell, to the 'Catholicism' which squared with the Decrees of the Council of Trent, it

[a] The quotations in this paragraph are from *Tract No. XC*.

[b] The assembly of Anglican clergy below the rank of bishop whose meetings were discontinued between 1717 and 1852.

[c] The council called by the Pope in 1545 to restore peace to the Church sat until 1563 and passed a number of decrees defining doctrines questioned by Protestants.

was rather a useless admonition, for the wit of man could hardly devise a sense of the Articles not to be found within such an extensive range as this. . . .

The reader will observe that in their use of the word 'Catholic,' the Tractators are directly opposed to our Reformers. Our Reformers were so far from thinking that Protestantism and Catholicism were opposed to each other, that one ground for their supporting the former was, their conviction that it best deserved the title of the latter. Bishop Jewell[a] believed that it was the Reformation that restored the 'antient religion' (to use the reviewer's phrase) to our Church. And both he and, I believe I may say, all the more learned reformers claimed the name 'Catholic,' as belonging more peculiarly to themselves, than to those who, both in the Western and Eastern Churches, had corrupted the pure faith and worship of the primitive Church. The Tractators, therefore, like the Romanists, are at issue with the Reformers as to *what is* 'Catholicism,' and the 'antient religion.' This the reader ought carefully to bear in mind, lest he be deceived, as too many suffer themselves to be, by words and phrases. And the same caution must be given as to the Tractators' repudiation of the charge of holding Romish tenets. Their repudiation of it is grounded merely upon their rejection of certain more gross impositions and practices of the Church of Rome; while, upon various most important points and leading features in that vast system of religious priestcraft, they are altogether in agreement with her. There is a previous question, then, to be determined, before their repudiation of the charge can be of any practical use, viz. What is Romanism? If, as our Archbishop Whitgift[2] tells us, their doctrine on the rule of faith is '*the ground of all Papistry*,' their verbal disclaimer of Papistry is mere idle talk. But unfortunately, to the ordinary reader, this equivocal use of terms throws the whole subject into inextricable confusion. It is very hard, he will say, that those should be accused of holding Romish doctrines, who have expressly repudiated and even abused Romanism. And is it not most desirable that we should hold 'Catholic' doctrines and the 'antient religion?' On these points, however, this is not the place to enlarge, as they will more properly come under our consideration in a subsequent page.

With these facts and statements before his eyes, the reader will not be surprised to learn that the Romanists are loudly hailing the efforts of the Tractators, as directly tending to the re-establishment

[a] See Simeon Endnote 19.

of their doctrines, as the doctrines of the Anglican Church. 'We may depend,' says Dr Wiseman, 'upon a willing, an able, and a most zealous co-operation [i.e. on the part of the Tractators] with any effort which we may make towards bringing her [i.e. the Anglican Church] into her rightful position in catholic unity with the Holy See, and the Churches of its obedience – in other words, with the Church Catholic.'[3] . . .

The object which the Tractators and the Romanists have in view in thus putting our Articles upon the rack to make them consistent with their views, is, from the foregoing extracts, sufficiently clear, namely, the more easy reduction of our Church, as a whole, to its former union with the Romish See, when the explanation, having served its purpose, would be, with the Articles themselves, indignantly thrown overboard, to make way for a truly 'Catholic' exposition of the faith, dictated at Rome. And then I suspect the poor remnant of the despised Protestants might sigh in vain for a 'Catholic' confession sufficiently indulgent to include an 'uncatholic' meaning, thankful as they would be to be indulged only with life. And if perchance the new light of another age should enable some gifted Protestant to show how easily Pope Pius's creed might be understood in a good Protestant sense, let us hope that Rome also would see in a new light her duty to her neighbour.

May God in his infinite mercy avert from us the evils which threaten us.

It would be difficult to overrate the responsibility resting at the present time upon the heads of our Church. There are those within the Church who, so far from being affectionately attached to her doctrines and practices, think that the very 'mark of being Christ's kingdom' is 'but faintly traced on her,' mourn over her Articles and services as framed by persons of a thoroughly uncatholic spirit, and framed '*for the establishment*' of a system which they believe to be even Antichristian, 'the religion of corrupt human nature;' and avow themselves 'ecclesiastical agitators,' purposing to avail themselves of every means of overturning that system, and 'unprotestantizing' the Church. There are others who, having adopted, with all the ardour of youth and inexperience, the same views, are seeking to enter our Church, that they may add their efforts to the accomplishment of the same end. All the oaths, declarations, and subscriptions required by the Protestant restorers of our Church as safeguards against the re-introduction of those doctrines and practices to which these persons are attached, form, in their view, no impediment to their either remaining or seeking to become ministers of a Protestant Church, for the purpose of 'unprotestantizing' it; the righteous end sanctifying, I suppose, (according to the well-known 'Catholic' doctrine) the unrighteous means.[4] This is no question, then, of high or low Churchmanship, of Calvinism or Arminianism, of this or that shade of doctrine, in which a latitude may justly be allowed. No, as the Tractators themselves tell us, '*very vital truths*' are concerned in the *change* they desire to effect in our Church, even '*matters of life or death*.'[5] It becomes not me to say more, than earnestly to pray that wisdom may be given to the rulers of our Church in this crisis in her history.

But it may be said, Surely there is some mistake in all this, for the Tractators have put forth their system as peculiarly entitled to the name of Anglicanism, and represented their doctrines as those of the great majority of our most illustrious divines, ever since the Reformation, and presented us with various 'Catenas,'[a] containing extracts from the writings of those divines in proof of this. This is one of the most extraordinary and painful features in the whole case. That such representations pervade the Tracts and works of the Tractators, is but too true; and too true is it also, that upon the strength of such statements they have gained a footing in our Protestant Church, which they could never otherwise have obtained. One great object, therefore, which I have kept in view in the following work has been to show, that so far from having the support they claim in the writings of our great divines, they are refuted and opposed in the most decisive way by all the best *even of their own chosen witnesses*; and that their appeal to those writings as in their favour is one of the most unaccountable, and painful, and culpable (however unintentional) misrepresentations with which history supplies us. The fact is, that almost the only witnesses to whom they could properly refer as at all supporting their *system*, are a few individuals, such as Brett, Hicks, Johnson, and others, forming a small and extreme section of a small and extreme party in our Church, namely, the Nonjurors;[6] and even among these it would be difficult to find one who agreed with their system as now developed. Their extracts from the works of our divines generally will be found to be, for the most part, general and loose and indefinite passages, whose meaning depends altogether upon the context, and which are *applied* by the Tractators in a sense which the views of the writers, gathered from their works as a whole, altogether repudiate.

[a] Collections of writings by different authors related to one topic.

Is this fair and ingenuous? Was there not a more candid course open to them? Might they not have said, There is much in the Church of England that we love, much in the writings of her great divines that we approve; but in the Articles and services of the one, and in the writings of the other, there are also various things of which we disapprove, conceiving them to be opposed to antiquity. We will not quit her communion till we see what effect a statement of our views may have upon the minds of her members, though ultimately, if such changes are not made, we shall be compelled to do so. For such a course an apology might perhaps be found. It might not, indeed, have gained for them so many adherents, but it would have been far more likely to have produced a permanent effect than their present conduct. In the place of this they have chosen to wiredraw[a] Protestant confession of faith, so as to make it appear to support Anti-protestant views, to publish extracts from staunch Protestant writers, to convert them, in the eye of the public, into opponents of Protestant principles; in a word, to represent our Church as being what it is *not*, in order to effect more easily the change they desire to bring about in it from what it *is*.

Almost equally incorrect and fallacious are their references to the early Fathers, of whose writings one might suppose, from the language they have used, that their knowledge was most accurate and extensive. I must be permitted to say, that the blunder Mr. Newman has made in the interpretation of a common phrase in a passage of Athanasius, the meaning of that phrase being a turning point in the bearing of many passages with relation to the present controversy, shows a want of acquaintance with the phraseology of the Fathers, which ought to make us receive his citations with considerable caution. Nor can I at all account for various other erroneous representations and allegations of passages from the Fathers, (to some of which I give a reference below, that the reader may at once see that there is ground for the remark),[b] but upon the supposition that much has been taken on trust from other and even Romish writers. And if the heads of the party are not free from such errors, it is not surprising that there are others among them still more deeply involved in them. Since public attention has been more directed to antiquity, we have been inundated with papers, and letters, and remarks, especially in the periodical publications, laying down this or that doctrine with all the calm dignity of an oracular

[a] To strain the interpretation by undue subtlety of argument.

[b] Goode here provides detailed references to the examination of these errors in the main body of his book.

response, as what everybody always everywhere in the primitive Church from the beginning proclaimed and maintained with one consent, and showing nothing more than that their authors need to go to school on the subject on which they would fain be teachers of others. One might suppose, from the tone of some of these writers, that all that has been done or said in all past ages of the Church was to be ascertained without the smallest difficulty or uncertainty, and could even be gathered second-hand from the notices of a few modern divines. For my own part, I freely confess to being in no small degree sceptical as to the possibility of any man knowing what 'everybody always everywhere' in the primitive Church thought on any point; even from a careful perusal of the records of antiquity themselves that remain to us. Indeed, though I can quite conceive a monk in his cell getting together the works of some few dozen authors of great name, and fancying himself able hence to vouch for the sentiments of 'everybody always everywhere,' I feel a difficulty in understanding how men of judgement and experience can allow themselves to be so deluded. But still less are such representations to be taken from those who have not even made themselves acquainted with those sources of information that are open to us. It would be amusing, were it a less important subject, to see the way in which, under the much-abused name of '*Catholic*,' mistakes and corruptions are recommended to public attention, almost as if our salvation depended upon them. Statements, indeed, more uncatholic than some that the Tractators themselves have made – as for instance that of Dr. Pusey, that 'to the decisions of the Church Universal we owe faith,'[7] – were never uttered. We appeal for proof to the writings of the early Church.

For myself, I make no pretensions to any superior knowledge of antiquity, nor desire to set up my own judgement of its verdict as a standard for others to go by, but only to place before the reader the testimonies upon which his conclusions should be formed. And though it is almost impossible to suppose that where so many references occur, there should not be some errors, I trust that the impartial reader will find that no labour has been spared to avoid them, and that the representation given of the sentiments of the Fathers is a fair, and, upon the whole, a correct one.

The success of the Tractators has been to many a subject of surprise, and among others, as it seems, to themselves.[8] For my own part, when I reflect upon the temporary success that has often attended heresies and delusions of the most extravagant nature, I cannot participate in such feelings. For the partial and temporary success that they have met with in the inculcation of their doctrines there are, I think, beyond the fact of novelty, several reasons, and I trust and believe many also that may be assigned, for the hope that, under the Divine blessing, that success may be *but* partial and temporary. Such trials from internal and external foes are the Church's predicted portion in this world, and the purer any Church is, the more may she expect that her great enemy will thus afflict her. If, however, she be upon the whole found faithful to her God, such trials will assuredly be overruled for her good; and there is perhaps nothing more inimical to her real welfare than a state of long and uninterrupted calm and prosperity.

One principal cause, then, of the temporary success of the movement made by the Tractators, has evidently been, that it fell in with the current of men's feelings in the Church at the time. At the period when they commenced their labours, the Church was beset with dangers. The various sects that have separated themselves from her communion had (with one honourable exception) risen up against her with all the bitterness and jealousy of a sordid spirit of worldly rivalry, and had avowed that nothing would satisfy them but her complete overthrow as the National Church, and the extinction of all her peculiar privileges. A Ministry which, if not directly hostile, was made so by its dependence upon the enemies of the Church, a hostile House of Commons, a country kept in agitation for party purposes, and from various causes excited against all its constituted authorities and antient institutions, combined to menace her welfare.[9] Such events had made all her friends anxious for her safety. That which might perhaps have been a permissible relaxation of principle in the conduct of her members towards the dissenters became so no longer, when it was clearly seen that the leading object of those dissenters *as a body* was to deprive the Church of all her peculiar privileges and opportunities for the promotion of Christianity throughout the land. Co-operation with bodies influenced by such views was no longer an act of Christian charity, but a direct breach of Christian duty. The ship was in a storm. Her existence was at stake. Everything conspired to show the importance, the necessity, of union, order, regularity, subordination, obedience to constituted authorities. In a word, the dangers that beset the Church, and the conduct and nature of the foes that assailed her, combined to lead all those who knew anything of Church principles, and had any regard for the Church, to serious reflection. There was in consequence a healthy reaction in favour of those principles. At this time, and under these circumstances, the Tractators commenced their labours. A more favourable moment could hardly have been found. Events had so completely prepared the way for them, that in the minds of many there was a strong predisposition in their favour. Their professions were those of warm friends of our Protestant Church. All that they blamed was 'ultra-Protestantism.' They claimed the support of all our great divines without exception. Antiquity was, beyond contradiction, wholly with them. Their language was cautious and plausible, and full of that self-confidence that is so influential with the popular mind. Is it surprising, then, that they should have pleased many ears, and gained many hearts, and that while they fell in with the current of feeling created by events, they should have succeeded in giving it an additional impetus in its own direction, tending to carry it to an unsalutary extreme? So far, alas! they have indeed succeeded, and thus in many cases have converted a healthy reaction into one which threatens to carry away its victims, and has indeed carried away several, into the bosom of Rome itself.

The circumstances of the times had evidently much influence upon the Tractators themselves in leading them to embrace the views they have taken up. They saw that the influence of the Church over the public mind was not such as it had been in former times, and might reasonably be expected to be. And, apparently, the great problem which they thought they had to solve was, how that influence might be restored. They have not unnaturally (whether wisely or not is another question) found the hope of regaining it in the assertion of those Church-principles which form the foundation of Popery. The abuses caused by the liberty of conscience and free use of private judgement, conceded by Protestantism, are to be cured by a re-establishment of the iron grasp with which Popery holds its votaries in subjection. And I must add, that their works bear such constant and manifest traces of their having been imposed upon and misled by Romish writers, that one cannot but fear that they suffered themselves to be prejudiced in favour of that system of doctrine to which the circumstances of the times had given them a favourable bias, before they had well studied the subject in a way which alone could have entitled them to assume the office of reformers and correctors of the Church. I am much mistaken if their 'Catenas' do not show either an unfairness, which I should be indeed pained at being obliged to charge them with, or a great want of acquaintance even with the works of our own great divines. And hence, instead of keeping within the bounds of that sound moderation that always characterized the Church of England, they have, while rejecting some of the most offensive practices in the Romish church, adopted almost all the doctrines and principles which have hitherto distinguished us as a body from that corrupt Church, and seem gradually progressing to the reception of the whole system; witness the remarks that have been more than once published by them in favour even of the fopperies of monkery itself. We have Dr. Hook's authority for saying that the extreme of high Church principles is Popery.[10] We beg the reader to ask himself whether those principles can well be carried further than they are stretched in the works of the Tractators.

And it must be added, (and this is *another reason* for their success,) that in the inculcation of their views they came upon those who were *generally, and, as a body,* unprepared by previous study for an impartial and judicious view of the subject. The low state of eccelesiastical learning among us for many past years is a truth so generally acknowledged and lamented, that it would be a waste of words to offer either an apology or a proof for the assertion. The consequences of such want of information could not fail to be seen under such circumstances. The slightest appearance of learning carried with it a weight which, in other times, would hardly have been conceded to that which had tenfold claims to it. And under the abused name of 'catholic,' by the aid of Romish sophisms, and partial and inaccurate citations from the Fathers, the corrupt doctrines and practices of which our truly learned Reformers were, by God's blessing, enabled to purge the Church, are urged upon us as veritable parts of that Divine revelation delivered to the world by the Apostles. And herein, be it observed, the Tractators are at issue with those whose learning it would be idle to dispute, not merely as to the foundation upon which their system rests, the authority of patristical tradition, but as to the *fact* whether that tradition, whatever its authority may be, is in their favour. Our reformers contended that the name *catholic*, and the support of the great body of the Fathers, belonged to that system of doctrine and practice which, from its opposition to the corruptions of Romanism, was called Protestantism. And as to any of the attempts hitherto made by the Tractators or their adherents to pluck the laurels from the brows of the Reformers, and to show the inaccuracy of their allegations from the Fathers, such as that of the British Critic in the case of Jewell, it reminds one but of the puny efforts of a dwarf to espy holes in the armour of a giant.

We may add also, as a still further reason for their success, that their doctrines are such as will always, as long as human nature remains what it is, attract many to them; of the clergy, from the power they give them over the minds of men; of the laity, from their greater suitability to the notions and feelings of the natural mind. To the clergy particularly such views will always be attractive. The system of the Tractators is a far more easy and simple one to work; likely also to produce more extended and visible results. Only bring men to acknowledge the authority thus claimed for the Church and the Clergy, and their instrumentality in the work of human salvation, and you wield a power over the minds both of the religious and the superstitious almost irresistible. But address a man merely as a witness for the truth, acknowledgeing your fallibility, and appealing to his judgement, 'I speak as to wise men, judge ye what I say,' and your personal influence over him is not to be compared with that which exists in the former case. The truth is left to work its way by its own intrinsic power, and faith is, as it ought to be, the result of a conviction of the heart. But the cases where such conviction is wrought will be much fewer than those in which a nominal adherence to the truth will be professed under the former system of teaching. And even were it not so, the personal influence of the clergy over their respective flocks in the two cases will not bear a comparison; in the one case, the voice of the pastor is almost like the voice of God himself, for an inspired messenger could hardly demand greater deference; in the other, the pastor himself merges his own claims in that of the message, and sends his hearers to search for themselves in the book of God, whether the things that he preaches unto them are so. It cannot be a question, then, which system is naturally the most attractive to the clergy. Nay, a zealous, earnest minister of Christ, who desires nothing more than to promote the best interests of mankind, may be so attracted by the influence given by the former, purposing to use that influence only for the good of his fellow-creatures, as to have at once a secret prejudice in its favour, which blinds his eyes to the baselessness of the claims upon which it rests.

All these causes have operated in favour of the Tractators.

But there are at the same time not a few reasons also for hoping that, in the mercy of God, their success may be *but* partial and temporary.

There are encouraging symptoms of a prevalent desire among us to search into the matter, especially since the recent publications of the Tractators have shown more fully their real views and aims. Now it is impossible for this desire to be carried into effect without their being detected in such inconsistencies, misrepresentations, and mistakes as will infallibly alter their position very materially in the eyes of many who may have been originally inclined to favour them. To some of these I have already alluded, and it would be easy to add to the list. While I am writing, my eye lights upon one in a late number of the British Critic (a number, by the way, which, for its flippant impertinences and gross personalities upon men who had the highest claims to at least respectful treatment, is unparalleled in such a work), made with all the coolness and confidence of one who is uttering an incontrovertible truth. For the sake of disparaging the Reformation, it is said, 'Nothing is more remarkable in the theology of the Reforming age (to speak generally) than the deficiency of all writings of a devotional, or even a practical cast.' (Brit. Crit. for July 1841, p. 3.) Now the writer of this is either profoundly ignorant of the ecclesiastical literature of that period, or he has misrepresented it for the sake of his party, and in either case is deserving of no little censure for thus misleading his readers, of whom few probably (speaking comparatively) would have the means of judging of the truth of his remark. Considering the character of the period, and the comparatively limited number of original works then published to what there are now, it is surprising how many practical works issued from the pens of our reformers and early divines, engaged as they were in the struggle with Popery. These things give reason to hope that such writers will ultimately find their level. Men do not like to be deceived, especially by those who put forth high claims to wisdom and learning. Their 'quiet, self-complacent, supercilious language,' as an able writer in the British Magazine has justly called it,[11] will be *doubly offensive* when found to be wanting in that which alone could afford the shadow of an apology for it. Their misrepresentations, in particular, of the sentiments of our great divines, by a few loose and indefinite extracts from their writings, though for a time they have (as might be expected) deceived many, can ultimately only recoil upon themselves. The disingenuousness also with which Articles of religion, drawn up by Protestant divines, 'for the establishment,' as is confessed, 'of Protestantism,' are tortured to an Antiprotestant sense, in order to enable Antiprotestants to retain their places in our Church, is so utterly irreconcilable with those common principles that hold society together, that it cannot fail ultimately, as indeed it has done already, to estrange the minds of simple and upright Christian men from such teaching. Indeed it is impossible not to see that it is a mere temporary expedient, which cannot long satisfy even those who have availed themselves of it, a hastily constructed refuge within the walls of our Church for those who are seeking to gain possession of the citadel, and who suppose that they have better opportunities to do so within the walls than without, but whose avowed objects make it clear that the present state of things cannot last, that one party or the other must give way. And when this becomes clearly appreciated by the Church at large, may we not justly hope that many who have been attracted to their standard while they were holding out, according to their own confession, 'false colours,' will, when they come to see the real state of the case, look upon them only as betrayers, and that their very best defences, their 'Catenas,' and high pretensions to learning and wisdom, antiquity and catholicism, will only be sources of moral weakness to their cause, and tend more than anything else to its overthrow.

That such a controversy should have arisen in our Church is deeply to be regretted. The agitation of such questions necessarily produces disunion and party spirit, the great causes of weakness, disorder, and ruin to any community that is afflicted by them. The powers of the Church are thus paralyzed, her energies spent in useless, and worse than useless, contentions; her friends are discouraged and perplexed, her enemies triumph; her God is displeased, and her strength departs from her. How great the responsibility of those who have raised such a strife within her, and made it a duty incumbent upon those who have any regard for her preservation, to arm themselves against their brethren for the defence of her very foundations! But when matters of such moment are at stake, when the question is, whether the true catholicism of our reformers is to give place to a system of doctrine and practice altogether unsound, and the corruptions from which our faith and worship have through the mercy of God been purged, are to be reintroduced into our Church, it would be culpable indeed to remain a neutral, a silent, or an indifferent spectator. It becomes the duty of all to do what may be in their power to prevent such a result. The zeal, and earnestness, and perseverance with which Popish views and principles are urged upon the public mind, under the abused name of catholicism, must be met with correspondent efforts to unmask their unsoundness and dangerous tendency. In a word, if the cause for which our martyrs laid down their lives was one worthy of their blood, it is the duty of those who have succeeded to the possession of privileges so dearly purchased, to contend with similar devotedness for their preservation and transmission unimpaired to their children. And we may humbly hope that He who out of evil oft educeth good, may grant that even this contoversy may not be without its good effects. The real principles of our Church will be better known and appreciated, even among its own members and ministers. The foundation upon which it stands will, we are convinced, bear examination, and therefore, if God's blessing rest upon it, we fear not for the result.

I am aware that it may be said, and with truth, that in the present day the majority need no arguments to induce them to slight human authority, and are scarcely willing to pay deference to any other guide than their own self-will. This I fully admit, and believe that judicious works, calculated to show the danger of such a disposition of mind, might, under the Divine blessing, be of essential service to the community, both as it respects their spiritual and temporal interests. But I see no reason hence to suppose that unfounded claims to their obedience would counteract the evil. Such doctrines as those of our opponents appear to me calculated to do anything rather than become a cure. I deny not, indeed, that to many minds they are likely to appear plausible, and calculated to act as remedy for the evils which internal dissensions have produced in the Protestant body. The liberty obtained by the Reformation has no doubt been in some cases abused. And the panacea for the evils so caused may appear to many to be the re-establishment of the iron tyranny under which the minds of men were held previous to that event. I believe this to be a growing impression in the minds of many both in this country and elsewhere, and Rome is largely availing herself of it. But whatever may be in store for this or other countries as a temporary dispensation, as a punishment for their sins, we trust that the substitution of a system in which 'the Church' and 'the priest' are thrust almost into the place of God and Christ, for the everlasting gospel, will be permitted to have but a very precarious and temporary hold upon the minds of men. Of this at least we are assured, that it is the duty of all who are interested in the real welfare of mankind to lay open the anti-christian nature and tendencies of such a system. Glad therefore as we should have been in being engaged in urging the just claims of antiquity and our Church to the deferential respect of mankind, and pointing out the evils and the guilt connected with that wild and lawless spirit of independence of constituted authorities now so prevalent, and painful as it is to have to point out the blemishes rather than the excellencies of the Church, and to appear in any degree as the apologist of irregularities against which on other occasions we should feel it a duty to protest, the unfounded claims to spiritual dominion set up by the Tractators on behalf of the clergy, make it more than equally a duty to guard men against such fatal errors. The clergy were appointed, not to be either individually or collectively, as Mr. Newman would have them, 'the sovereign lord of conscience,' but witnesses for the truth, not lords over God's heritage, but examples to the flock, not to be mediators between God and men, but to point men to the one Mediator Christ Jesus.

The Romanists and the Tractators both tell us that the divisions among Protestants are all owing to the free use of the Bible as the sole authoritative rule of faith. Not to stop to retort the charge of internal divisions, or to say that unity obtained by impositions upon the credulity of mankind is as little to be boasted of as the peace that exists among the ashes of the dead, let me ask those who for so many centuries kept the Bible as a sealed book from the hands of the people, seriously to put it to their own consciences, how far the blame rests upon their own heads. Would it be any matter for surprise if youths long debarred from their just rights should, upon finding themselves free agents, run into extremes, and not find the middle path until age and experience had enabled them to take a calm and dispassionate view of things? Why, then, should we feel surprised that the Church, upon her emancipation from the Papal yoke, should for a long time suffer from the excesses into which the restoration of her liberty has ensnared some of her members? Such divisions, indeed, are now likely to exist more or less to the end. And would that the evils caused by such divisions might lead those who are aiding in their perpetuation, to serious reflection upon the necessary consequences of their vagaries, and to a remembrance of the words of our Divine Master, that a house divided against itself falleth! But let the blame be shared by those whose conduct has tended, more than anything else, to produce such a result. The unchristian usurpations of Popery have done more than any other cause that can be named to destroy the unity of the Church, and subvert the moral influence of the clergy over the minds of men. Nor let it ever be forgotten by the Romanists, when complaining of the divided state of the Protestant body, that they have themselves, by the imposition of unchristian terms of communion, rendered themselves the most schismatical portion of all Christendom. When men are cast out of the Church by a Diotrephes,[12] the brand of schism rests not upon the excommunicated, but the excommunicator.

For presenting to the public the following work, an apology can hardly, I suppose, be needed. It was impossible to see the deadly leaven of Popery insinuating itself into the very vitals of our Church, and that too under the venerable names of those whose lives were spent in purging it out of her, or preserving her from re-infection, without feeling that any warning (from whatever quarter it might proceed) could not be mistimed; that any effort, however it might fall short of doing full justice to the subject, could not be misplaced. I trust I shall not be misunderstood by the amiable authors of the works upon which I have here ventured to animadvert, when I say that it appeared to me to be – certainly it is equivalent in its *effects* to – treason in the camp. They have surrendered to Rome the *principles* upon which that vast system of religious fraud and imposition is built, and while they give themselves out to be the opponents, nay the best opponents, of Romanism, though limiting their opposition to a few of her most crying sins and practical abuses, they are in fact paving the way for her by upholding those *first principles* of Popery, upon which her dominion over the minds of men principally rests.

In the prosecution of the work, I have spared neither time nor labour in endeavouring to place before the reader the facts and arguments upon which his conclusions ought to rest, and further, to put him in possession of the views of the best and most able and pious writers upon the subject, both of the primitive Church and of our own. That more might have been done in this respect I freely own. But it was not composed in the calm quietude of the College, with every literary aid at hand, but (I may say it *emphatically*) amidst the cares and trials of active life. For the proper execution moreover of such a work many things are required; facilities of which the great body of the parochial clergy are destitute. Those who know what opportunities such have of supplying themselves with the original sources of information, will understand the difficulties to be encountered in the performance of such a task. I trust, however, that the work will be found, upon the whole, to contain a fair and correct representation of the facts upon which the question rests, and of the sentiments of those referred to; and that if there are some slighter inaccuracies, they are such as will not be found to affect the main argument of the work – a circumstance which those who are *in search of truth* will appreciate, when drawing their conclusions upon the points at issue.

And here I would, once for all, acknowledge my obligations to those who have laboured in the same field before me, for many references to the Fathers, of which I have freely availed myself, when I have found them, on viewing them in their context, to afford good proof of that for which they are cited. The authorities our earlier divines have adduced in their works against the Romanists have no doubt enabled me to push my researches much beyond what my own unassisted labours would have enabled me to do. I may be permitted to say, however, that I have endeavoured to explore the ground again with more attention to the original sources of information than has usually been paid to them here of late years, and trust that by so doing I have been enabled to add somewhat to what has been done by previous labourers in the same field.

Of the replies already published to the writings of the Tractators, I have abstained almost wholly from the perusal; the principal of them, indeed, I have not seen; any similarity, therefore, of views or statements is wholly accidental.

I appear before the public as the advocate of no particular party or system, but that of the Church of England itself. As far as human infirmity (to the effects of which no man ought to shut his eyes) may permit the remark to be made, truth has been my only object, and I have followed where it appeared to lead me. And but for the establishment of great and important truths, I trust I shall never be found upon the field of controversy. It is one which nothing but a sense of duty should ever induce me to enter.

In conclusion, I would express my sincere hope that there is nothing in the tone, or spirit, or language of the following work, of which my opponents can justly complain. If there is, I most sincerely regret it. On such important points as are there discussed, one cannot but feel warmly, and he who feels warmly is apt to express himself warmly. I must beg pardon, however, for saying, that there are some circumstances in the present controversy which appear to me to justify, and indeed to require, strong language. There are many points in the system itself of our opponents, which it is impossible too strongly to denounce and reprobate. The means also by which that system has been enforced and recommended, are such as to require grave reprehension. Our opponents appear to me like men who, thinking that a great change is needed in the views and practices of their Church, endeavour, by explaining away its formularies, and bringing forward a few isolated passages from the works of some of its great divines, to persuade people that it is no change at all; for while they admit and bewail the fact, that their system has been nowhere and at no time put in practice in our Church, they persist in calling it the Anglican system. They must not then be surprised if this (however well intentioned) is not considered plain and fair dealing. Nor can I help adding, that the anonymous publications of the party more particularly are, many of them, characterized by a self-complacent spirit, and scornful tone towards their opponents, such as intimate, more plainly than words could do, that the only possible reason for men not holding the views of the Tractators must be sheer ignorance; a spirit and tone which, I will venture to say, the degree of learning and research shown in those productions renders worse than ridiculous. These are circumstances that would well justify strong language. We are far from disputing the piety or the learning of the Tractators, but (let us not conceal from ourselves the fact) neither can we dispute the piety or learning of many others who have at various times misled portions of the Church. Such recommendations, then, are wholly insufficient as proofs of the truth of their doctrines. These evidences are to be found with many different parties. The question, therefore, must be determined by an impartial investigation, in which all prejudices derived from such sources must be laid aside. To enable the reader to conduct such an inquiry, is the object of the following work; and thankful indeed shall I be, if it shall tend to bring back into the old paths of our Church any who have been misled, or preserve any who are in danger of being misled, by the specious arguments and plausible statements of the Tractators. I commend it humbly to His blessing who alone can make it instrumental to the good of His Church.

WILLIAM GOODE

London,
November 20, 1841.

7. *Address delivered at a Public Meeting of the Inhabitants of Allhallows the Great and Less, London. Convened for the Purpose of considering the propriety of Presenting an Address to the Crown on the Recent Act of Papal Aggression, Nov. 15, 1850* (1850)

On 29 September 1850 the Papal Brief recreating a Roman Catholic hierarchy in England was issued and on 17 October the newly elevated Cardinal Wiseman's exultant Pastoral read in the parish churches of his diocese. The fifth of November that year saw an outbreak of English anti-Popery with leading Catholics burnt in effigy. Popular anti-Catholicism was based upon a number of fears and prejudices: suspicion of Catholics as potential subversives since they owed a double and possibly conflicting allegiance to the Pope and the Crown; the evidence of such potential sedition as seen in Ireland; working-class economic fears of migrant Irish labourers flooding the English labour market in increasing numbers after the 1845 Irish famine; upper-class distaste at the incongruity in the Papal States between the baroque extravagance and appalling poverty. This brief extract from Goode's address shows how the usually well-balanced intellectual heavyweight of the Evangelical party could be roused to voice in emotional tones the popular prejudices of a Protestant country threatened by a foreign aggressor, who combines the roles of degenerate tyrant and mountebank.

The connection made here between 'No Popery' and 'No Tractarianism' had been fostered by watching Wiseman's and Newman's recent attempts to win over those Tractarians disillusioned by the apparent victory for Erastianism and Protestantism that the Gorham Case implied. A letter, published on 7 November, from the Whig Prime Minister, Lord John Russell, to the Bishop of Durham, abusing traitors within the Anglican Church and promising any legal action necessary, looked like further confirmation for the triumph of Protestant Erastianism.

I think, then, that I have now pointed out sufficient reason to the most strenuous supporters of the principles of religious liberty (which I for one should be sorry to infringe) why this act of Papal aggression should meet with our earnest and uncompromising resistance.

Upon the theological errors of the Church of Rome, I have not enlarged, because I do not think that they form the grounds, certainly not the chief grounds, upon which our opposition to the late acts of the Pope and his emissaries ought to rest. At the same time, I cannot conclude my remarks on this subject, without observing, that there are parts of the Roman Catholic system of theology which may well justify the jealous supervision (to use a mild phrase) of those who are interested in promoting the peace, the welfare, the morality of their country. To learn the genuine influence of Popery we must look to the state of things in Italy – to the condition of Ireland. Can there be more convincing evidence than we find in those two countries of the state of moral degradation, and consequent misery, to which Popery reduces those who are under its yoke? The abominations of the Confessional, the encouragement given to crime by the way in which the true doctrine of the ministerial privilege of declaring God's forgiveness of a true penitent is metamorphosed into a priestly power to give absolution, the impositions practised upon the people through the doctrine of purgatory, the image-worship and idolatry of the Church of Rome, clearly point her out as standing upon very different ground from that occupied by other religious communions. The real character of that Church has been (I fear), by many of our fellow-countrymen, greatly misunderstood. They have found it impossible to believe that Popery in the present day could be such as it was represented to be. The stronger the evidences afforded of the contrariety of many of the tenets and practices of the Church of

Rome to religion and morality, the more the minds of men seemed to revolt from the belief that such tenets and practices were rightly ascribed to it. I would ask those who have indulged themselves in such incredulity, whether the time is not now come for them to pause, and inquire whether they have duly weighed the proofs laid before them, and whether experience shows that religious systems are necessarily free from doctrines and practices directly opposed to the spirit and principles both of religion and morality.

But I will not enlarge on this point, because it opens too large a field of observation for the present occasion.

Of the Pope himself, I know nothing to the contrary, but that he may be (so far as the principles of Popery permit) an upright, conscientious, and well-intentioned personage, who believes that he is only doing his duty; and therefore I shall say nothing in depreciation of him. An open, straightforward, professed antagonist deserves respect. Certainly he has done nothing but what is quite consistent with the principles he professes to hold; and in this respect stands in honourable contrast with some in our own Church, who, while they have been solemnly professing to maintain its principles, and availing themselves of its influence and resources, have been, some more, some less, some directly, some indirectly, sapping the foundations upon which that Church is built. So far as this question concerns the Church of England, it is impossible not to feel, that these internal enemies to the genuine doctrines and principles of that Church are far more dangerous to its peace and welfare than its open antagonists; and it is the position they have assumed in our Church that has been (I am convinced) one leading inducement to the Pope and his adherents to take the step which we are met to resist. And I must add, that the rights of the Royal Supremacy have been equally, and more criminally, outraged by some of those who have solemnly pledged themselves to respect and maintain them, than by the Pope and his adherents, who have always openly repudiated them.

On this part of the subject, however, I will not dwell. Let us hope that when the enemy is before the gates, all but those who are in heart with him will unite in repelling the advances of a common foe. Let us hope that there will be more caution exercised in accepting his presents, – his books, his legends, his toys; less love for his livery in aping his ceremonial mummeries; and a firmer adherence to, and maintenance of, our own *distinctive* doctrines and principles – albeit we have been recently told, by one who yet lingers among us, that we have none.[13]

William Goode (1801–1868)

Let me add, in conclusion, that I trust that this aggression of the Papacy will only have the effect of placing more distinctly before us the unscriptural character and claims of that corrupt Church, and of causing us to put a higher value upon the blessings we enjoy as a Protestant nation. Our privileges have been obtained for us, under God's favour, by the blood of martyrs, who loved not their lives unto the death to bear witness for the truth. Let us prove ourselves worthy of the benefits we derive from their sufferings, by inscribing upon our banners the same testimony to the truth, the same protest against the Bishop of Rome and all his enormities.

Edward Miall

(1809–1881)

8. *The British Churches in Relation to the British People* (1849),

pp. 196–200, 206–13, 292–303, 348–51, 361–2, 367–71

Before Miall's ordination in 1831 he had read classics and English literature at Wymondley Theological College: a course which, no doubt, developed those oratorical skills which he was subsequently to display as journalist and politician. Eight years spent as a Congregational pastor acquainted him with the conditions of the working classes and made him acutely aware of Dissenting disabilities. The event that precipitated his resignation from the ministry was the imprisonment, in 1840, of a member of his Leicester congregation for refusal to pay an Anglican Church rate. In 1841 Miall took up the editorship of the *Nonconformist*: a post which he was to occupy until 1878. Although the *Nonconformist* reported news of general secular interest, its chief function was declared in the motto, derived from a speech by Burke, 'the Dissidence of Dissent and the Protestantism of the Protestant religion'.

The single-mindedness of Miall's campaign for Church disestablishment won him a public reputation for narrow, rancorous bitterness, comprehensible in view of the savagery with which he denounced his opponents, but personally unmerited. Matthew Arnold repeatedly used 'Mialism' (*sic*) and the *Nonconformist* to epitomize those parochial and divisive forces of 'Sub-Hebraism and Philistinism' which he perceived as undermining the 'ideal of complete harmonious human perfection' or Culture, whilst admitting Miall himself to be a man of 'character and culture too' (*The Complete Prose Works of Matthew Arnold*, ed. R. H. Super (10 vols., Ann Arbor, 1960–74), vol. ii, p. 323; vol. v, pp. 101, 128–9; vol. vi, p. 126). In 1844, encouraged by the break-up of the Established Church in Scotland over the issue of Erastianism, Miall created the British Anti-State Church Association, renamed in 1853 the Society for the Liberation of Religion from State Control. The Liberation Society drew upon all those with a grudge against the Established Church – militant Dissenters, Chartists, political reformers and Free Traders – but, for Miall, the focus of all this radical activity remained the aim of Church disestablishment. The political nature of his ensuing activities, as Liberation Society leaders toured Britain, strengthened the division between and within the various forms of Dissent, splitting the radicals from the more conservatively inclined who disavowed political agitation. Opposing such sectarian or separatist thinking Miall embraced secular means to secure religious ends. He first stood for Parliament in 1845 and was finally elected M.P. for Rochdale in 1852.

The revelation of Dissent's numerical strength in the 1851 Religious Census encouraged the growth of the Liberation Society into the most powerful political pressure group of the 1860s. Yet, when Miall retired from Parliament in 1874, his ultimate objective was no nearer realization than it had been in the 1840s. Many specific Dissenting grievances had been removed – these had been the price exacted for support for Liberalism – but ultimately Miall had lost. Between 1871 and 1873 he unsuccessfully introduced three disestablishment motions in Parliament. Although his society had provided a local platform and organization for Liberalism, Nonconformists had not managed to gain control of the Liberal Party. Moreover Miall's much-criticized readiness to embrace secular means in pursuit of his religious programme was perhaps the seed of failure for his great ambition, for the younger men whom he had stirred came to see social and political reforms as ends in themselves.

The census suggestions of working-class religious alienation came as no surprise to a Dissenter like Miall. He had invited the expression of working-class opinion in the letter page of the *Nonconformist* and gave a course of lectures at the City of London Literary Institute examining the problem. The following extracts come from the volume subsequently prepared for publication as *The British Churches in Relation to the British People*. Miall did not confine himself to berating the Established Church. His genuinely radical temperament, nurtured in the Congregational tradition of independence, led him to deplore the social stratification and loss of spiritually revolutionary zeal which had characterized the development of the Dissenting churches. Despite the Dissenting habit of preaching without text or notes Miall nevertheless detected the growth of an 'etiquette of preaching' which had created its own conventions, impenetrable to the uninitiated.

The distance separating Miall's response to a religion failing in its responsibilities from that of the Tractarians' can be estimated at this point. Miall and Keble offer us two strongly contrasted 'handmaids of Religion', Trade and Poetry: the former characterized by the possibilities it affords for 'pushing the spirit of the gospel into notice', the latter by its habit of delivering truth by means of indirection and reserve. Two almost mutually incomprehensible modes of life are also sharply illuminated by this contrast. Miall's panegyric upon the nobility and enormous responsibilities of trade, drawn from close knowledge of northern towns and the great Nonconformist businessmen with whom he became associated, is reminiscent of Elizabeth Gaskell's Dissenting character Mrs Thornton, encouraging her aspiring industrialist son with the text, 'Her merchants be like princes' (*North and South* (1855), ch. 50). To men like Keble, bred in the conservative traditions of the landed southern squirearchy, both pictures would have seemed equally strange and remote. Miall's positive exploration of the trade metaphor is striking because it challenges the frequent pictures of Dissent as 'nothing more than low-pitched gables up dingy streets, sleek grocers, sponging preachers, and hypocritical jargon' (George Eliot, *Adam Bede* (1858), ch. 3). With the first of these phrases in mind, and recollecting constant jibes about mean Dissenting architecture, it is interesting to watch Miall's refusal to fall back on easy puritan anti-aestheticism (p. 211).

Miall's criticisms of contemporary religious life have much in common with those of less sympathetic commentators. Compare, for instance, his complaints about foreign missions with Carlyle, 'Occasional Discourse on the Nigger Question', *Fraser's Town and Country Magazine*, 40 (1849), 670–9; or Dickens, *Bleak House* (1852). Indeed his outbursts over the degradations of poverty and the complacency of the religious sects bear notable similarity to the rhetorical oratory of Carlyle, Dickens or Kingsley. The *Nonconformist*, it is worth remembering, carried considered reviews of contemporary fiction. The way in which Miall can be seen appropriating and reshaping the distinctive metaphors of Carlyle, e.g. endemic disease, both physical and moral, slowly permeating all levels of society (below, p. 101), and the vision of a society subjugated to the compulsive tyranny of the steam-engine trade spirit (below, p. 100) bears comparison with Dickens. The second passage particularly repays attention. Miall employs the devices to which Carlyle and Dickens have accustomed us: cumulative phrases, suggestion rather than analysis, calculated alterations of rhythm, catalogues to suggest a meaningless confusion of values, but here the didactic purpose is always foremost. Miall repeatedly intervenes in the image he is creating to offer us points for contemplation, to ensure that we have taken the true implications from his analogy. Despite his clear creative energy and declamatory, not to say denunciatory verve, Miall's integrity, his subordination of artistry to message, emerge as he sacrifices dramatic impetus to a concept of 'fairness'.

Readers will note that I have frequently footnoted Biblical quotations to draw attention to the way in which Miall's criticism of his society was deeply rooted in Scriptural vision. It is not, in his case, over-familiar, casual use of jargon, denounced alike by Dickens in his portrait of Chadband and by the Tractarians, but a proof that he was constantly mindful of how relevant Christ's or His disciples' examples and searching questions were to his own times.

The Aristocratic sentiment

It is not without a sense of pain that I am obliged, in passing on to an examination of the state of the British Churches, in reference to this matter, to furnish a melancholy contrast to what expectation might have pictured. The aristocratic sentiment has taken such hold upon them, has diffused itself so generally through them, and has modified to such a wide extent their opinions, habits, and practices, that illustrations of its presence and its power are difficult of selection simply because they are everywhere to be met with. All denominations are affected – some, perhaps, more than others – none so little as not to detract from their influence and impede their usefulness. Allowing, as we are bound to do, for considerable differences of degree in the culpability of different churches, it may be stated roughly, that between the numerous and various associated bodies of Christian disciples, and worldly society at large, there is very little distinction visible in reference to this evil. The same pride of class, the same exclusiveness, the same deference to rank and wealth, the same depreciating view of poverty, the same struggle to keep up appearances, the same notions of respectability, the same frigid reserve on the one hand, and shrinking timidity on the other, proceeding from the same cause, and that cause having nothing whatever moral in its character, are to be found inside, as outside, the Christian Churches of our land. There is a slight modification of the aristocratic sentiment by religious sympathies, of course – more marked, however, in individual cases than in organized communities – and the type of the mischief may be milder – but, substantially, the same features of it are plainly discernible in the Church as in the world. And, alas! it touches and taints well-nigh everything that can be affected by it – opinion, feeling, intercourse, worship, work. It would almost seem to have been naturalized amongst us, and really to be considered part and parcel of Christianity. It is, indeed, a national characteristic – the formation and growth of a long series of generations – and so deeply inwrought is it into our social structure, so insidiously does it insinuate itself into our judgements, and so tenaciously cling to our feelings, that we find it difficult to admit either the necessity or the wisdom of utterly eradicating it. And yet it is in itself as absurd, it is in its effects as pernicious, as the prejudice against colour in the United States of America, which we who have it not are at a loss to conceive how Christian men can entertain.[1] Nay! this is not the whole, nor the worst. Men of eminence amongst us, ministers of the gospel, which was to be preached to the poor, exponents of God's word, to whom Churches have given wistful and reverential heed, losing sight of the apostolic declaration, that 'God hath chosen the foolish things of the world to confound the wise – and God hath chosen the weak things of the world to confound things that are mighty – and base things of the world, and things which are despised, hath God chosen, and things which are not, to bring to naught things that are'[a] – have seriously contended for the necessity of adopting means for raising the respectability of evangelical bodies, and thus adapting them to the taste of the higher classes of society. Let me not, however, in these strictures, be misunderstood. I am aware that there has lately sprung up a cant on this subject, against which the thoughtful will do well to be upon their guard. The many and serious evils resulting from the action of the aristocratic sentiment in the British Churches, have provoked in some minds a re-action running to the opposite extreme, and a spurious and mawkish sentimentalism has sought to elevate poverty to a virtue, and to insist upon the rights of toiling and hard-handed industry so exclusively, as to suggest the idea that no other rights exist. We must not, however, allow ourselves to forget that God's good tidings by his Son are for the rich as well as the poor – the cultivated as well as the unlettered – the refined as well as the rude – and that in the external form of their promulgation, adaptation to habits, taste, and modes of mental intercourse, is as necessary for the one class as for the other. That which appears to me to merit

[a] I Corinthians 1:27–8.

severest censure is, the strong disposition evinced, and sometimes justified, to treat as unbecoming, and even as a desecration of revealed truth, all methods of exhibiting and enforcing it which are not approved of by those who call themselves the respectable section of society, and the fear seemingly entertained by some who ought to know better, that there is little hope of progress for Truth, until she is dressed in fashionable attire. 'To the weak, I became as weak,' says the Apostle Paul, 'that I might win some'[a] – but, surely, to the weak only. To those who move in the more refined and elevated circles, refinement in the outer habiliments of the gospel may be fittingly and wisely attended to – but it would appear to be lost sight of that that which renders it commendable, in regard to spiritual agency, is *adaptation* to the wants of an important class; and that the desire to raise the entire system of means up to the highest standard of worldly taste, is open to the reproving inquiries of Paul, 'If the whole body were an eye, where were the hearing? If the whole were hearing, where were the smelling? And if they were all one member, where were the body?'[b] . . .

Scarcely less fertile of illustration are the *enterprises* of the British Churches – the general character of their plans of usefulness. Foreign missions, which at first blush might seem to represent a noble exception, present such an exception only as confirms the rule. Extreme distance conceals the vulgarity of human wretchedness, and invests every effort to meet and relieve it with a tinted atmosphere of romance. Hence many a man who yearns for the conversion of the heathen at the antipodes, and subscribes liberally to send the gospel amongst them, evinces little or no compassion for the scarcely less degraded heathen at home. Foreign missions have passed through the stage of contempt, and have even reached that of fashionable patronage. Bishops and nobles, the wealthy and the wise, merchants and mariners, almost all classes have united their testimony in favour of religious enterprise in this direction – and not to be interested in it, is, in effect, to declare the good opinion of the world a matter of indifference. But exceptions there are, although this be not one, and we have reason to be grateful that they are fast multiplying. Let me mention, as the most striking of them, and as destined apparently to be amongst the most useful – city missions, ragged schools, and ragged kirks.[2] Perhaps, indeed, we should be justified in adding – that in no department of religious manifestation has the tide of improvement set in with greater force.

[a] I Corinthians 9:22. [b] I Corinthians 12:17–19.

Still, I apprehend, we are bound to confess that the leading characteristics of modern spiritual enterprise exhibit largely the injurious operation of the aristocratic sentiment. The sphere of them has been predominantly bounded by the outermost limits of the middle classes – the machinery they have brought into play, such as is adapted to tell only within those limits – and the standard of success, one which takes worldly respectability fully into account. Certainly the Churches have not so systematically 'gone out into the highways and hedges,'[a] bearing with them the message of salvation, as to warrant us in referring to it as their habitual practice. On the contrary, in large towns – for the description is not so applicable to the rural districts – the supply of direct religious means is regulated, not by the wants of the population, but by prospects of pecuniary support. The thriving neighbourhood attracts all denominations; the poor are comparatively overlooked. . . . In regard to the use of the press, as an instrument of religious instruction and impression, we have exhibited the same preference of quality over numbers. Had we conjoined the wisdom of the serpent with the harmlessness of the dove,[b] we should have been to the full as anxious to extend the range of our Christian literature as to heighten its tone; but our efforts at adaptation have pretty uniformly had a look upwards. I acknowledge, not only the existence, but the usefulness of the Religious Tract Society.[3] But what is this amongst so many?[c] The utmost effected, or even attempted, by this and similar agency, amounts to but little more than a bare confession of our responsibility in the matter, and, as compared with what is done to make the press available for the service of the middle classes, proves that enterprise seldom looks beneath them. Had it done so, and done so with sagacity as well as determination, the British Churches would not have left till now to individual zeal, all effort to abolish the monopoly of printing the sacred Scriptures[4] a restriction upon the liberty of the subject, and a practical impediment in the way of divine knowledge, which would never have been tolerated but for the sanction given to it by the ruling class of the community. Had it done so, it would have rung remonstrance in the ears of the legislature against the continuance of taxes on knowledge,[5] the repressive influence of which upon popular literature, spiritual as well as secular, useful as well as pernicious, it is impossible fairly to estimate until they have been wholly removed. Had it done so, the masses of our countrymen

[a] Luke 14:23. [b] Matthew 10:16. [c] Adapted from John 6:9.

would not have been so long neglected, or when specifically addressed, addressed in a style so utterly unsuited to attract their interest, or to lay hold upon their sympathy – nor should we have been compelled to deplore, as now we must, that the children of this world, wiser in their generation than the children of light,[a] have been beforehand with us, and have sown a crop of pernicious sentiments, and infidel opinions, which the best directed efforts of all the Churches during the next quarter of a century, will hardly succeed in rooting out of the soil. The state of things to which I have now adverted appears to my mind evidence but too decisive that the religious enterprise of the British Churches has not been deeply interested in seeking the welfare of the children of toil or the victims of indigence. It has spent its strength chiefly upon the classes above them, seemingly satisfied with allowing them permission to pick up 'the crumbs which fall from the master's table.'[b] The insidious power of the aristocratic sentiment has left its traces upon most of the Churches' attempts to evangelize the country, and to win the heart for God.

As might have been anticipated, *practice* follows in the same track as project; and what the Churches do, bears a close resemblance in character to what they plan. I profess here, as, indeed, throughout, to describe only what is general. Exceptions, and, in this instance, large ones, I cheerfully admit. But I am bound to say, that in watching the operations of our religious institutions, whenever I have endeavoured to put myself in the position of the humbler classes, and have asked myself, 'What is there here to interest such?' I have been at a loss for a reply. I do not arraign architectural magnificence – we cannot, indeed, boast much of it outside of the Establishment – for in continental countries I am not aware that it discourages the humblest worshipper. But here, in Great Britain, we carry our class distinctions into the house of God, whether the edifice be a splendid monument of art, or whether it be nothing superior to a barn. The poor man is made to feel that he is a poor man, the rich is reminded that he is rich, in the great majority of our churches and chapels. The square pew, carpeted, perhaps, and curtained, the graduated scale of other pews, the free-sittings, if there are any, keep up the separation between class and class; and even where the meanly-clad are not conscious of intrusion, as is sometimes painfully the case, the arrangements are generally such as to preclude in their bosoms any momentary feeling of essential

[a] Luke 16:8. [b] Matthew 15:27.

equality. We have no negro pews, for we have no prejudice against colour – but we have distinct places for the pennyless, for we have a morbid horror of poverty. Into a temple of worship thus mapped out for varying grades of worshippers, in which the lowly and the unfortunate are forbidden to lose sight of their worldly circumstances, some such, spite of all discouragements, find their way. In the singing, it may be, they can join, and mingle their voices and their sympathies with those around them – unless, indeed, the more respectable tenants of the pews, deeming it ill-bred to let themselves be heard, leave the psalmody to the Sunday-school children, and the vulgar. Possibly, their emotions may be elicited by prayer – seldom, we should think, by the discourse. It may be excellent, persuasive, pungent – but, in multitudes of cases, it will also be cast in a mould which none but the educated can appreciate. Let it not be said that this is owing exclusively to their ignorance. 'The common people heard' our Lord 'gladly'[a] – the early reformers won their way to the inmost hearts of the lowliest of men – and even those who in our day are judged to be too uncultured to profit by the ministry of God's word from the pulpit, are sufficiently intelligent to derive interest from a public political meeting, to appreciate the points of a speech from the hustings, and to feel the force of an argument when put to them in private. No! it is not altogether ignorance which prevents them from following the generality of preachers. It is the entire absence of coloquialism from the discourse – an absence imposed upon the speaker by that sense of propriety which the aristocratic sentiment engenders. The etiquette of preaching prescribes an exclusively didactic style – and an address, the aim of which is to save souls, is supposed to approximate towards perfection, in proportion as it is free from conversational blemishes and inaccuracies, satisfies a fastidious and classical taste, and flows on in one unbroken stream from its commencement to its close. The consequence is, that whilst some few are pleased, and, perhaps, profited, the mass remain utterly untouched. Oh! for some revolution to break down for ever, and scatter to the four winds of heaven, our pulpit formulas and proprieties, and leave men at liberty to discourse on the sublime verities of the Christian faith, with the same freedom, variety, and naturalness, with which they would treat other subjects in other places! . . .

The trade spirit

One of the radical mistakes which men have been prone to make respecting Christianity is the idea that it claims so large a propor-

[a] Mark 12:37.

tion of our being for the things of eternity, as to leave us comparatively little for the things of time – as though what is given to *it* must needs be abstracted from something else. They seldom commit this error in regard to other objects. This individual may identify his life with military glory – that, with the sway of kingdoms – a third, with intellectual pre-eminence – a fourth, with scientific discovery. All are known to be filled with a dominant purpose not yet realized – to 'live and move and have their being'[a] in it – to have given themselves up, indeed, to an imaginary future. And yet no one sees in this fact a necessary withdrawal of their energies from present engagements. The soldier whose dream is of universal conquest and world-wide fame, is not deemed to be thereby incapacitated from intense study of whatever will practically fit him for his work. The ruler who aspires to dominion over his fellow-men, however intent upon the yet distant object, is stimulated to give, rather than precluded from giving, the most earnest attention to immediate duties; and whether he observes human nature in its individual manifestations, or in its national idiosyncrasies – whether he turns over the leaves of history, or ponders the meaning of those pages which passing life presents to his notice – he flings, not less, but more energy into his daily pursuits, in consequence of his self-consecration to a governing idea. Christianity opens up to us the glorious prospect of a future state of entire sympathy, intellectual and moral, with the happy God – a state of conscious, perfect, unchangeable, unending oneness of will with him – an eternal harmony of our being with his character, his expressions of it, and his purposes. Why should the resignation of our entire life to the expectation thus excited, unfit us for taking a deep interest in the affairs of time? They are not contrary the one to the other. Nay – the things of the present exist but with a view to the future. Everything we have to do here, is part of the process necessary to the full realization of the hereafter. Christianity gives us another meaning during our sojourn on earth – not another sphere. It elevates, by imparting a moral to, every thing connected with our passage through life – it destroys nothing whatever but sin. The pursuits of trade, for example, are not only not inconsistent with the absorption of our whole being by Christianity, but if trade is the path appointed for us to travel along through our career of probation, our interest and activity in it will be in proportion to

[a] Acts 17:28.

our self surrender to the gospel of salvation. Life in the end will put life in the means.

About to enter upon an examination of the depraving influence of the trade spirit upon religious life in the British Churches, I deem it expedient, in order to prevent any misapprehension of my object, to state, as clearly as I am able, the views I hold on the relationship of trade to religion. Trade, then – employing the term in the broadest sense of which it is susceptible – is not only not antagonistic in its own nature to the main object of Christianity, but is eminently auxiliary to it. It constitutes one of the principal schools, ordained by the wisdom of Providence, for eliciting, training, exercising, and maturing, the spiritual principle implanted in the heart of man by the gospel. It opens to us one of the most accessible, and one of the largest spheres in which to develop the new and heaven-born character. Affectionate sympathy with truth, rightness, temperance, benevolence, forbearance, meekness – in a word, with all the moral attributes the love of which divine revelation is adapted to inspire and nourish – may here find ample scope for exerting, proving, and invigorating its strength. Trade multiplies our relations with our fellow-men. It puts us into close contact with others, at innumerable points. It furnishes us with a quick succession and an endless variety of occasions for the action of the governing principle begotten in our souls. It shifts our position with every passing hour, calling incessantly for new manifestations of the spiritual life, correspondent with every change. The scenes into which it introduces us, and in which it requires us to take a part, rapidly vary, and call out, consequently, a vigilance of spirit, a promptitude of judgement, and a repeated reference to first principles, not needed elsewhere. It increases almost indefinitely the number of ties by which man is linked to man, and through which mind may transmit influence to mind. It creates countless grades of mutual dependence, and necessitates mutual trust in all its stages. It places our earthly lot so far within our own reach as to hold out an almost certain reward to diligence and frugality – and yet its issues are so far beyond our individual control, and its vicissitudes so incapable of being accurately foreseen, as to throw us most sensibly upon the overruling providence of God. It accustoms us to subordination – for 'method,' as is proverbial, 'is the soul of business.' It raises us to posts of responsibility and government – for few men can prosecute trade through a lifetime without occupying, occasionally or statedly, a position of authority. It offers all kinds of facilities for pushing the spirit of the gospel into notice – an intricate and all-pervading ramification of channels, along which to propel the waters of eternal life. It gives us, at one and the same time, scope, means, opportunities, and motives, for the lively exemplification of every characteristic of the spiritual man. Suppose trade to be annihilated, and every individual of our teeming population sustained by simple labour upon his own spot of land – and the monotony of social life, so far from favouring the development of Christian virtues, would necessarily impart to them very much of its own insipidity and listlessness. I can scarcely conceive of a high cultivation of spiritual life in this world – a rich growth of Christian character – an intelligent manhood of religion in the soul – save by means and arrangements partaking very closely of the nature of trade. If our present state of existence is emphatically one of education – if what we are to be hereafter, in mind, morals, and spirit, is to result from what we are now – I can imagine no arrangement of such exquisite contrivance for subjecting all our powers to salutary discipline, for breathing our young capabilities, and giving to right principles such meet and daily exercise, as that which passes under the generic name of trade. It is as much God's ordination as is the culture of the soil. It bears upon it the unequivocal marks of his wisdom and his benevolence. Intrinsically, and in its own nature, it is the handmaid of Christianity; a humble but useful helpmate to religion – smiled upon by it, and greatly promotive of it.

It will be manifest, however, even to momentary reflection, that trade can only be ancillary to spiritual life, when made subordinate to a dominant spiritual purpose. Its use to us, religiously, depends upon the end to which we are determined to turn it to account. It may be entered upon as a sphere for the discipline of character, or as one for the attainment of a much lower order of gratification. It is quite possible to traverse it – in company, too, with moral principles of a high grade – without the remotest moral intention. It displays numberless attractions to men, viewed simply in their relation to the present life. It is occupation – and that alone is desirable to active and energetic spirits. The variety of it is pleasing. The excitement it quickens soon becomes grateful – in many cases, necessary. The facilities it furnishes for the indulgence of social tendencies are alluring. It stimulates intelligence – gives scope for the exercise of ingenuity, contrivance, forethought, calculation. It is an excellent stage for the observation of human nature. To many it is a pastime of the graver sort. To most it is a necessity, between which and ruin there is no other alternative. It is the condition exacted from the large proportion of our fellow-countrymen for their livelihood – it is the only means to a numerous class of compassing the gratification of their passions and their tastes. Trade, resorted to for any of these purposes exclusively, is an impediment to spiritual life. Whether the end be bare subsistence, decent comfort, extravagant display, pleasurable excitement, or the love of money, there is the same absence of Christian morality from it. The object aimed at falls short of spiritual good – is acquisition, not development – the gain of somewhat external to us, not the ripening of somewhat inherent in us – and, inasmuch as the means to that object are in no sense religious, all activity, all self-sacrifice, all expenditure of our powers, in that direction, must be set down, in relation to the divine life, as constituting so much dead loss. And this is what I mean by the trade spirit. The phrase, in the sense I attach to it, does not necessarily imply a reigning desire of wealth, a hard-hearted, mean-spirited, all-grasping cupidity, although it comprehends them. But under this term I wish to expose and condemn, as fatally suppressive of religious vitality, the disposition to pursue trade with an exclusive, or even a predominant view to the worldly advantage to be got by it – making it its own end, or at least proposing in it something distinct and apart from, and infinitely inferior to, the nourishment of our sympathies with God and his government. I believe this to be the greatest and most pernicious practical error of the present day. Partly from misapprehension, partly from habit, and partly from motives which conscience must condemn, the sphere of trade is frequented by Christian men, as one in which they are to serve themselves mainly, and their Divine Master incidentally only, and by the way. This is supposed to be their own ground, on which, if the character exemplified must be in some measure accordant with their spiritual profession, the end pursued is chiefly their own temporal good. They seem to have no notion that business is allotted to them as one of the means of grace, and one that might be rendered most efficient. At least, they do not resort to it as such. They speak of it sometimes as a hindrance, sometimes as a snare – often as a trying necessity – occasionally as an instrument of gratification – never, hardly, as a school for the education of their spiritual nature. They can understand communion with God in direct religious exercises, in the sanctuary, in the outspread works of his hands – but not in trade. They go to the house of God to seek him there – to their factories, counting-houses, and shops, they repair for no such purpose. In this direction, few, indeed, look for him – some, it is to be feared, do not even take him there. Much of what they know of him they forget within these precincts of secular engagement – to learn more of him in such places, they do not expect. Their Christianity is rather of the nature of a branch of occupation, than a principle of life and action. They may be honest – they may be diligent – they may be truthful – they may be frugal – they may economize their time – but their purpose in business is distinct from their purpose in the place of worship. Here it is specially their own – there it is specially God's. Hence the double pursuit is sometimes bemoaned as if antagonistic; whereas the only thing wanting in order to render their trade a means to their religion, is their own determination to make it so. Business as well as nature yields fruits after the kind of seed we sow. The results we reap will correspond with the objects we desire. Things are secular or spiritual as we make them such. The difference originates in our own intention.

Religious life in this country is peculiarly liable to the unfriendly action upon it of the trade spirit. Without imputing to the British people generally a more selfish or sordid spirit than may be found elsewhere, there can be no doubt that devotion to the pursuits of trade is our national characteristic. Gain, in one shape or another, is 'the great goddess' most assiduously worshipped in these realms. Business is everything with us – the power to which all others are secondary. The phenomenon may, perhaps, be fairly accounted for. Something may be set down to the score of race – something to climate – something to geographical position. Our political history may have done much to mould our character into the form it has taken – possibly our religious faith may have exerted some influence upon it. But the intensity of the trade spirit has, I think, been much increased by an artificial pressure upon its energies – and, just as population in the presence of poverty multiplies in a higher ratio than in the enjoyment of ease and abundance, so, I apprehend, restrictions of one sort and another upon our industrial commercial energies, have forced them to re-act with unnatural vigour. For many years a monopoly of food[6] – to this day an enormous weight of taxation, and a population expanding so rapidly as to feel the terrible inconveniences resulting to them from the law of primogeniture and entail[7] – the land, as it were, too strait for its inhabitants,[a] and every profession, every trade, every industrial pursuit overcrowded with hands – the sharpest competition, consequently, in every branch of employment, and the absolute necessity,

[a] Adapted from II Kings 6:2.

in order to moderate success, of great diligence, promptitude, and, in some cases, pushing – the increased value, in such a struggle for a livelihood, of minutes and of pence, and the absorption of undivided attention by details, by means of which only can a man hope to realize a tolerable income – these are causes in daily operation well calculated to stimulate into excessive development the trade spirit. And, certainly, it has been raised to a pitch which it is scarcely possible to sustain without great moral deterioration. The national wear and tear under this high-pressure system of business is frightful. As a people, it is clear we are living too fast. Ours is the rush of railway life. We see nothing by the way. Health, comfort, affections, intellectual culture, reflection, devotion, – they scarcely fill a more important space in our plans, scarcely detain our attention longer, than the trees and churches, the homesteads and meadows, which seem to dance past us as we gaze through the window of a carriage in an 'express train.' And we are always on the line. True! we stop at appointed stations – most of which, however, are simply for convenience, not for refreshment. We are whirled along from early youth in most cases to the hour of death, with no other pause or break than the weariness of exhausted nature absolutely requires. The march of trade is like the irresistible career of a locomotive – and even they who most delight in rapid movement are compelled to ask themselves, at times, 'Can such speed as this be safe?'

It must in fairness be admitted, I think, that the religious life involved in this incessant whirl and scamble, has done something to check the progression of the evil. . . .

Social and political hindrances to the success of the churches

There lies at the bottom of society in this country, and especially in the metropolis and the more populous towns, a thick sediment of physical destitution, which it is morally impossible for the light of Christianity to penetrate and purify. Far be it from my thoughts to limit the power of the grace of God. I rejoice in the belief that with him 'all things are possible.'[a] But it does not become us to overlook the general laws by which he regulates the proceedings of his remedial economy – and foremost amongst those laws we find a strict adaptation of means to ends. Individual and isolated instances

[a] Matthew 19:26.

may be discovered of the triumph of the divine message in the soul of man, even where it has had to encounter the disadvantage of the most squalid poverty. But the few exceptions only serve to prove the rule. It may be safely laid down that there are positions of physical depression and degradation which disqualify human nature for the appreciation of the gospel. Men exiled by want from the sympathy, and even notice, of the great mass of their fellows – driven to subsist precariously and scantily on garbage – clothed in rags, loathsome both to sight and smell – preyed upon by vermin – herding for shelter in dark, damp cellars, or dilapidated and filthy garrets, or, still worse, packed nightly, in nakedness, body to body, along the noisome dormitories of cheap lodging-houses – to whom the next wretched meal is always an uncertainty – in whom a sense of cleanliness can scarcely ever, by any chance, have been realized – whose mode of life precludes order, comfort, prudence, reflection – who live half their time in an atmosphere of poison – who cannot, if they would, escape close and familiar contact with obscenity and vice – devoid of all moral motive, because divorced from hope, and denuded of self-respect – men in this frightful abyss are, as a class, as much below the immediate reach of the gospel, as the better tended cattle that are driven to the shambles. And to the shame of philanthropy in our land be it spoken, these festering heaps of misery have gone on until just lately, increasing in bulk, unnoticed by society, until they comprehend hundreds of thousands of individuals. Their numbers alone might well alarm us – but there is something more appalling than their numbers. Out of this slimy bed of physical destitution rises perpetually a pestiferous moral exhalation dangerous to all other classes of society – most dangerous to those immediately contiguous to it. Swarms of thieves, trained from infancy to their business of plunder, and of prostitutes turned nightly into our thoroughfares to ply their deadly seduction, carry with them the taint of demoralization into all other sections of the social body. That physical wretchedness which we have selfishly allowed to accumulate, passing by it, like the Levite, on the other side of the road,[a] avenges itself upon our supineness and neglect, by permeating the entire mass of uplying humanity with a moral typhus, perilous to every family in the land, and carrying into not a few the germ of death.

What can Christianity do with this terrific mass of rottenness? Ragged schools and ragged kirks are admirable institutions in their way – but alone they will never Christianize this region of the shadow

[a] Luke 10:32.

of death. Most efficient they are as pioneers of benevolence into the heart of this matted jungle of poverty, ignorance, vice, and crime – but they are pioneers only. They may heroically carry religious truth into the haunts of desperation – but religious truth cannot well abide there. The spiritual man must be, in some measure, at least, contemplative, and contemplation asks privacy – but with the class to which we refer there is scarcely a possibility of retirement. In order to [develop] religious emotions there must be some maintenance of self-respect – but self-respect cannot linger amidst the dirt, brutality, and hopelessness, the vicious and polluting sights and sounds of scenes like these. The culture of piety requires a frequent reference of the mind and heart to God, in his works and word – but here almost all the facts met with are embodiments, not of the divine, but the human, and radiate, not purity, but corruption. Where is the city missionary who has not felt this? What single instance of the power of revealed truth has he met with in these outcast parts, that has not suggested to him the necessity, in order to the completion of its triumph, of rescuing the subject of it, if possible, from the appalling depths, and insurmountable disadvantages, of his social position? . . .

I come now to political religionism – or, in other words, that state of sentiment in reference to Christianity, its object, spirit, and means, created and fostered by State interference with its institutions and operations. Many of my readers may wonder that this question was not once adverted to in my examination and exposure of the mischievous sentiments which mingle with and enervate the religion of the British Churches. The truth is, I cannot recognize civil establishments of Christianity as organizations for the extension of Christ's kingdom, in any sense. They are not Churches – they are merely political arrangements for the real, or ostensible, attainment of spiritual objects. They are machinery invented, constructed, put in motion, and presided over by 'the powers that be,'[a] professedly for imparting religious instruction, and dispensing gospel ordinances, to all the subjects of the empire – but they want all the characteristics of the machinery appointed by God. They comprehend all the inhabitants of the land without distinction of character. They may be devoid of a single member whose heart is in living sympathy with God, as mirrored in the person and life of his Son, without losing one essential feature of their constitution. They are not an association, but an aggregation merely – for the bond of their union is only nominal.

[a] Romans 13:1.

8. *The British Churches*

We have already cordially admitted that there are many ministers in the Church Establishment in England whose religious character ranks deservedly high. But of three-fourths of them it may be remarked, without the smallest breach of charity, that they are practically ignorant of the great spiritual principles of the gospel, the purifying power of which they have never felt, nor even professed to feel. The office they sustain allies them with the aristocracy, and a benefice ensures to them, in most cases, a certain, and, in not a few, an ample income. The Establishment south of the Tweed has its prizes to attract, and its honours to distribute amongst the sons of our nobility and gentry. Moved by impulses of the most worldy kind, these flock to our universities to prepare themselves for 'holy orders'. The training they undergo is in perfect keeping with the main object they have in view. Theology is the last thing to which their attention is directed – spiritual religion, in any sense worthy of the name, almost the only influence with which they never come in contact. Oxford and Cambridge are notorious as centres of abandoned profligacy.[8] Immorality walks their streets unabashed, and fills the surrounding villages with victims, whose self-respect is destroyed, and whose reputation is for ever blasted. In these places human depravity, heaped up in masses, reeks out its most offensive exhalations. From these schools of corruption go forth, year by year, the legally authorized expositors of Christianity, carrying with them, for the most part, habits imbued to the core with worldliness, and understandings and hearts alike ignorant of 'the things which pertain to life and godliness.'[a] What is the general consequence? The flocks over whom they preside learn nothing from their lips of 'the unsearchable riches of Christ,'[b] see nothing in their lives illustrative of 'the beauties of holiness.'[c] They go through their dull routine of formality, where necessary, in person – where practicable, by proxy, and for the rest, they are – gentlemen. Can it be wondered at that amongst such men, filling such a position, the worst absurdities of priestism should find high and extensive favour? Could they be otherwise than predisposed to take the *virus*, when all their previous practices and habits had been of a character to virtually reduce religion to outward rites, priestly manipulations, and senseless dogmas? Yet these men, like a tissue of net-work, overspread the land from end to end, and, in the dread name of Him whose authority they so little revere, assume to themselves an exclusive right to be regarded as 'the ministers of Jesus Christ'.[d]

[a] II Peter 1:3. [b] Ephesians 3:8. [c] Psalms 110:3. [d] I Corinthians 4:1.

Such a state of things, even if it went no further, places in the way of the British Churches a fearful impediment to the successful prosecution of their spiritual enterprise. It is the substitution, on a national scale, of a name for a reality – a formal pretence for a living power. But the evil does not rest here. This legalized ecclesiasticism, claiming exclusive right to dispense God's gospel to the people of these realms, and casting contempt upon all unauthorized efforts, puts itself into jealous and active antagonism to the Christian zeal which sends forth into our neglected towns, and amongst our stolid peasantry, labourers of various denominations, for the purpose of rescuing immortal souls from a cruel and fatal bondage. Every one familiarly acquainted with our rural districts can bear witness to facts in proof of this position. Go into almost any village in the empire, and set yourself down there to win souls to Christ, and your bitterest foe, your most energetic and untiring opponent, will prove to be the clergyman – the State-appointed minister of Jesus Christ. The very first symptoms of spiritual life which show themselves among his parishioners – social meetings for prayer, anxious inquiries for the way of salvation, eager attention to the proclamations of the gospel – will attract his vigilant notice, and provoke his severest censure. The thing is so common, and has been so from time immemorial, as to cease to excite surprise. Would you stir up in men's minds serious concern respecting their highest interests, the parish 'priest' will be sure to cross your path at every step. Gather around you the children of the poor, to instil into their young and susceptible hearts the truths of the gospel, and instantly, their parents are threatened with a forfeiture of all claims upon parochial charity. Circulate from house to house plain, pungent, religious tracts, and in your second or third visit you will learn that the vicar has forbidden their reception. Assemble a few men and women 'perishing for lack of knowledge,'[a] that you may preach to them the message of reconciliation, and ten to one you will be informed, in the course of a few weeks, that the occupant of the house in which you laboured has been served with a notice to quit. It matters nothing that your efforts are free from all tinge of sectarianism – they are regarded as intrusive, irregular, and mischievous. How many villages are there in this country in which, through clerical influence, it is impossible to hire a room, within the narrow walls of which to proclaim to rustic ignorance the tidings of eternal life! How many more in which, from the same cause, misrepresentation,

[a] Hosea 4:6.

intimidation, and oppressive power, are brought to bear upon miserable and helpless dependents, to scare them beyond the reach of the gladsome sound of mercy! How many millions of souls, hemmed in on all sides by this worldly system of religion, cry aloud from the depths of their ruin to earnest Christians for help, whom, nevertheless, State churchism renders it impossible to reach! It was, doubtless, with this melancholy picture before his eyes, that Mr Binney so emphatically pronounced his opinion – an opinion fully justified, I think, by the facts of the case – that 'the Church of England destroys more souls than she saves.'[9]

Isaac Williams

(1802–1865)

9. *Tract No. 87 On Reserve in Communicating Religious Knowledge* (1840), pp. 40–9, 51–7, 58–61, 73–81

A brief summary of the major events of Williams's life suggests why he has been treated by many historians of the Oxford Movement as an also-ran. Even to himself this must sometimes have appeared true. He failed, after a nervous breakdown, to get the anticipated first at Oxford, he failed to achieve the coveted Oriel fellowship, failed to be elected as Professor of Poetry at Oxford, left Oxford in 1842, spent six years as Thomas Keble's curate before illness again struck and he spent the next seventeen years in semi-retirement from active clerical duties. There is, however, nothing of the valetudinarian in his writing: his autobiographical record of the Oxford Movement, compiled in 1851, reveals an astute and sometimes stern judge of human nature.

Tract No. 80 (1838), of which *Tract No. 87* (1840), represented below, is a continuation, was entitled *On Reserve in Communicating Religious Knowledge*. Designed to be read at Pusey's theological society it displays, as does *Tract No. 87*, something of the coterie's use of nicknames. Keble asked for the paper to be included in the Tract series and Newman, Williams claimed, suggested its title. 'I mention this circumstance', he wrote later, 'because some were more alarmed at the name than anything else . . . I afterwards wrote Tract No. 87 in explanation, which I believe quite did away with all reasonable objections excepting those of the Low Church.' (*The Autobiography of Isaac Williams*, ed. Sir G. Prevost (1892), pp. 90–2). In 1851 Williams was able to write thus calmly of the events of 1838 and 1840, but on the eve of *Tract No. 87*'s publication he had been less sanguine. 'The state of things reconciles me in some degree to my throwing stones at the Peculiars, but I do not think at all with comfort upon this Tract I have just finished and fear it may do more harm than good, and hope never again to touch on controversy' (quoted by O. Jones, *Isaac Williams and His Circle* (1971), p. 34).

This remark is illuminating, both of the times and of the person. Hindsight may suggest the inappropriateness of recommending the caution necessary to the early persecuted Church in a nineteenth-century Christian State, but this criticism misses the sense of urgency which compelled a man of Williams's quiet disposition to declare himself. Such a remark also helps to explain how Williams found himself at the heart of the contested election for the Oxford Professorship of Poetry to succeed his friend Keble in 1841. Whilst most accounts of the affair, in which the poet Williams, nominated by the fellows of Trinity, was opposed by Garbett, a critic, put forward by Brasenose, stress Pusey's role in fanning the flames by issuing a circular claiming that the contest was in essence a religious one, fewer allude to the candidate's own pertinacity. Williams finally decided to accept nomination when it was put to him by the brothers of another would-be candidate that he would undoubtedly be opposed as a Tractarian. 'On this threat', Williams replied, 'I cannot retire' (*Autobiography*, ed. Prevost, p. 138). Williams finally did retire after a comparison of promised votes revealed that he would lose honourably (921 for Garbett; 621 for Williams), but not before the undignified wrangle had ensured that for the next few years every Oxford appointment would be seen in terms of party warfare. Indeed Williams had regarded it as 'all right and natural' that the Low Church should be opposed to his candidature.

He had been born and bred a High Churchman, by disposition and training antipathetic to Evangelicalism and implacable against Roman Catholicism. An instinctive reserve, which was encouraged by his admiration for this aspect of John Keble's character, prompted his dislike of Evangelicalism's reliance on popular tools ('popular' is a pejorative adjective in Williams's vocabulary) and emotional witness, and a high respect for the Church Visible taught him to distrust the carelessness of divinely appointed order implied in the term 'Low Church'. The natural hauteur of the life-long High Churchman is detectable in the suspicion with which he treated the ex-Evangelical, Newman. Newman's restless temperament, fast-moving mind and lack of automatic obedience to the authority of bishops rendered his final conversion, or apostasy, explicable to Williams.

'Obedience' and 'religious caution', Williams told the clergy to whom this Tract was addressed, should characterize their teaching and practice. Almost alone amongst the leading Tractarians Williams recognized the dangers of publishing Froude's *Remains* (see Goode Endnote 1) and making public the excessive penances of his late friend. In William's emphasis upon humility, obedience and private acts of self-denial he comes nearest to Pusey. For both of them the theology of the Cross of Christ was a central truth: a personal espousal of the suffering and humiliation of Christ rather than the resting in Christ's labours which some Evangelicals preached.

Williams's style, as one might expect, provides no easy route to his personality. As a prolific devotional poet Williams never found a truly distinctive voice. The Tracts printed in this selection by Keble and Williams, both practising poets, touch on common ground, but Williams's is almost devoid of the metaphors and fanciful pursuit of images which characterize Keble's: those images he does use in the pursuit of his argument stand out because of their comparative rarity. Yet one has no hesitation in seconding Pusey's encomium: 'You can do what few can, and now still fewer – write' (Jones, *Isaac Williams and His Circle*, p. 145). As one might expect from Trinity College's Lecturer in Rhetoric, Williams's style provides a model of clarity in argument. Observe for instance the opening section of the extract where he swiftly summarizes the argument of the previous forty pages. Clarity is, in Williams's case, the fruit of conviction. Quiet but absolute confidence in his, or the Church's, teaching pervades the extract. 'Indeed', 'the fact is' and 'doubtless' are typical devices; words which can aim either to reinforce the truth of an argument's soundness, or to indicate that all possible objections have been considered and ultimately dismissed as worthless or beside the point. Opponents' arguments are frequently undermined by the phrase 'they are supposed to', implying either feckless lack of logic or sheer insubstantiality. This severe clarity carries a cutting edge only redeemed from the charge of sarcasm by the terrible seriousness underlying the argument (e.g. first paragraph, p. 116). Williams has no time to waste in playing cat-and-mouse games with adversaries when souls are at stake. The very real moral earnestness of the man is observable in the close attention he pays to those key texts and jargon which had become the small change of Evangelicalism and something of the poet emerges in his desire to re-invest language with its full original significance.

Part IV. The testimony of the ancient church

The practice and principle of the Antient Church perfectly analogous to our Lord's *example*

The evidence therefore of Catholic Antiquity affords the fullest and most complete confirmation, in every point of principle and detail, to all that has been said in the former treatise respecting the conduct of our Lord when seen in the flesh. And as our Lord has vouchsafed His presence to be with His Church, and the condition of that His presence is union and agreement; therefore in this concurrent acknowledgement to this principle we have again in the eyes of Faith our Lord's presence, His spiritual as before His bodily presence. There is a wonderful analogy in all God's dealings with mankind; in the conclusion of Part II. (Tract No. 80.) it was observed that a perfect parallel might be found throughout our moral nature, wherein He who is 'the light which lighteth every man that cometh into the world' discloses Himself. The same exact parallel may now be shown as He is revealed in His Church. (And that independently of the occasional testimony which the foregoing extracts bear to the conduct of our Lord having been as we describe, in the way of historical allusion to the fact.)

First of all, as our Lord in the flesh concealed His divinity and His miracles, so did the Disciplina Arcani[a] of the early Church do the same. It was that high doctrine that this system concealed, and the nature of those Sacraments, which are as it were a continued miracle in His Church.

Secondly, it appears that, as our Lord spake by parable things hard to be understood to the multitude, and explained them to His chosen disciples, so does the Catholic and Primitive mode of interpreting Scripture imply that all the Holy Word is like a parable, containing within it Divine wisdom, such as is disclosed to the faithful and good Christian. – That, if we are inclined to feel surprise at our Lord's not making Himself publicly known to His enemies in His power and Wisdom, the early Church suffered herself to be under the same obloquy and misinterpretation among heathens, who were singularly ignorant of the nature of Christian-

[a] The practice of the Early Church, when teaching pagans and catechumens, of holding back the most sacred rites and some doctrines until they had shown themselves ready to receive them.

ity. – That, as our Lord implied that there was great and increasing danger to those who knew His will, so, in a manner quite different to our modern notions, do the Ancients imply, that great danger is to be apprehended from knowing the Gospels, and not acting suitably to that knowledge. – That, as the Gospels indicate throughout that the benefit conferred on every individual was exactly according to his faith, to the effort he made to ask, or to touch the hem of our Saviour's garment, so do the Fathers also teach that exactly according to the advancement in holiness of life, or the effort to advance, does Christ disclose the Eternal Father. That, as our Lord continually pointed out to natural objects, as conveying spiritual instruction and the Wisdom of God, – the birds as teaching filial confidence, the lilies of the field humility, the seed sown the nature of the eternal kingdom, – so do the Fathers speak of nature itself being also but a clothing, by which the Almighty was concealed from us, and revealed to those who read His works with faith. Finally, it would appear that, as the mortification of the Cross, and keeping the commandments, was our Lord's teaching to all indiscriminately, and to those who were thus brought to Him that He made known His Divinity; so the object of the Disciplina Arcani was to effect this purpose, to procure a preparation of the heart previous to the imparting of the highest knowledge. That such is throughout the teaching of the Fathers, that the Doctrine of the cross is among them one of extensive meaning, containing both the humiliation of the natural man, and in conjunction with it the knowledge of our Lord's Divinity and Atonement.

Part V. The principle opposed to certain modern religious opinions

The nature of the objections which have been made

It is very evident that the mere mention of such a principle as this subject indicates would immediately be met with the very strongest objections, before it is at all considered what is really meant by it. For let it be only suggested that Holy Scripture observes a rule of reserve, it may be answered at once by the strong and distinct contradiction, that the very word *Revelation*, directly declares the contrary; for is it not the very purpose of Scripture to communicate knowledge, not to conceal it? Does not, it may be said, its very graciousness depend on this very circumstance, that it reveals God's goodness to His creatures, sitting in darkness and the shadow of death; as well might it be said that the very object of light is to darken, of communication to conceal. And this argument, when not thus stated, might be put at great length, by adducing passages of Holy Writ which declare expressly their very object, – that its purpose is to reveal. But all these texts, thus adduced, need not be separately referred to, or answered, as the whole argument which they are brought to prove runs up into, and is contained in, this very simple statement, viz., that Scripture is a system of revelation, to imply therefore that it is a system of reserve, is at once a palpable contradiction.

And it is curious that the very texts, adduced in this mode of treating the subjects, often imply or suggest all that we maintain. To refer to figurative language, it is said, does not God 'deck Himself with light, like as with a garment?' Whereas this very expression conveys it; for does not a garment veil in some measure that which it clothes? is not the very light concealment? The revelations of God must ever be to mankind in one sense mysteries; whatever He makes known opens to view far more which we know not. Not light only, but the 'cloud' also, is the especial emblem of the Spirit's presence. 'God is light,' but 'clouds and darkness,' also 'are round about Him;' 'His pavilion is in dark waters, with thick clouds to cover Him.' The comings and goings of our Lord are often significantly said to be with clouds; of Wisdom, that hath made her dwelling in Jacob, it is said, that she 'dwells in high places, and her throne is in a cloudy pillar. She alone compasses the circuit of the heaven, and walks in the bottom of the deep.'[a]

In the same manner of considering the subject, which we have spoken of, it might be said, that St. Paul, a person of all others the most laborious in preaching, had no other object than that of declaring the Gospel to the world; and what did the Gospel contain of good tidings, but the Atonement? It might further be stated, (though I am not aware it has been,) that a certain *παῤῥησία*, or openness in confessing the truth, was the very characteristic of St. Paul; it was the very object of his prayers; and his request, that it might be that of others for him, (Eph. vi. 19. Phil. i. 20,) that this free utterance and boldness of speech might be given him. It was his boasting that he had thus spoken; he appealed to his converts that he had kept back nothing from them that it was expedient for them to know. 'With great boldness to speak the truth,' is one of the first

[a] Ecclesiasticus 24.

gifts of the Spirit, as bestowed on the Apostles on the day of Pentecost; and 'utterance' is numbered among the highest Christian graces.[a] Now all this is not only granted, but also that if any thing here maintained would imply conduct different from that of the Apostle, would in any way derogate from the necessity of that *παῤῥησία*, it would of course be to be condemned in the strongest manner: of this there could be no doubt. It is needless to observe, that to withhold the truth from fear or false shame or pride is to be ashamed of Christ, to which that awful warning is denounced. Let it therefore, if necessary, be explicitly stated that if any conduct is supposed to be here taught different from that which would have been practised by St. Paul, among inspired Apostles, by St. Chrysostom, among the Ancient Fathers, and by the earnest and single-hearted Bishop Wilson,[1] in our own Church, such is far from being the intention of this treatise.

With regard to that mode of argument alluded to, it is evident that in this manner Holy Scripture might be quoted against itself, and a principle based on one command utterly repudiated without consideration, on account of its supposed discrepancy with another apparently opposed to it. But in such cases, it is by reconciling and explaining such apparent contradictions that we obtain the most life-giving principles contained within them, and the most important rules of conduct; thus we derive them best and most safely. These difficulties are like the hardness of an external covering, which preserves and guards the most precious fruits of nature, and affords trouble at arriving at them. That this reserve is not incompatible with such a declaration of the truth is evident from this, that the two persons whom we should select as most remarkable for fulness and freedom of speech, St. Paul and St. Chrysostom, are equally as much so for their reserve. For the Fathers speak of its being most observable in St. Paul; and it is evident how it marks his writings, especially when he touches on the subject of mysteries. Perhaps the most obvious passage that could be adduced, which seems at first against this supposition, is that in which St. Paul says, he 'had kept back nothing that was profitable;'[b] and it is remarkable of this text, so often quoted against us, first of all, that it was spoken to the Ephesians, to whom we know that St. Paul beyond all others revealed spiritual knowledge; secondly, that they were not the Church at large, but the elders of Ephesus; and, thirdly, to show how differently the ancients viewed these things, on referring to St.

[a] I Corinthians 1:5. II Corinthians 8:7. [b] Acts 20:20.

Chrysostom, we find he marks as emphatic the word 'that was profitable, *τῶν συμφερόντων*;[a] for there were some things,' he says, 'which it was not expedient for them to learn; to speak every thing would have been folly.' And as to St. Chrysostom himself, he often refers to this reserve, as an acknowledged principle, and it is observable that though he sometimes shows he is fully impressed with the secret senses of Scripture, yet in his Homilies he seldom alludes to them.

On preaching the word most effectually

But with regard to that short and summary manner in which the whole subject may be got rid of by saying, that, notwithstanding all such speculative and abstract principles, it is nevertheless our duty to 'preach the Word' (i.e. Christ Crucified) 'in season, and out of season,'[b] and woe be to us, if we do it not. Doubtless it is so; a 'dispensation is committed' unto us, a talent which it would be death to hide. And to this it must be said, that the principle of Reserve which we mention is so far from being in any way inconsistent with this duty, that it is but the more effectual way of fulfilling it. And this may be shown by another case very similar. It is our bounden duty to 'let our light shine before men,' to set a good example, that they 'may see our good works:'[c] but nevertheless it is true notwithstanding, that the great Christian rule of conduct, as the very foundation of all holiness, is that our religious actions should be in secret as much as possible. These two therefore are perfectly compatible. And unless we do act upon this latter principle, that of hiding our good works, our example will be quite empty and valueless. So also may it not be the case, that our 'preaching Christ Crucified' may be in vain and hollow, unless it be founded on this principle of natural modesty, which we have maintained will always accompany the preaching of a good man under the teaching of God?

But without considering the subject in the light of a holy and religious principle, if we put it on the very lowest ground, why, it may be asked, in religion are all truths to be taught at once? in all other matters there is a gradual inculcation, something must be withheld, something taught first; and is not the knowledge of religion as much a matter of degrees as any human science? But we have rather treated it here in the higher point of view, in order to

[a] Literally 'of those things being profitable'. [b] II Timothy 4:2. [c] Matthew 5:16.

show that our efforts to do good will be worse than fruitless, unless in doing so we act on this principle, to sanctify and strengthen our intentions, that the contrary mode of proceeding is not an indifferent matter, but very injurious. If any one acts on the pure love of God, there is no occasion to command this secrecy; for God will doubtless 'reveal even this unto him;' and if we preach Christ from the highest motives there is no occasion to teach this reserve; but if we are liable to be influenced by new religious schemes, and indirect motives, we have great need of the warning.

And the fact is, that all we say is so natural, so obvious to natural modesty, if men would but seriously consider it, that those who are most opposed to all we maintain, do in themselves practise it unconsciously in other points. But when they hear of this Tract, without waiting to know what it intends, they hasten to the attack: like the hasty servant in Aristotle, *ἀκούει μέν τι τοῦ λόγου, παρακούει δὲ,* and *ἀκούσας μὲν, οὐκ ἐπίταγμα δὲ ἀκούσας, ὁρμᾷ πρὸς τὴν τιμωρίαν.*[a]

It is asked with some degree of impatience, 'Is not knowledge good for man?' Doubtless we have maintained it most especially by making it the very highest of all things, as a talent of exquisite work, the very jewel of great price, infinitely divine and sacred. We do not lower the doctrine of the Atonement, but heighten and exalt it, and all we say is, that it should be looked upon and spoken of with reverential holiness. If it is the name of Reserve only which is objectionable, then let the substance of this article be expressed by any other which may be found equally to serve the purpose, whether it be forbearance, or reverence, or seriousness, or religious caution, as long as the full intention of it is equally preserved.

A rule of moral and religious teaching of such a nature as this of course requires a little attention: there is no subject with which the generality of persons are so little acquainted, or which they have so little considered, as that of practical moral principles. And there often may be something in their mode of life, which peculiarly indisposes them to enter into the one now under discussion. If a person has never been engaged in religious teaching, where his object has been to bring men to a serious consideration of the truth; if he is known to look upon theology rather in a political than a religious point of view; if he is much used to popular speaking, and the applause that accompanies it; if he allows himself to discuss the most sacred subjects in the daily periodical; if he has never been

[a] *Nicomachean Ethics*, VII. 6: 'hears the word of reason to some extent, but mishears it, and having heard, but not having heard the actual order given, rushes away to exact vengeance'.

trained to any reverence for holy places; if he consider Christianity as a mere popular system; if he disparages sacraments: then of course we cannot consider such an one as an adequate and fair judge on a subject the very nature of which is opposed to his own practice; for the discernment of every moral principle depends on conduct regulated with regard to it.

On teaching the doctrine of the Atonement

But there is another reason, more pervading and deeply rooted than any of these, although in various ways connected with them, which remains to be considered. All the objections are made without reference to the case we adduce, and without attention to the arguments, on account of a previously conceived strong bias against it; which makes it necessary that we inquire more at length into the system of the day which has claimed for itself the inmost sanctuary of religion, and at once predisposes men so strongly to be thoroughly opposed to all that we can urge. All the arguments adduced, and the principles maintained, are at once looked upon with respect to that system; all other matters to which it applies, and all the circumstances on which it is founded, are immediately set aside as unworthy of consideration, because this system of late years and of human invention is through all its branches thoroughly opposed to it: and many, and more than are aware of it, have taken up their position in these opinions, and consider it so impregnable, that whatever opposes it must necessarily be false. The system of which I speak is characterized by these circumstances, an opinion that it is necessary to obtrude and 'bring forward *prominently* and *explicitly* on all occasions the doctrine of the Atonement.' This one thing it puts in the place of all the principles held by the Church Catholic, dropping all proportion of the faith. It disparages comparatively, nay, in some cases has even blasphemed, the most blessed Sacraments. It is very jealously afraid of Church authority, of fasting and mortification being recommended, of works of holiness being insisted on, of the doctrine of the universal judgement. It is marked by an unreserved discourse on the holiest subjects. To this system all that we have said is thoroughly opposed.

Now it is evident that this system is throughout *peculiar*,[a] in distinction from what is Catholic: by the term Catholic we of course mean a combination of both what the Universal Church and the

[a] A nickname used in Oxford from about 1837 to allude to members of the Evangelical party.

Holy Scripture teach *conjointly*, the former as interpreting the latter. It is a plan thoroughly un-Scriptural, un-Catholic, unreal: we will therefore at once allow that this maxim of Reserve is directly opposed to it throughout, in its tone and spirit, in its tendencies and effects, in its principles and practices. Where Christians so thoroughly differ, what appeal can there be? When inspired Apostles, when even Paul and Barnabas, had a dissension and disputation betweeen them, they were sent up to Jerusalem unto the Apostles and Elders about the question, to decide the point in dispute. We appeal to Scripture and the Church.[2] Now those who hold these opinions will allow that the Church Catholic holds them not. Neither does Scripture warrant them; which may be easily shown, even though we allow not the Church as its interpreter. Nor, indeed, are they grounded on Holy Scripture, but on a supposed expediency. For in fact the advocates of these opinions will not allow an unreserved appeal to the written Word, but they maintain, that then only, when the Holy Spirit was given, did Holy Scripture set forth the Atonement with that fulness which they require. Thus have they contrived to take a position which sets aside almost the whole of Holy Writ, including the Gospels themselves, from any appeal on this subject. In fact, this system is nothing else but a method of human device, which is able to quote a part of Scripture for its purpose. It is not according to the general tenor or the analogy of Scripture, nor is it founded or based on Scripture as its origin. They consider, like the Romanists, that they infallibly hold the truth, which must therefore be a fuller development of Scripture in a later age; thus, in fact, do they make the Word of God of none effect through their tradition. These opinions, indeed, are grounded on nothing else but certain effects, which this system is thought to produce.

It is supposed that there is something particularly life-giving and heart-searching in these modes of teaching, which thrust forth exclusively and indiscriminately the doctrine of the ever blessed Atonement, and inculcate loudly the necessity of our dependence on the good Spirit of God: and these are so considered in distinction from those, which in connexion with them inculcate also practical duties, and the various departments of public and private religious worship. In which opinion there is indeed something true, but not so in the mode in which it is put forward and understood. There is indeed a great truth, of which these peculiar statements catch at the shadow, and it is their connexion with this great truth itself, which has caused them to be received as the whole of Religion. And perhaps many, who have appeared to themselves and others to have been embracing these popular opinions, have, in fact, by God's mercy thought of, and practically embraced, nothing else but that great truth itself. . . .

With regard to the notion that it is necessary to 'bring forward the doctrine of the Atonement on all occasions, prominently and exclusively,' it is really difficult to say any thing in answer to an opinion, however popular, when one is quite at a loss to know on what grounds the opinion is maintained. Is it from its supposed effects? pious frauds might be supported on the same principle: but let us observe these effects as they become more fully developed: the fruits of the system have shown themselves in the disobedience of ministers to their ecclesiastical superiors, of individuals to their appointed ministers, of whole bodies of Christians to the Church. Is it the popularity of the opinion? this is not a test of truth, but an argument of the contrary; Christian truth is in itself essentially unpopular; and even were it otherwise, what is popularity when it is opposed to Catholic antiquity? Is it from Scripture? we have shown that the tone and Spirit of Holy Scripture is quite opposed to it.

Do we then maintain that it is to be intentionally and designedly withdrawn from all public mention? nothing of this kind has been ever suggested or practised by us; this would of course be as unnatural as the other. Why should we not be content to act naturally, with the Church and Divine Scripture for our guides? why should not a conscience exercised therein, and practised in the discernment of good and evil, be content to act as our common sense and judgment, or, if we may reverently use such words, as the Holy Spirit, ever enlightening the path of obedience, dictates, without shaping our conduct into this mould? Why should one who thus acts be thought unworthy of the Christian name? Why should it be thought necessary to bring proof and induction, and, as it were by a stretch of charity, to obtain some indication that such an one denies not the doctrine of the Atonement? which has been done in the case of the Fathers and Saints of old, and of Bishop Butler and others in our own Church.[3]

It may be said, are we not saved by the faith alone in Christ, and if so, what else have we to preach? It may be answered by another question, was it not the very office of the Baptist to be the herald of Christ, and yet, so little did he publicly make a practice of declaring this, that there was a doubt whether he was not himself the Christ: but instead of proclaiming Him aloud, he taught Repentance, and to each individual amendment of life. The Baptist declared, 'I came that He might be manifested,' but how was He to be manifested, excepting, as our Lord said, that He would manifest Himself unto him that kept His commandments. Therefore the Forerunner preached repentance. When he did allude to the Atonement, in the expression of 'the Lamb of God,' it was secretly and obscurely, and probably only to a few chosen and favoured disciples, who themselves could not have understood the clear meaning of the allusion, to whom it must have been a dark saying. Doubtless, we are saved by faith in Christ alone; but to come to know this in all its power, is the very perfection of the Christian; not to be instilled or obtained by lifting up the voice in the street, but by obedience and penitence, so that, as each man advances in holiness of life, and comes the more to know what God is, the more does he feel himself, with the Saints of all ages, to be the chief of sinners. But as for that assurance[a] and sensible confidence, with which it is thought necessary that the doctrine should be preached and received, it would seem as if there was scarcely any thing against the subtle effect of which we are so much guarded in Holy Scripture as this: all those who are recorded as being most approved, were remarkable for the absence of it; as in the case of the Centurion,[b] the Canaanitish woman,[c] and others; above all, of those who at the last day shall be surprised with the welcome tidings that they are accepted: on the contrary, those who are rejected shall come with that plea of confidence, because they have prophesied in Christ's name, and He has taught in their street, and will be condemned with emphatic words, as they that *work* iniquity; whereby the whole stress is thrown on that single point, which those who hold these opinions are most studious to make of secondary importance, the necessity of *working* righteousness.

Surely the doctrine of the Atonement may be taught in all its fulness, on all occasions, and all seasons, more effectually, more really, and truly, according to the proportion of the faith, or the need of circumstances, without being brought out from the context of Holy Scripture into prominent and explicit mention. Did not St. James preach the Gospel most effectually under the guidance of God's good Spirit? Did not St. Paul preach the Gospel to the Thessalonians, when he spoke of the day of Judgement, as well as to the Galatians, when in answer to certain Jewish prejudices, he set forth the only remission of sins to be found in the Cross of Christ? May not we regulate our teaching according to the case of the persons we address, as they did? But above all, did not our Lord preach the Gospel? did He not say to the two disciples who came

[a] See Extract 2, pp. 35–7. [b] Matthew 8:15–13. [c] Matthew 15:22–8.

from St. John the Baptist, 'To the poor the Gospel is preached?' But how was it preached? We know what His preaching was; He taught the Atonement always, but never openly: He taught it always; He taught it in the Beatitudes, in the parables, in His miracles, in His commands, in His warnings, in His promises; He taught it always, but always covertly, never at all in the manner now required, but quite the opposite. And as it pervaded all our Lord's teaching; and ought to do, as we have stated, (Tract, No. 80 pp. 76, and 81,) the teaching of every good Christian; so surely it may do so in a way to be more effectually impressed on others, and to indicate its thorough reception into the character of the speaker, by one who might have even never prominently and explicitly declared it, any more than our Lord does in His own teaching. It may be impressed on others by the tone of a person's whole thoughts, by the silent instruction of his penitent and merciful demeanour, by immediate inference and implication from his sayings, by the only interpretation which his words will bear; but above all things, by the doctrine of the Sacraments ever influencing his life; He may thus ever bear about in the body the marks of the Lord Jesus, and preach Christ Crucified. Whereas, on the contrary, another who expressed this doctrine with all the fulness which is now required, might in all the tone of his disposition, his teaching, his whole bearing and observation, be as far from it as one who had never heard of it; and adopt this tone to the great injury of himself and others. The important thing needed consists in those preparations of the heart, which may lead men to humiliation and contrition; when this is done, He who 'dwells with the humble and the contrite,'[a] will never fail to lead them to all the consolations of Religion. Let us consider the case of a friend who consulted us on a matter that afflicted his conscience, how tender and careful should we be in such a case for fear of administering consolation too speedily, lest by so doing we check the workings of God's good Spirit, and heal too slightly His wounds to our friend's great detriment: and shall we do this to all indiscriminately?

But besides this, the awful name of the blessed Spirit, without whom we can neither think nor do any thing that is right, is, as is supposed, ever in like manner to be proclaimed as it were in the market-place, and those who do not do so, are supposed to deny His power, the power of the ever blessed Spirit of God, in whose Name we were baptized, Whom in the doxology we confess daily,

[a] Isaiah 57:15.

in Whom we live and move. Let these sacred words be introduced in our teaching, as they are in Holy Scripture. But even from this we almost shrink at feeling that they have been used in an unreal manner, and 'taken in vain;' for these holiest of words may be constantly used by us, when we are not at all affected and influenced by so concerning a doctrine, which may be seen by the whole of our character in daily life, and tone of our teaching; by self-confidence, and an absence of that fear and trembling, which ever follows the consciousness, that it is God that worketh in us both to will and to do. And what is done in such a case? Is the effect merely nugatory? Surely not: great injury is done by this irreverence to that most sacred Name. There is far less chance of real repentance in such a case.

Surely this great and life-giving doctrine might be taught more truly by one who practised no obtrusive system of this sort; to say nothing of his practical intructions, every word of which might be calculated to teach a person dependence on God; but even by his silence. For instance, might not one like holy Simeon,[a] (whom sacred Scripture has so strongly marked as one under the gracious guidance of the good Spirit, by the expression, thrice repeated, that 'the Holy Spirit was upon him,' that it was 'revealed unto him of the Holy Spirit,' that 'he came by the Spirit into the temple;') might not such a one, by daily frequenting 'the House of Prayer,' with that earnestness and assiduity which showed that he felt himself unable to stand for a day without assistance from above, learn and teach so affecting a truth, as well as by set declarations concerning it? Might he not, by these habitual practices, be rendered meet to find Christ in His Temple, and to prophesy in His name?

Danger in forming a plan of our own different from that of Scripture

Surely we know not what we do, when we venture to make a scheme and system of our own respecting the revelations of God. His ways are so vast and mysterious, that there may be some great presumption in our taking one truth, and forming around it a scheme from notions of our own. It may not be the way to arrive at even that truth; and also it may counteract some others, which it is equally important that we should be impressed with. The very idea of forming such a scheme, arises from a want of a due sense of the depth and vastness of the Divine counsels, as if we could com-

[a] Luke 2:25–35.

prehend them. It is with states of society as with individuals; those whose thoughts and knowledge are most superficial, are most apt to systematize; and it is very little considered what awful things in the economy of God may be thus habitually kept out of sight – kept out of sight, perhaps, by many quite unconsciously; for the secret influence of these opinions is more extensive than they are aware of, who are subject to them. It is not an uncommon thing to hear sermons which are throughout specious and plausible, which seem at first sight Scriptural, and are received as such without hesitation, and yet, on a little consideration, it will appear that they are but partial views of the truth, that they are quite inconsistent with the much forgotten doctrine of a future judgement. What effect, therefore, must this system have upon an age and whole nation?

Nor is it only in its not supporting the analogy of the faith, that this system is opposed to Scripture; but its spirit and mode of teaching is quite different. It may be observed in this, that this scheme puts knowledge first, and obedience afterwards: let this doctrine, they say, be received, and good works will necessarily follow. Holy Scripture throughout adopts the opposite course.[4] In many and extensive senses, the language it adopts, and the plan it pursues, is on the principle that 'the law is the schoolmaster, to bring us to Christ;' 'that he who will do the will shall know of the doctrine;' whereas this teaching is, 'receive only this doctrine, and you will do the will.' The kind of secondary way, and as it were in the back ground, in which the necessity of obedience is put in this system, is the very opposite to Scriptural teaching. Scripture ever introduces the warning clause, 'If ye keep the commandments;' they, on the contrary, 'If ye do not think of them too much.' . . .

Statement of the case from plain moral principles

Religious doctrines and articles of faith can only be received according to certain dispositions of the heart; these dispositions can only be formed by a repetition of certain actions.[5] And therefore a certain course of action can alone dispose us to receive certain doctrines; and hence it is evident that these doctrines are in vain preached, unless these actions are at the same time practised and insisted on as most essential.

For instance, charitable works alone will make a man charitable, and the more any one does charitable works, the more charitable will he become; that is to say, the more will he love his neighbour and love God; for a charitable work is a work that proceeds from charity or the love of God, and which can only be done by the good Spirit of God: and the more he does these works therefore, the more will he love his neighbour and love God: and he who does not (in heart and intention at least) perform these works, will not be a charitable man, i.e., will not love God or his neighbour: and those are not charitable works which have not this effect; for no external act, such as the giving away of money, is necessarily a work of charity, but only such as consists in the exercise of the principle of charity. He therefore will most of all, love God and love Christ, who does these works most; and he will most bring men to Christ, who most effectually, with God's blessing, induces them to do these works in the way that God has required them to be done.

Or again, he only will be humble in heart who does humble actions; and no action is (morally speaking) an humble action but such as proceeds from the spirit of humility; and he who does humble actions most will be most humble; and he who is most humble will be most emptied of self-righteousness, and therefore will most of all value the Cross of Christ, being least of all sensible of his own good deeds: and the more he does these works, the more will the Holy Spirit dwell with him, according to the promises of Scripture, and the more fully will he come to the knowledge of that mystery which is hid in Christ. That teacher, therefore, who will most induce men to do these works, will most of all bring men unto Christ, though he speaks not most fully and loudly of His ever blessed Atonement.

Or again, good works consist especially in Prayers. He who does most of these good works, i.e. he who prays most, seeks most of all for an assistance out of, and beyond himself, and therefore relies least of all on himself and most of all upon God; and the more he does these good works, the more does he rely upon God's good Spirit, for which he seeks. He, therefore, who, by preaching the judgement to come, or by recommending alms and fasting, or by impressing men with a sense of the shortness of life and the value of eternity, or by any such practical appeals which the occasion suggests, will lead men most to pray, will do most towards leading them to lean on God's good Spirit, although he may not repeat in express words the necessity of aid from that good Spirit, without whom we cannot please God.

To say, therefore, that such works, which alone are good works, tend to foster pride, and are a seeking for expiations beyond the one great Atonement, conveys a most dangerous fallacy; when the works which are intended, if the words can be applied to anything worthy of condemnation, must be bad works, those of ostentation, of hypocrisy, or superstition, and the like, which, of course, the oftener they are repeated, the more do they make men ostentatious, hypocritical, or superstitious; and so do take them from the Cross of Christ. They are sins against which we cannot warn men too much; sins repeatedly condemned by Christ, who never condemns or disparages good works, but insists upon them always and throughout most earnestly. Let hypocrisy, in all its shapes, be condemned as Scripture condemns, and we shall fully understand such teaching. Or again, consider the case morally with regard to the teaching of Repentance. For instance, take the deceivable sin of covetousness, of which we are all in danger. A covetous man is he who trusts in riches; and so far as any one trusts in riches, in that degree he cannot trust in God, and therefore can have no saving sense of the atonement of Christ, or dependence on the good Spirit of God. And if his feelings are excited on the subject of these doctrines, while he is under the influence of this vice, it cannot be any thing better than a mere delusion of the fancy; and therefore that teacher who will most of all lead men to abandon and get rid of covetousness, will render their minds most open to receive these two great doctrines of the Gospel; as seen in the case of Zaccheus, when salvation came to his house as a true child of faith; and in our Lord's advice to all to sell and give alms.[a] The same inference may be drawn with regard to the love of praise, in which case it may likewise be shown that it follows as a plain moral consequence, what our Lord has declared, that they cannot 'believe who receive honour one of another.' So also with respect to impurity of heart; for a man of impure heart may be very sensibly affected by these touching and vital doctrines of the Gospel; and yet it is certain that he cannot receive them rightly; for the pure in heart alone can see God; and therefore can alone see, so as rightly to understand, those doctrines in which God is manifested. That minister, therefore, who, by preaching the terrors of the judgement day, or by any other Scriptural means, induces men to repent of these crimes, will necessarily, and by a plain moral consequence, open their eyes, their ears, their heart, to receive the high saving principles of the Gospel; though he speaks not explicitly of them any more than the Baptist did, or our Lord, or His Apostles. So palpably absurd, even on the plain grounds of moral principles, is it to speak of the teaching of repentance being opposed to the preaching of Christ.

[a] Luke 19:2–9; 12:33.

9. *On Reserve*

This is an explanation of some obvious reasons why Holy Scripture should connect our own cross with the Cross of Christ, as it so often does, and emblematically typified of the Church, in him who bore the cross after Christ; for it is said to us all, 'whosoever doth not take up his cross and come after Me cannot be My disciple.'[a] Now there can be no repentance, and no progress in religious duties without self-denial. These duties, therefore, are a bearing of our own cross, which will alone bring us to a right sense of the Cross of Christ. It is not setting aside the Cross of Christ, nor disparaging it; it is only showing the mode by which alone we may be brought to know its inestimable value. . . .

On eloquent preaching and delivery

There is another important point in which the modern system is opposed to Scripture in breaking the spirit of reserve, viz., in attaching so great a value to preaching as to disparage Prayer and Sacraments in comparison. According to this the Church of God would be the House of Preaching; but Scripture calls it the House of Prayer. But with regard to the subject of preaching altogether, it is, in the present day, taken for granted, that eloquence in speech is the most powerful means of promoting religion in the world. But if this be the case, it occurs to one as remarkable, that there is no intimation of this in Scripture: perhaps no single expression can be found in any part of it that implies it: there is no recommendation of rhetoric in precept, or example, or prophecy. There is no instance of it; no part of Scripture itself appears in this shape, as the remains of what was delivered with powerful eloquence. Many parts of it consist of poetry, none of oratory; and it is remarkable that the former partakes more of this reserve, the latter less so. It speaks of instruction, 'precept upon precept, line upon line, here a little and there a little,' but never of powerful appeals of speech. The great teacher of the Gentiles, in whom we would most of all have expected to find it, was 'weak in bodily presence, and in speech contemptible;' and rendered so, it is supposed, by 'a thorn in the flesh.'[b] Whereas, it would be thought by many now, that the great requisites for a successful minister are a powerful bodily presence and eloquent speech. Indeed, St. Paul says, that the effect of words of men's wisdom would be to render the Cross of Christ of none effect. It is, moreover, observable, that in Scripture all the words

[a] Luke 14:27. [b] II Corinthians 12:7.

denoting a minister of the Gospel throw us back on the commission. Such, for instance, is the word 'Apostle,' or 'the Sent,' which title is repeated with a remarkable frequency and emphasis, and united, in one instance, with the awful and high expression, 'As my Father hath sent me, even so send I you.'[a] And the word 'preaching,' as now used, has a meaning attached to it derived from modern notions, which we shall not find in Scripture. 'A preacher,' indeed, properly conveys the same idea as 'Apostle,' and really signifies the same thing – 'a herald;' for, of course, all the office of a herald depends on him that sent him, not so much on himself, or his mode of delivering his message. All other words, in like manner adopted in the Church, speak the same; they all designate him as one *ministering* or *serving* at God's altar, not as one whose first object is to be useful to men; such, for instance, are the appellations of *diaconus*,[b] *sacerdos*.[c] It is curious that our word 'minister,' implying also the same, comes to be commonly used in the other sense, being applied, like that of preacher, to self-created teachers. Thus do men's opinions invest sacred appellations[6] with new meanings, according to the change in their own views.

If people in general were now asked what was the most powerful means of advancing the cause of religion in the world, we should be told that it was eloquence of speech or preaching: and the excellency of speech we know consists in delivery; that is the first, the second, and the third requisite. Whereas, if we were to judge from Holy Scripture, of what were the best means of promoting Christianity in the world, we should say obedience; and if we were to be asked the second, we should say obedience; and if we were to be asked the third, we should say obedience. And it is evident, that if the spirit of obedience exists, simple and calm statement of truth will go far. Not that we would be thought entirely to depreciate preaching as a mode of doing good: it may be necessary in a weak and languishing state; but it is the characteristic of this system as opposed to that of the Church, and we fear undue exaltation of an instrument which Scripture, to say the least, has never much recommended. And, indeed, if from Revelation we turn to the great teachers of morals which have been in the world, we shall be surprised to find how little they esteemed it useful for their purpose. The exceeding jealous apprehension of rhetoric which Socrates evinces is remarkable, as shown throughout the Gorgias. Nor does it ever seem to have occurred to the sages of old, as a means of

[a] John 20:21. [b] Servant of the church. [c] A priest who offers sacrifice.

promoting morality; and yet some of them, as Pythagoras and Socrates, made this purpose, viz., that of improving the principles of men, the object of their lives: and the former was remarkable for his mysterious discipline, and the silence he imposed; the latter for a mode of questioning, which may be considered as entirely an instance of this kind of reserve in teaching.[7]

And here again, if we are referred to expediency and visible effects, let us ask what these effects are. They have the effect of bringing people together in crowds, of creating strong religious impressions: so far it may be well; but even then, to all strong feelings the saying may be justly applied, 'quod est violentum non est diuturnum,'[a] But does this system make men more desirous to learn, and more exact in adhering to truth? Does this system in the long run make men more humble and obedient to their appointed ministers, more frequent in attending the daily prayers, more honest and just in their dealings with mankind? Does it lead men to think more of God and His appointments, and less of men and their gifts. Does it produce a healthful and reverential tone of feeling respecting the blessed Sacraments? Are persons who have been used to popular preaching more submissive to Divine ordinances, and more easily moved to the self-denying duties of repentance and prayer? But on this point, with regard to religious effects, even did they appear satisfactory yet we are, in fact, no judges at all on this subject; the next world only can show this: here we walk by faith, not by sight. Certainly the silence of Scripture should make us cautious how we allow too much to this instrument. The great importance now attributed to these means is sufficient to show the tendency of the system; it is one of expediency, it looks to man: that of the Church is one of faith, and looks to God. Their principle is to speak much and loud, because it is to man; that of the Church is founded on this, 'that God is in Heaven, and we on earth;' therefore, 'keep thy foot in the House of God,' and 'let thy words be few.'

This system a worldly system

It is very remarkable, how much this new scheme of religion is an instance of an observation which has been made, that they who set out with the profession of principles holier, or wiser, or purer than those of Holy Scripture, do ultimately tend to the virtual denial of those very truths which they professed most strictly to uphold.

[a] Whatever is violent is also short-lived.

They who maintain that the Church does not sufficiently preach the dependence of man upon God, and trust in the Atonement, do practically, in their whole system, tend to derogate from those truths themselves, while the Church continues to hold them. They consider, for instance, that the efficacy of a preacher consists in human eloquence and activity, and not in the power of his Divine commission, which is, in fact, to set up something else, which may be sensibly felt, for the Divine gifts of the Spirit. By disparaging the efficacy of the Sacraments, they have come to substitute for them something like a meritorious act, or opinion, on the part of an individual. Professing to be guided exclusively by the written Word, they have established a method so opposed to it, as to render the greater part of it superfluous. Requiring us to speak loudly of Spiritual assistance, they have set at nought all those practices, whose sole end and object was to live in that invisible world, and to partake of its gifts. For men have been led to reflect, censure, and even ridicule, not on the superstitious and wrong observance of Sacramental Ordinances, and Creeds, and Prayers, but on the punctual observance of them at all; and sentiments are expressed which would brand with superstition the devout Daniel for his unbending adherence to times and circumstances of devotion;[a] and the widow Anna, who departed not from the temple, with formalism.[b8] And all this arises from the fact, that these opinions are not thoroughly and unreservedly based on Holy Scripture, and therefore look too much to external support.

The very principle of sound Religion is that the world 'knoweth it not, as it knew Him not:' its rules of action are so essentially opposed, that they cannot understand each other, from something of an essential nature different. The system, on the contrary, of which we speak, has ever the indirect object of making a league with it, – not externally, on the contrary, it has devised externally strongly-marked lines of demarcation and distinctions, which do not extend to the thoughts or character; and in every way has substituted a great unreal system, nominal, superficial, formal, though in name spiritual, and the more formal in reality, because in name spiritual. Where God is, there must be the fear of Him.

For this reason it has come to pass that names of the most awful and holy import have been so used habitually, that they carry not with them their own high and awful meaning, even the Names of the ever-blessed Trinity. Not only have they become used without

[a] Daniel 6:10. [b] Luke 2:36–8.

reverence, and very much as the distinctive signs of a party, – but the very use of them tends to keep up this feeling of unreality, and without bearing on the heart and conduct. Whereas homefelt natural expressions in which any one who is in earnest is apt to clothe his sentiments, and which touch the heart and conscience of another, as they come from his own, are disliked; because they break through this unreal web, and bear more upon the daily life and conscience.

All this is substituting a system of man's own creation for that which God has given. Instead of the Sacraments and external ordinances, it has put forth prominently a supposed sense of the Atonement, as the badge of a profession. That which is most thoroughly internal, most thoroughly spiritual, secret, and holy, it has made the external symbol of agreement; and therefore has completely (so to speak) turned people inside out, wherever it is received: and thus it has lost the essential peculiarity of Christianity, that purity of heart which is directed to 'the Eye that seeth in secret.' This spirit has thoroughly imbued their whole system, in the same manner that it has prevailed in the corruptions of Rome. In the case of the latter, the use of external symbols the most sacred, has lost much of its power, by rude exposure to the gaze of the world; so is it with this system in the use of words; they have lost their proper sense and meaning, and have a peculiar signification. That dread doctrine so essential as received into the heart, the very foundation of life and actions, has come with them to consist in that which can be called up from time to time, and satisfy the professor in sensible emotions and satisfactions. Works as performed strictly in secret, and directed to the eye of God, cannot but be life-giving and good: the corruptions of Rome have substituted for these external actions; and this system external professions. The eye of man is on both, unhallowing the holy things of God, and engendering pride. Hence has arisen among them that rejection of natural modesty, and sacred reserve, on the subject of religion in discourse and writing: – attempts to remedy certain effects and symptoms of the want of religion, instead of that want itself. Much indeed of this may arise from a natural craving after sympathy on the highest of all subjects, and from having lost the legitimate expressions of it. External visible Communion must be preserved by external visible means; when these are withdrawn, sacred principles or sacred feelings will be outwardly substituted. In proof of this, it may be observed, that a Sect which has least of all to distinguish it in doctrine or discipline as a separate body, the Wesleyans, are most under the influence of what is here condemned, to the great injury of their moral character: words with them do not signify what they do with others. Instead of visible means of grace, and participation in the same Sacraments, being the bonds of union, something in external speech or demeanour becomes substituted.[9] A still more remarkable instance may be seen in the Sect denominated the Society of Friends, who, after labouring to divest themselves of all the appearances of a visible Church and visible Sacraments, have become from external garb and mode of speech, the most visible of all Societies.

It must be allowed that this modern system did for a time partake of 'the reproach of Christ,' and did in that strength prevail for a season. In that reproach, all good Christians will be glad to share with them. Doubtless the very name of Christ must ever carry with it a blessing; and earnestness in religion, in views however mistaken, seems ever to have annexed to it the reward of God. And for a time this earnestness of mind carried with it incidentally much good, and led me to embrace other great truths of Christianity, and perhaps that of Christ Crucified, in reality as well as in name; being far better themselves than their system, and better in their practice than in their opinions, which they held rather speculatively and controversially, than practically: but these things for a while corrected by the sincerity of individuals have gone by, and left the legitimate fruits of the system. The evils it has led to in various forms of dissent are too evident wherever we turn our eyes, leading men to the neglect of honesty and plain dealing, and at length to indifference, unsettledness, and infidelity. In the Church it excludes with jealous eagerness all things that may alarm the consciences of those who heartily adopt the system, obedience to Church authority, practices of mortification, the fear of God, and the doctrine of judgement to come. It sets forth religion in colours attractive to the world, by stimulating the affections, and by stifling the conscience, rather than by purifying and humbling the heart. Hence its great prevalence in places of fashionable resort. And to those who have in any way forfeited their character for religion and morality or sound doctrine, instead of the process of painful secret self-discipline and gradual restoration, or the open and salutary penance of the Ancient Church, it affords an instant and ready mode for assuming at once all the privileges and authority of advanced piety. And the consequence is, that real humility of heart, and a quiet walking in the ordinances of God, finds not only the world in array against it, but that which considers itself as Christianity also. Through all its appearances it is marked by a want of reverence; and therefore it can use worldly instruments and worldly organs. It may serve as a ready cloak to cover an unsubdued temper and a worldly spirit, concealing them as well from the individual himself as from others. It may offer a convenient refuge to those who would cling to the Establishment, rather than the Church, if she should be spoiled and persecuted. But the effect of these opinions is not confined to those who profess and receive them; but as a great part of the office of the Gospel is to be a witness to all nations, even to those who receive it not, the witness itself, or the voice which is heard from it, becomes altered in its character. One or two great truths are thus put forth exclusively as the whole of religion; and this has a vast effect on the whole of society, among those who do not openly avow, nor are even secretly conscious of, these opinions: the world accepts them, not even as the professors of them would themselves intend, but as palliatives to an uneasy conscience, as an assistance to throw off the sense of responsibility, and as false easy notions of repentance. Therefore it is that these peculiar views in religion amalgamate so readily with the liberal notions of the world, and both will be found readily to unite against principles of a more unbending nature. There exists a secret affinity between them.

There was one impediment in the Jews throughout, which prevented their receiving the truth; they trusted in their being of the seed of Abraham. From this point as a centre, the evil one wove around them a web of external and specious observances, from which the great Teacher of repentance, and our Lord Himself, and St. Paul, in vain endeavoured to extricate them: they bore leaves, but not fruit. The Baptist had laid the axe to the root of the tree: our Lord had interceded for three years with the Father, till He should dig around it and dung it: St. Paul had endeavoured to graft within it the better stock; but in vain; it still bore leaves, but not fruit. The present age is one of affected refinement in sentiment combined with loose morals; one of expediency rather than principle, of rationalism rather than faith; one that will take all that is agreeable and beautiful and benevolent in religion, and reject what is stern and self-denying and awful. Now the whole truth in its just proportions we have in the Creed, which God has given us as a key to Scripture, the depository of the faith in the Church, to each individual a guide and safeguard. But it is very evident that if we take one point only in religion, instead of this analogy of the Faith, we may produce a religion which may please ourselves and others, and yet may be very far from the truth as it is in Scripture, and from the principles of that new world wherein dwelleth righteousness. And it is an awful and trying question for a man to ask himself, whether the reason why he sets aside the Day of Judgement, the severe discipline of the Church, and above all the two Sacraments, in his public teaching, is not this, that in the secret core of himself he does not consider them: and whether the strong controversial party feeling, exhibited on these points, does not arise from the dislike he has to be disturbed in these easy convictions, into the truth of which he will not seriously enquire.

Now against all this leaven of a worldly system, the reserve that is here inculcated seems at once the remedy; for its strips off at once all those external indications of a religion which exists not in the heart, as rather hindrances to true piety than the promoters of it; and requires one to be reverential and considerate in all that regards it.

John Keble

(1792–1866)

10. *Tract No. 89 On the Mysticism attributed to the Early Fathers of the Church* (1840), pp. 1, 3–7, 8–10, 134–6, 137, 143–4, 145–8, 165–7, 169–71, 185–6

Keble's personal influence with pupils and later with parishioners and friends, church dignitaries and statesmen, was always profound and when plans were being set afoot for concerted action in 1833 Newman wrote to Froude, 'I think we ought to puff Keble as our head' (*The Letters and Diaries of John Henry Newman, 1801–34*, ed. I. Ker and T. Gornall (4 vols., Oxford, 1978–80), vol. IV, p. 17). Characteristically Keble voiced his preference for a bishop to head the movement (*ibid.*, p. 22). Unsuited by inclination and belief for the leadership of any movement, Keble's natural reticence here received reinforcement from his High Churchman's regard for the divinely ordered episcopal ministry. An utterly consistent conservative respect for orthodox pieties marked his thought and behaviour both as man and pastor. 'Yes, that is exactly what my father taught me', was the highest praise Keble could vouchsafe to an idea from a younger Tractarian collaborator, and his participation in the Oxford Movement was throughout based upon the belief that he was defending the best of Anglican High Church *tradition*. Despite his academic attainments Keble's contribution to the Oxford Movement was not as an intellectual, but like his revered George Herbert, as an exemplar of moral and pastoral values.

The first extract is composed of passages from Keble's *Tract No. 89*, published in 1840, although in private circulation in 1837. Of the four points outlined by Keble (pp. 137–8) he covered only the first two before the Tracts as a whole were abruptly curtailed by the appearance and ensuing row over Newman's *Tract No. XC*. This selection concentrates upon the theory behind Keble's defence of the Fathers' mystical mode of interpreting Scripture by analogy with poetical imagery as more interesting than the laborious and, at times, whimsically far-fetched illustration of his theories from their writings.

The suggestion of arcane scholarship in this Tract's title should not blind us to the absolute centrality of its thought to Tractarian teaching. Mysticism builds upon the habit of reserve, discussed in the previous extract, in its assumption that the initiated will be able to see through the moral, allegorical and parabolic teaching to the reserved truth at its core. Like Newman, Keble was distressed by the rationalistic spirit of the age, but the difference in their discussion of the problem indicates two very distinct minds and personalities. Keble wholly eschews the forensic, sceptical element of Newman's mode of thought, displaying none of the enjoyment Newman clearly experienced in following an opponent's argument until he had his prey cornered. Keble's distrust of cleverness or personal charisma that might distract men from the worship of God is reflected in his writings. Sparkling aphorisms, flashes of wit, brilliantly executed logical pirouettes, inflammatory denunciations or emotional appeals to conversion are wholly alien to his work. Indeed the caution with which so many of his propositions are hedged about ('I had almost said' is a representative mannerism), and the intricacy of many of his sentences, make the argument at times laborious to follow. Such a style is, however, directly based on his determination to eschew the 'smoothness of phrase', the glib explanations and reductionist analysis so favoured by 'the present generation'. Yet the overall effect is not dry, crabbed or cold. At the heart of the writing lies positive emotional commitment, an awed reverence of 'the beauty of holiness'. His prose may be regarded as poetic, not in the composition of individual lines or elaborately contrived metaphors but, to use his own definition, 'If we suppose Poetry in general to mean the expression of an overflowing mind, relieving itself, more or less indirectly and reservedly, of the thoughts and passions which most oppress it.' Without sympathy of feeling, this Tract demonstrates, reason is useless. The premise of the appeal to antiquity must first be accepted since the value of Tradition is unlikely to be apparent either to those who believe that Revelation is progressive and that knowledge has advanced as the human race has matured, or to those Rationalists whose commitment to empirical inquiry makes them suspicious of authority. Keble's manner of argument here helps us understand why he remarked that 'neologists are too wicked to argue with' and why he sometimes terminated friendships after an argument.

It is in this Tract that Keble made as clear as his notions of reserve permitted the Sacramentalism implicit in his poetry. When Newman acknowledged the debt he owed to Keble for his sacramental view of Nature he also made clear the philosophical inheritance behind it (*Apologia*, p. 29). In *The Analogy of Religion* (1736) Bishop Butler had looked at the evidence of the natural world, not as logical proof for the existence of God, but as hints of, or analogies for, the more perfect future state towards which humanity can move. This provided Keble, who thoroughly distrusted the Rationalist manner of thought employed by Natural Theology, with another way of perceiving Nature – a way reinforced by the Romanticism of Wordsworth and Coleridge. Their apprehension was congenial to Keble in that it emphasized man's capacity for an active response to such correspondences. Indeed Keble's vocabulary is indicative of the extent to which he has assimilated certain Romantic concepts. When Keble refers to those Rationalists 'who would reduce all Mysticism to the mere workings of human fancy' (p. 145), 'fancy' here does not merely imply whimsical invention but rests upon such a distinction as Coleridge made between imagination and fancy. In rejecting the Church's tradition of mystical interpretation as primitive and therefore obsolete, Rationalists fail to see how such a mode of human perception is essential to the present life of the Church precisely because it is God-given, or to use Coleridge's definition, such an imaginative mode of perception is 'a repetition in the finite mind of the eternal act of creation in the infinite I AM' (*Biographia Literaria*, ch. 13). In more narrowly theological terms Keble's poetic interpretation of the Bible can be seen as a reaction to the literal-minded, allegorical, moral, or merely denunciatory prophetical studies of the Evangelical school.

Occasion, Grounds, and Limits of the Present Inquiry

It is curious, and may be not uninstructive, to observe how from time to time the assailants of Primitive Antiquity have shifted their ground, since the beginning of the seventeenth century. During the struggle of the Reformation, men had felt instinctively, if they did not clearly see, that the Fathers were against them, so far as they had begun to rationalize, whether in ecclesiastical practice, or in theological inquiry. But it was many years before they ventured to avow this feeling distinctly to themselves, much more to maintain and propagate it. . . . [I]n our day, perhaps, the more usual course is, for persons, who do not even profess any acquaintance with those writers, beyond vague impressions received from report or quotation, to dispose of their authority in any controverted point, under the notion, understood or expressed, that 'the Fathers were Mystics, and need not be regarded at all.'

Now, if it were indeed an object with the Evil Spirit, to decry the relics of Christian Antiquity, and divert men's attention from them, it is difficult to say what single word he could have chosen, so critically adapted to his purpose in our days, as this same word, Mysticism. In the first place, it is not a *hard* word, having been customarily applied to such writers as Fenelon[1] and William Law,[2] whom all parties have generally agreed to praise and admire. So far it suits well with the smoothness of phrase, on which the present generation especially prides itself. It seems to set down the Fathers gently, and so is readily acquiesced in by many who would shrink from the coarse sneers of Middleton[3] or Gibbon.[4]

In the next place, it touches the very string, which most certainly moves contemptuous thought, in those who have imbibed the peculiar spirit of our time. Mysticism, implies a sort of confusion between physical and moral, visible and spiritual agency, most abhorrent to the minds of those, who pique themselves on having thoroughly clear ideas, and on their power of distinctly analyzing effects into their proper causes, whether in matter or in mind.

Again, Mysticism conveys the notion of something essentially and altogether remote from common sense and practical utility: but common sense and practical utility are the very idols of this age.

Further, that which is stigmatized as Mysticism, is almost always something which at once makes itself discerned by internal evidence. The man of the world, the practical man, the inductive experimental philosopher, commonly persuades himself that he can perceive by instinct, when a train of thought, or mode of speaking, is mere religious dreaming, indistinct fanciful theory; and he rejects it accordingly, and is saved all trouble of research. Here, again, is no small temptation, in the eyes of a world full of hurry and business, to acquiesce over lightly in any censure of that kind.

John Keble (1792–1866)

Yet, again, if any man be disposed to speak and think more harshly of the early Christian writers, this same term, Mysticism, may serve his purpose also; for it is easy, by a dexterous enunciation, or choice of context, to insinuate through it a charge of deliberate fraud. It is an instance, therefore, of a mode of speaking, equally convenient for all shades and degrees of enmity to, or contempt of, Antiquity. We see what its power is in a kindred instance; how meanly even respectable persons allow themselves to think of the highest sort of poetry, – that which invests all things, great and small, with the noblest of all associations, – when once they have come to annex to it the notion of Mysticism. And perhaps its mischievous effects on theology are as great as any attributable to a single word.

It may, therefore, be of some use to consider, as distinctly as we can, what people really mean when they charge the Fathers with Mysticism; which being done, we may perhaps have a better chance of making out to our satisfaction, whether, and how far, as a body, they deserve the charge.

By the term Mysticism, then, as applied to the writers in question, I understand to be denoted, a disposition, first, to regard things as supernatural which are not really such; and secondly, to press and strain what may perhaps be really supernatural in an undue and extravagant way.

Upon which bare statement, without going any further, a devout mind will probably at once acknowledge, on which side in the present question the peril of erring will be greatest. The question is like that of the general evidences of religion: a person who would go into it with advantage, should be imbued beforehand with a kind of natural piety, which will cause him to remember all along, that perhaps, when he comes to the end of his inquiry, he will find that God was all the while really there. He will 'put off his shoes from off his feet,' if he do but think it possible that an angel may tell him, by and by, 'The place where thou standest is holy ground.' So it must be, in some measure, with every right-minded person, in the examination of every practice and opinion, against which the charge of Mysticism is brought. Whatever may appear in the case at first sight, likely to move scorn or ridicule, or tempt to mere lightness of thought; it will be an exercise of faith, a trial of a serious heart, to repress for the time any tendency of that kind: the loss and error being infinitely greater, if we are found trifling with a really sacred subject, than if we merely prove to have been a little more serious than was necessary. In this sense, that is to say in regard of the reverent or irreverent *temper*, in which such inquiries may be approached, superstition is surely a great deal better than irreligion: whatever may be thought of the abstract question, Whether it be the safer extreme to believe too much, or too little?

It may be said, that the Fathers themselves indicate an exception to this rule, by the light and sarcastic way, in which they often allow themselves to treat the pretended mysteries, sometimes of heathens, sometimes of heretics as bad as heathens. But the case is not strictly in point. For I am speaking of pretensions unexamined, and therefore, as yet, more or less doubtful: but the Fathers had, or accounted themselves to have, good grounds for believing that the mysteries and miracles which they held up to scorn were, in part at least, the work of evil spirits, with whom they thus most effectually renounced communion. Before we indulge the like feeling in our treatment of any claim to supernatural powers, we had need have the like assurance of diabolical agency in them: and that to show them any reverence would seem like imparting of God's honour to the Evil One. Although even in such a case deep fear and humiliation of heart would seem the more appropriate sentiment for ordinary Christians. For is it not a fearful and humbling thought, that mankind, that we ourselves, are, or have been, in danger of mistaking the work of God's enemy for His own?

Further, it may be well to bear in mind, that the noblest and most refined devotional tendencies have always had to bear the imputation of Mysticism, or some other equivalent word; as if to cultivate them were a mere indulgence of a dreamy, soaring, indistinct fancy. In this use of it, the word Mysticism has done probably as much harm in checking high contemplative devotion, as the kindred term, Asceticism, in discouraging Christian self-discipline.

Thus much for the first impression, which the very application of the term to the Fathers would make on a considerate person, as yet ignorant of their writings. He would expect, almost certainly, to find them imbued with devotional feelings of an unusually high order; and he would be prepared for the possibility, that even those views of theirs, which might seem at first glance overstrained, fantastic, or unnatural, might turn out in the end to be portions of true Christian wisdom.

What now are the particulars of the Fathers' imputed Mysticism? i.e. in what respects would they be commonly charged with an undue anxiety to make out supernatural meanings and interferences? The following heads would seem to comprehend the greater part of their supposed delinquencies in this kind: –

1. Their interpretations of Scripture are said to be far-fetched and extravagant; extracting figurative, theological allusions out of the most irrelevant or insignificant details of language or history.

2. Correspondent to this is their mode of treating natural objects, and the truths of philosophy and common life; fancying every where indications of that system, on which their own hearts were set.

3. They were mystics in their notions of providential interference, whether in the way of judgement, deliverance, or warning. To which head may be referred whatever they state of the exercise of the gift of prophecy in their times; as also their accounts of reputed miracles, and of the sensible agency of evil spirits, and of their own and others' warfare with them.

4. Finally, they are blamed for Mysticism, properly so called, in their moral and devotional rules; i.e. for dwelling too much on counsels of perfection, tending (as is affirmed) to contemplation rather than action, to monastic rather than social and practical virtue.

These are the sort of imputations on which the changes have been rung, for the two last centuries, by those who have wished to evade the testimony of the Fathers, without setting them down distinctly as deliberate impostors.

It may be added, that many of their professed advocates, (Warburton for example),[5] have in fact given up their cause, as far as concerns every one of these representations. For what, in reality, does his defence of them come to, even when he is led to state their case most favourably; e.g. in the Preface to Julian? Just to this, and no more: that they might be trusted in their relations of things which came within the scope of their own knowledge, provided there was no room for surmising any thing miraculous: and again, that on other subjects, whether as reasoners or as narrators, they were not weaker, but a little wiser, than Pagan and Jewish writers of the same date.

It is true that Warburton belonged to a school, which has a temptation of its own for slighting the Fathers, over and above differences in particular doctrines; a school, whose leading principle is, that theology, like other sciences, improves by time: or, (to use the words of one of its most plausible advocates) that 'Christianity was in its infancy, at most in its childhood, when these men wrote; and therefore it is no wonder that they *spake as children*, that they *understood as children*, that they *thought as children*. This was according to the economy they were then under.'[6] . . .

May it not with reason be suspected, that the root of the matter lies deeper, and that in order to arrive at it, we must make up our minds thoroughly to consider the whole subject *ab initio*? It may perhaps turn out that the boldest way of meeting the difficulty is the most rational, and ultimately the most consoling. We must not be startled, though we find ourselves compelled to own, that modern and ancient theology are to a great extent irreconcileable; that if popular notions are right, the Fathers are indeed 'mystical' in a bad sense, and that, in all the several departments above mentioned.

Thus, in respect, first, of Scripture *interpretation*, the received doctrine of this age seems to be, that nothing ought to be figuratively or typically explained, except on the authority of Scripture itself; it being assumed, that we can no otherwise be certified of the divinely intended relation, necessary to make up the nature of a real Type. Now those who hold this rule must necessarily think meanly of the Fathers as expounders of Scripture, since in every paragraph almost we find some allegory, not scriptural according to the required test.

Secondly, in respect of *allusions* moral or theological, regularly and uniformly deduced from the contemplation of the creatures of God, in the manner, e.g. of Boyle's Occasional Reflections;[7] it would probably be considered a candid judgement, in our time, which should allow that such might constitute tolerable *poetry*: but to consider them as a part of *theology*, to regard them as having been from the beginning intended by the Creator, and the creation ordered with a view to them; – who is there among us, that would not at first be tempted to reject such a theory as overstrained and merely fanciful?

Thirdly, consider the tone of thought, which is accounted safest and meets with most encouragement in our days, concerning the intimations of God's mysterious *providence*, whether national or individual. Is it not a subject, that, as things are, even sincere-minded persons shrink from? They are afraid of trusting themselves with it, though but in thought. What is meant will be perceived in a moment, if people will reflect what their first impressions were, on reading, e.g., the Journal of Archbishop Laud,[8] those portions of it which detail supposed providential warnings. Or, again, how backward we all find ourselves in confessing our sense of God's judgements, public and private, when in our thoughts we can hardly fail to perceive them. I am far from asserting that this backwardness is not both pious and reasonable, taking all circumstances into account: but does it not imply a great change, either in men's condition or opinions, or in both, since the days of St. Ignatius and St. Cyprian?[a]

[a] Early Christian Fathers of the first and third centuries respectively.

Lastly, the difference in *moral sentiments* is too obvious to be denied. The cheerful, liberal, indulgent side is the popular one, now, in all questions of ethics: severity, strictness, self-denial, are but so far approved, as their immediate good effect is seen and understood. Need it be remarked, that the direct contrary is the case of the Primitive Church?

On the whole, the discrepancies between the two ages, occasioning the imputation of Mysticism to the ancients, are far beyond being accounted for by local, accidental, or temporary circumstances; they must be referred to some difference in first principles: and unless we are prepared to say positively, with the philosophic theologians above mentioned, that theology is, like other sciences, really advancing, of course, as the world grows older; we cannot but in candour allow it at least possible, before examination, that the ancients may have been in the right, and we in the wrong. . . .

Ancient Mysticism as applied to the Interpretation of the New Testament

It is most true, there *is* a great danger in the mystical contemplation of the Scriptures, more especially of the Gospels, by how much the Word of Life is there brought nearer to us, to be not only heard of, but also to be seen with our eyes, to be looked upon and handled with our hands. There is a great, an unspeakable danger, if our practice be not conformable. But this danger is not peculiar to the process of spiritual interpretation; it belongs equally to all ways of communicating the secrets of the Kingdom of Heaven; to the Creeds and Prayers of the Church; to the Catechisms which all children learn. And the remedy for it is not, in this or any other instance, to hide our eyes indolently from the light, which we know shines round us, but to strengthen them gradually, that they may be able to bear it; and this can only be done by moral means; i.e. by repentance, devotion, and self-denial. As we train ourselves, so also, according to our means, should we endeavour to prepare others, for the right study of the Bible. He who looks no deeper than the latter, may simply recommended candour, and patient investigation, and freedom from sensual and other disturbing thoughts: but he who knows beforehand, that the Personal Word is every where in the written Word, could we but discern Him, will feel it an awful thing to open his Bible; fasting, and prayer, and scupulous self-denial, and all the ways by which the flesh is tamed to the Spirit, will seem to him no more than natural, when he is to sanctify himself, and draw near, with Moses, to the darkness where God is. And this so much the more, the more that darkness is mingled with evangelical light; for so much the more he may hope to see of God; and we know Who it is, that has inseparably connected seeing God with purity of heart.[a]

As therefore God's people are continually to be told, concerning the Blessed Sacrament of the Eucharist, that it is infinitely dangerous to come near it unworthily, but they are not therefore to leave it out of their minds, but rather to think of it night and day, they may prepare themselves, and come as God would have them: so is it with this mystical presence of Jesus Christ in every part of the Scriptures. We are not to shrink from the thought of it for fear of irreverence, but bearing it continually in mind, we are to train ourselves so, that we may have grace to discern it, according to our measure, in particulars. This training is no matter of intellectual acuteness, industry, and memory: they will only mislead into some wrong kind of Mysticism, if separated from a single mind, and a heart full of reverence: but he that is willing indeed to do His will, he shall know *περὶ τῆς διδαχῆς*,[b] 'concerning the manner of teaching,' as well as the substance, 'whether it be of God.' Common sense surely will add, that one necessary sign of this willing reverence of heart, will be our religiously walking by the clue, which the ancient Church has given us, wherever we can keep satisfactory hold of it; never daring to contradict the unanimous voice of the Fathers, still less to treat with scorn and mockery the serious opinion, though it be but of one among them.

On the other hand, no ignorance, not even inability to read, disqualifies men from thus receiving our Lord in His Scriptures. It does not hinder them from seeing God's hand in His *natural* Providence, in His care of their own and others' welfare: why should it make them incapable of perceiving His *supernatural* Providence, (if one may so call it) – the presence of His Christ, – in all those works of His, the record of which they hear from time to time in Church, or at home out of their Bibles? Such perception of our Lord's presence, through the veil of the letter, is in fact the religious improvement of the fondness for type and parable, natural to all, but often most developed in those who have least means of acquiring literal instruction. From which it would seem, that we need not fear to inure even poor unlearned persons, having the fear of God, and leading good lives, with the ancient

[a] Matthew 5:6. [b] Literally 'with regard to the teaching'.

mode of exposition. Humanly speaking, their habits of thought make them for the most part apter to receive it, than persons of greater learning and refinement.

But whether to wise or simple, to learned or unlearned, the great and certain advantage of this method, (over and above its positive truth) is this: that it tends so directly in every part and parcel of the Scriptures, to keep up the conviction that God in Christ is there, ready to reveal Himself to us with a blessing, if we seek Him religiously and worthily. This conviction, continually realized and acted on, will prove to be of unspeakable value, though we never were conscious of a single discovery, a single new interpretation, in the ordinary sense of that term. Such faithful self denying labour will be worth a double 'hidden treasure' to us, bringing us secretly into closer Communion with Him, in whom are now hidden, one day to be revealed, '*all* the treasures of wisdom and knowledge.'

These remarks may suffice, on the manner of the Fathers as Mystical Interpreters of the Bible. We shall next have to consider them as Mystical Observers of natural and providential things, and of the visible world around us: a kindred subject, as a little inquiry will show.

Mysticism as applied to the works of nature, and generally to the external world

We know how very large a part of modern literature and education, nay, and of modern theology too, is occupied by instruction and research on physical subjects, and in what a tone of self-complacency men praise their times and one another, for the great and rapidly increasing proficiency of the two or three last generations in their knowledge and command of the powers of nature. But when we turn to the first ages of Christian literature, the very first sentiment which strikes us is, the care taken every where to exclude views merely scientific and physical, – to prevent our acquiescing in that kind of knowledge, as though in itself it were any great thing. . . .

[T]he one great and effectual safeguard against such idolizing of the material world, or rather of our own minds acting upon it, is the habit of considering it in that other point of view, to which Christian Antiquity would guide us, as earnestly as it would withdraw us from the speculations of the mere natural philosopher. I mean the way of regarding external things, either as fraught with imaginative associations, or as parabolical lessons of conduct, or as a symbolical language in which God speaks to us of a world out of sight: which three might, perhaps, be not quite inaptly entitled, the Poetical, the Moral, and the Mystical, phases or aspects of this visible world.

Of these, the Poetical comes first in order, as the natural groundwork or rudiment of the other two. This is indicated by all languages, and by the conversation of uneducated persons in all countries. There is every where a tendency to make the things we see represent the things we do not see, to invent or remark mutual associations between them, to call the one sort by the names of the other.

The second, the Moral use of the material world, is the improvement of the poetical or imaginative use of it, for the good of human life and conduct, by considerate persons, according to the best of their own judgement, antecedent to, or apart from, all revealed information on the subject.

In like manner, the Mystical, or Christian, or Theological use of it is the reducing it to a particular set of symbols and associations, which we have reason to believe has, more or less, the authority of the Great Creator Himself.

Now the first peculiarity of the Fathers' teaching on this head having been shown to be their jealousy of the merely scientific use of the external world, the next appears to be their instinctively substituting the mystical use in its room; not a merely *poetical*, or a merely *moral*, but a *mystical*, use of things visible; according to the exposition of the word *mystical* just above given.

To state the matter somewhat differently: If we suppose Poetry in general to mean the expression of an overflowing mind, relieving itself, more or less indirectly and reservedly, of the thoughts and passions which most oppress it: – on which hypothesis each person will have a Poetry of his own, a set of associations appropriate to himself for the works of nature and other visible objects, in themselves common to him with others: – if this be so, what follows will not perhaps be thought altogether an unwarrantable conjecture; proposed, as it ought, and is wished to be, with all fear and religious reverence. May it not, then, be so, that our Blessed Lord, in union and communion with all His members, is represented to us as constituting, in a certain sense, one great and manifold Person, into which, by degrees, all souls of men, who do not cast themselves away, are to be absorbed? and as it is a scriptural and ecclesiastical way of speaking, to say, Christ suffers in our flesh, is put to shame in our sins, our members are part of Him; so may it not be affirmed that He condescends in like manner to have a Poetry of His own, a set of holy and divine associations and meanings, wherewith it is His will to invest all material things? And the authentic records of His will, in this, as in all other truths supernatural, are, of course, Holy Scripture, and the consent of ecclesiastical writers. . . .

There is a wonderful agreement among the Fathers, in the symbolical meanings, which they assign to most of the great objects in nature; such an agreement as completely negatives the supposition of the whole having sprung from mere poetical association. It were against all calculation of probabilities, that so many writers, of various times, nations, and tempers, and in such different lines of life, should either light on the same set of figures independently of one another, or coincide in imitating any one who had gone before them with no special authority; more especially, as many of the symbols are far from possessing, at first sight, that exquisite poetical fitness, which would be required, regarding the whole as a matter of taste; on the contrary, not a few of them are blamed, by the disparagers of Antiquity, on this very account, that they are so forced, overstrained, and irrelevant, and what classical judges might perhaps call *ψυχϱά*.[a]

Thus they complain, not perceiving that the fact on which they rest, if it were granted, tends on the whole to make us suppose a higher origin for the imagery in question, than any man's poetical or imaginative taste. Such writers, for example, as St. Ambrose or St. Cyprian, St. Chrysostom, or St. Gregory Nazianzen,[b] who evince in their remains the most vivid sense of poetical delicacy and beauty; – when we find them all concurring in the use of symbols, such as have now been described, must we not suppose that they drew from a common source, and were guided in their selection by something deeper than imaginative delight in the beauties of nature, and in the exercise of their own ingenuity?

The same may be said of the hypothesis (if such should occur to any one) which would make these allusions of the old writers *merely moral*; i.e. so many analogies or similitudes *selected by themselves*, from the course of human life or external nature, to render some truth or precept more forcible and vivid. I do not deny that such analogies occur; especially when they are employed, as by St. Basil

[a] Baseless.

[b] Together with St. Basil, these were third and fourth century Fathers of the Christian Church renowned for the eloquence of their writings.

and St. Ambrose, in their Hexaëmeron before mentioned, in descanting on the works of Creation. For example, we may take St. Basil's account of a mode which the gardeners had of correcting the insipid wateriness of certain fruits.

'Some plant the wild figs close to the cultivated: others bind the fruit of the forest fig to the mild and cultivated sort, and so heal its insipidity, the juice of the wilder having the effect of keeping the other from melting and falling away. Would you know what this riddle, presented to you by nature, signifies? That we should often do well to resort even to those who are aliens from the faith, and from them assume a kind of steady vigour, for the performance of good works. I mean, should you see any one either living as a heathen, or separated from the Church by perverse heresy, yet behaving soberly and observing discipline generally in his moral conduct, do thou draw more strictly the bands of thine own goodness, and so become like the fruitful fig-tree, gathering energy to itself from the presence of its wild kindred, so as both to stay its fruit from falling, and cherish it more effectually to its full size.'

It is easy to see that St. Basil produces this particular parable as an invention of his own, claiming no particular authority for it. And this I call the *moral* way of symbolizing natural objects.

At the same time, it may appear from the phrase, *τί σοι τὸ παρὰ τῆς συκῆς αἴνιγμα βούλεται;*[a] that he was speaking as one himself aware, and among persons who made no question, that every part of nature has its appropriate *αἴνιγμα*,[b] if we could but find it out. Now this, was an opinion which St. Basil was little likely to frame for himself, through excessive indulgence to his own fancy, since he of all the Fathers most earnestly protests against the unrestrained use of allegory. We must then conclude that the sacramental or symbolical view of nature which he implies in the last-mentioned clause, had been received by him as an acknowledged truth, not struck out as a speculation of his own.

In other places indeed he avows it more distinctly: e.g. where he speaks of the heavenly bodies: 'If the heaven is vast beyond the measure of human understanding, what mind then shall have power to trace out the nature of the invisible things? If the sun, which is subject to decay, is so fair, so large, so swiftly moving, yet so regular in fulfilling its courses, – being both for magnitude proportioned to the universe, so as not to exceed the due relation to the whole system, and for beauty a sort of clear eye to nature, the

[a] 'Would you know what this riddle derived from the fig tree signifies.'
[b] Riddle; hidden meaning.

ornament of all creation, – if I say this be a sight of which one can never have too much, what must He be for beauty, who is the Sun of Righteousness! If the blind have a loss in not beholding this our sun, how great is the sinner's loss in being deprived of the TRUE LIGHT.' Of this epithet, True, thus applied, more will be said by and by; I will but suggest here, that on consideration it may possibly be found to involve the whole theory here contended for.

In the next paragraph, St. Basil speaks thus of the heavenly bodies in general: 'As the fire is one thing and the lamp another, the one properly having power to enlighten, the other made to conduct the light according to our needs; so were the lights of heaven now framed as a vehicle for that purest and unmingled and immaterial light. Even as the Apostle calls certain, 'Lights in the world,' although the True Light of the world is other than they; – such as that by participation of It the Saints became lights of the souls whom they disciplined, delivering them from the gloom of ignorance: – so also in the creation was this visible sun, stored with that brightest light, by the Maker of all, and kindled in the world.'

These, and similar divine parables, so to call them, are evidently introduced in somewhat of a different tone from that before quoted about the cultivation of figs, which was introduced expressly and formally as a new thing; whereas these assume a certain familiarity, on the hearer's part, with the symbolical imagery.

If one were to call these latter, of the sun and stars, examples of a symbolical or sacramental view of nature, it would perhaps be no improper mode of expressing the fact here intended; *viz.* that the works of God in creation and providence, besides their immediate uses in this life appeared to the old writers as so many intended tokens from the Almighty, to assure us of some spiritual fact or other, which it concerns us in some way to know. So far, therefore, they fulfilled half at least of the nature of sacraments, according to the strict definition of our Catechism: they were pledges to assure us of some spiritual thing, if they were not means to convey it to us. They were, in a very sufficient sense, *Verba visibilia.*[9] . . .

Warrant of scripture for the Mystical view of things natural

Now it would seem, that to one large class at least, of those to whom the writings of St. John were at first addressed, – the

Hellenistical Jews of Alexandria, – this doctrine of correspondence between things seen and unseen was familiar and very acceptable.

But not to pursue this topic further at present; let it be considered, whether there are not, on the face of Scripture itself, other obvious appearances in its favour. In the first place, there is the broad fact, that the revealed oracles deal so largely, I had almost said so unreservedly, in symbolical language taken from natural objects: and next, what is equally obvious, that the chosen vehicle for the most direct divine communications has always been that form of speech, which most readily adopts and invites such imagery; viz. the Poetical. These are undeniable and surely most significant circumstances, and hardly to be accounted for by the sayings of those, who would reduce all Mysticism to the mere workings of human fancy. Let us reflect, distinctly and at large, on each of them.

And first, as to the symbolical language of Scripture, is there not something very striking, to a thoughtful reverential mind, in the simple fact of such language occurring there at all? This is not meant of merely metaphorical and figurative language, expressing one human and temporal matter by another; but the case intended is, when truths *supernatural* are represented in Scripture by visible and sensible imagery. Consider what this really comes to. The Author of Scripture is the Author of Nature. He made His Creatures what they are, upholds them in their being, modifies it at His will, knows all their secret relations, associations, and properties. We know not how much there may be, far beyond mere metaphor and similitude, in His using the name of any one of His creatures, in a translated sense, to shadow out some thing invisible. But thus far we may seem to understand, that the object thus spoken of by Him is so far taken out of the number of ordinary figures of speech, and resources of language, and partakes thenceforth of the nature of a Type.

For what is it, wherein our idea of a Scriptural Type differs from that of a mere illustration or analogy? It appears to lie chiefly in these two things: first, that the event or observance itself, to which we annex the figurative meaning, was ordered, we know, from the beginning, with reference to that meaning: next, that the ideas having been once associated with each other, by authority of God's own Word, reverential minds shall never thereafter be able to part with that association; the sign will to them habitually prove a remembrance and token of the thing signified: and this also must have been intended in the first sanctioning of the type, being the inevitable result, in all minds that fear God, and watch for the signs of His presence. Thus Abraham's sacrifice of Isaac, for example, had it been related only by Josephus, might well have been used by way of similitude or comparison to illustrate the sacrifice of God's only begotten Son, on the same mountain, two thousand years after: but it is not clear that we could have positively called it a Type. That which warrants us in doing so, is the constant interpretation of the Church, confirming the thought which would naturally enter into good and considerate hearts on reading of it in the Scriptures. . . .

Now considering to what an extent nature (so to speak,) delights in pairs and groupings, and relations; how 'one thing' – as the son of Sirach[a] observes, is everywhere 'set against another;' how impossible it is to find an object single and uncombined with all others, or to limit the extent of the associations and connexions, which manifest themselves one after another, when we set about tracing any one of the works of creation, through all its influences and aspects on the rest; it ought not perhaps to seem over strange, if the symbolical and mystical use of any one thing were thought to imply the possibility at least of a similar use and bearing in all things.

And this presumption will evidently be strengthened, as the instances which Holy Scripture furnishes multiply, and as we find, on more and more acquaintance with it, that its typical allusions are more developed, and come out on its surface, as stars meet the eye more abundantly, when we continue gazing for any time on what seemed at first merely a space of open sky. St. Augustin appears to have been particularly gifted with the power of discerning this kind of holy imagery. It is really wonderful, as one reads his descants, on the Psalms more especially, how many allusions he detects and brings out, with more or less ingenuity in the particular instance; so that it must require, one would think, a mind prepossessed altogether with dislike of the principle of Mysticism, not to be carried away with him. But even without stopping to discern these more latent allusions, it should seem that on the very surface of Scripture so many of the chief visible objects are invested with spiritual meanings, that to affirm the same of the whole world of sense ought not to sound too hard a saying. The symbols which are mentioned are almost enough to make up between them 'a new heaven and a new earth,' and to complete the proof, that 'the first heaven and the first earth' are to be regarded both generally and in their parts, as types and shadows of those which are out of sight.

[a] Or Ecclesiasticus, *Apocrypha*, but the quotation is from Ecclesiastes 7:14.

10. *On Mysticism*

On this head there appears something instructive in the circumstance that the phrase just referred to, 'a new heaven and a new earth,' occurs both in the Old and in the New Testament at the very conclusion of a great body of Prophecy,[a] in the course of which the imagery of the visible world has been, one may say, unreservedly employed to represent the scenes and transactions of the invisible one. That is, after the devout mind has been accustomed in detail to associations of that kind, comes in the most comprehensive phrase that could be employed, apparently confirming, by the Creator's authority, the view of creation, thus become familiar. Perhaps it adds something to the argument, that in the second instance the phrase occurs within a few sentences of the conclusion of the whole Bible.

Nominalists however of various classes are ready enough with their solutions of these appearances. They say, 'it is the imperfection of language; the Almighty Himself condescending to employ human words and idioms, could no otherwise convey ideas of the spiritual world, than by images and terms taken from objects of sense.' Or again, 'it is the genius of Orientalism: if God vouchsafed to address the men of any particular time or country, he would adopt the modes of speech suited to that time and country.' Or 'the whole is mere poetical ornament, the vehicle of moral or historical truth, framed to be beautified and engaging in its kind, in mere indulgence to the infirmity of human nature.'

But as to the particular point in question, would it not be enough to say, in answer to all these statements together, that even if granted in fact, they fail as explanations? since the question would immediately occur, Who made Language, or Orientalism, or Poetry, what they respectively are? Was it not One, who knew beforehand that He should adopt them one day, as the channel and conveyance of His truth and His will to mankind? Surely, reason and piety teach us, that God's providence prepared language in general, and especially the languages of Holy Scripture, and the human styles of its several writers, as fit *media* through which His supernatural glories and dealings might be discerned: and if they be so formed as necessarily to give us notions of a certain correspondence between the super-natural and the visible, we can hardly help concluding that such notions were intended to be formed by us; except there be some direct text, or strong analogy of faith, against it. . . .

[a] Isaiah 65:17. Revelation 27:7.

So much for the direct encouragement given in the Bible to the symbolical use of things natural. There is, as was mentioned above, another indirect yet real presumption to the same effect, which at present can only just be adverted to: and that is, the studied preference of *poetical* forms of thought and language, as the channel of supernatural knowledge to mankind. Poetry, traced as high up as we can go, may almost seem to be God's gift from the beginning, vouchsafed to us for this very purpose: at any rate the fact is unquestionable, that it was the ordained vehicle of revelation, until God Himself was made manifest in the flesh. And since the characteristic tendency of poetical minds is to make the world of sense, from beginning to end, symbolical of the absent and unseen, any instance of divine favour shewn to Poetry, any divine use of it in the training of God's people, would seem, as far as it goes, to warrant that tendency; to set God's seal upon it, and witness it as reasonable and true.

Much might be said on this head: but it is enough now to have just indicated it, as one among the many reasons for thinking that Christian Antiquity was far more scriptural, than at first we might be apt to imagine, as in many other things, so in the deep mystical import, which it unreservedly attributes to the whole material world, and to all parts of it.

11. *Lectures on Poetry*, translated by E. K. Francis (2 vols., 1912), vol. II, pp. 477, 480–3

If readers had found Plato lurking behind Keble's poetic conception of a universe of symbols rather than a mechanist world of material order or behind his concept of reserve in God's manner of communicating truth, Keble would not have been offended. Since God was not merely deducible from the evidence but immanent in His universe, then the analogies and correspondences by which He was revealed were not the result of human cleverness but created by Him to be glimpsed even by pagans.

As Oxford's Professor of Poetry, Keble gave a series of lectures in Latin dealing with classical poetry which were first published, with a dedication to Wordsworth, in 1844. These two very brief extracts from his final lecture expand upon his idea of Revelation as essentially poetic and demonstrate the consistency of Keble's thought – a quality he admired in writers as apparently diverse as Sir Walter Scott and Aeschylus.

There is, then, nothing in their [the Fathers'] teaching inconsistent with the belief that all that array of poets and poetry, upon which Greeks and Romans prided themselves, pointed forward in God's

Providence to a coming order of things, even though the writers themselves were unconscious of it.

And if they truly possess this quality, we may heartily approve the policy of our forefathers in assigning so great a share and influence in the education of youth to the ancient Greek and Latin poets. In this they do no more than follow in the footsteps of the Providence which, so many ages ago, saw fit to train the opening minds of God's own people in studies of the same kind: and, just as it gave to the Jews the oracles of the prophets, so to the rest of the world, though under a different dispensation, accorded Homer, Plato, and Virgil as first elements of wisdom and truth. Finally, let us be well assured of this: it vitally concerns the interests of sacred truth to maintain the usage which has survived in our Universities up to the present time, of requiring from our students a close and constant study of the writings of the classic poets, philosophers, and historians: who may all be considered poets, so far at least as they are wont to elevate the mind by the clear light either of memory or lofty speculation. . . .

And here, as so often before, we must go back to the very beginning and foundation of all Poetry. Our conclusion was, that this divine art essentially consisted in a power of healing and restoring overburdened and passionate minds. It follows that the more deeply any feeling penetrates human affections, and the more permanently it influences them, the closer are its relationships and associations with Poetry. Now, partly the very nature of religion in itself, partly the actual confession of all who can be supposed to have the faintest sense of true piety, impress on us the fact that nothing takes such entire possession of the human heart, and, in a way, concentrates its feeling, as the thought of God and an eternity to come: nowhere is our feeble mortal nature more conscious of its helplessness; nothing so powerfully impels it, sadly and anxiously, to look round on all sides for remedy and relief. As a result of this, Religion freely and gladly avails itself of every comfort and assistance which Poetry may afford: such as the regularity, the modulations, the changes of rhythm; the use of language sometimes restrained, sometimes eager and passionate; and all those other methods which all men feel after, but only a few can express. Moreover, a true and holy religion will turn such aids to the fullest account, because it, most of all, feels itself overwhelmed in the presence of the boundless vastness of the Universe: and this is so both when in early days, before Truth itself was fully revealed, simple untrained races were being taught by some dim outlines and types, and when more advanced believers are being trained to find utterance and language worthy to express their gratitude for God's great mercies to them.

Moreover, from this common weakness there springs a common use of this external world and of all objects which appeal to the senses. And in this regard it is marvellous how Piety and Poetry are able to help each other. For, while Religion seeks out, as I said, on all sides, not merely language but also anything which may perform the office of language and help to express the emotions of the soul; what aid can be imagined more grateful and more timely than the presence of Poetry, which leads men to the secret sources of Nature, and supplies a rich wealth of similes whereby a pious mind may supply and remedy, in some sort, its powerlessness of speech; and may express many things more touchingly, many things more seriously and weightily, all things more truly, than had been possible without this aid? Conversely, should we ask how, pre-eminently, 'came honour and renown to prophetic bards and their poems',[a] it is Religion that has most to be thanked for this. For, once let that magic wand, as the phrase goes, touch any region of Nature, forthwith all that before seemed secular and profane is illumined with a new and celestial light: men come to realize that the various images and similes of things, and all other poetic charms, are not merely the play of a keen and clever mind, nor to be put down as empty fancies: but rather they guide us by gentle hints and no uncertain signs, to the very utterances of Nature, or we may more truly say, of the Author of Nature. And thus it has come to pass, that great and pre-eminent poets have almost been ranked as the representatives of religion, and their sphere has been treated with religious reverence. In short, Poetry lends Religion her wealth of symbols and similes: Religion restores these again to Poetry, clothed with so splendid a radiance that they appear to be no longer merely symbols, but to partake (I might almost say) of the nature of sacraments.

There is, too, another strong tie of kinship which binds these two together, in that each is controlled by a tone of modest and religious reserve. For, on the one hand, all who carefully try to imitate Nature are forced to observe a certain restraint and reserve: at least thus far, that, like her, they approach each stage of beauty by a quiet and well-ordered movement, not suddenly or, to use a mathematical phrase, *per saltum*[b] (as do those who have no scruple in appearing

[a] Horace, *Ars Poetica* 400. [b] By a sudden leap.

boldly in public); and, on the other hand, the whole principle of piety, such at least as is wisely governed, is ordered by the rule divinely laid down in Holy Scripture, that things of highest worth should, for the most part, not be offered to listless and unprepared minds; but only be brought into the light when the eyes of those who gaze on them have been disciplined and purified. Thus the controlling Power which tempers and orders all things has compelled each, by a kind of decree, not to permit any one to have full fruition of the beauteous form and features of Truth, except his devotion be such as leads him to take zealous pains to search her out. Certainly no one who has been trained in this principle from his earliest years and into whose mind it has sunk deeply will ever allow himself to expose the sacred mysteries either of Nature or Religion to public view without regard to the temper and training of his hearers. He would rather be charged with obscureness than pour forth all truths, secret and open alike, without restraint; he would rather be criticized as wanting in ability than wanting in reserve.

Lastly, both in Poetry and in Religion, an indefinably tender and keen feeling for what is past or out of sight or yet to come, will ever assert and claim a high place of honour for itself. For those who, from their very heart, either burst into poetry, or seek the Deity in prayer, must needs ever cherish with their whole spirit the vision of something more beautiful, greater and more lovable, than all that mortal eye can see. Thus the very practice and cultivation of Poetry will be found to possess, in some sort, the power of guiding and composing the mind to worship and prayer: provided indeed the poems contain nothing hurtful either to religion or morality.

John Henry Newman

(1801–1890)

12. 'The Tamworth Reading Room', *Discussions and Arguments* (1872), pp. 254–305

'Who could resist the charm of that spiritual apparition, gliding in the dim afternoon light through the aisles of St Mary's, rising into the pulpit, and then, in the most entrancing of voices, breaking the silence with words and thoughts which were a religious music – subtle, sweet, mournful?' (*Complete Prose Works of Matthew Arnold*, vol. x, p. 165).

Matthew Arnold's analysis of his society demanded that Newman be used to represent the sweetness and light of Oxford which had been overcome by the successive currents of liberalism and democracy. His nostalgic portrait, therefore, allows Newman ghostly beauty and magnetism but subtly distorts by ignoring the energy and sharpness of thought and the apparent informality of the brilliant conversationalist seen in the following piece.

In 1841 Newman wrote a series of letters to *The Times* on 5, 9, 10, 12, 20, 22 and 27 February: the first was unsigned, but the remainder appeared over the name 'Catholicus'. Later that year the letters were published in pamphlet form as *The Tamorth Reading Room. Letters on an Address delivered by Sir Robert Peel, Bart. M.P. on the Establishment of a Reading Room at Tamworth.* In the pamphlet Newman made numerous corrections of punctuation and a few verbal changes. His only major addition was the paragraph in Letter 4 beginning, 'I will make this fair offer to both of them . . .', responding to a letter to *The Times* on 9 February which pointed out that the Vicar of Tamworth was to be an *ex officio* member of the committee. The further revised edition printed here is found in *Discussions and Arguments*, where Newman extended the quotations from works he was attacking. Such revision between editions was the habitual practice of writers on controversial subjects and makes Newman's opening jibe at a politician exercising his immemorial right to emend between speech and pamphlet appear even more cavalier.

In this work, however, we see Newman enjoying the pleasures and weapons of attack. He is under no obligation to undertake a systematic defence of his ideology, nor to formulate constructive proposals about the place of education as he was to do in *The Idea of a University* (1852–9). Rather he is free to answer assertion with counter-assertion, crush his opponent with the weight of accumulated parallel clauses, or slay with an epigram. *The Times*'s invitation to polemical journalism must have come as a welcome relief from the writing of *Tract No. XC* where the onus of proof lay so heavily upon Newman.

Newman uses the unfortunate Peel as his stalking-horse for an attack on the secular liberal ideology of the Age of Reform, which he believed to be wholly opposed to the

Catholic mind and temperament. The utilitarian philosophy of self-improvement seems to have become so pervasive that Newman catches the foremost Conservative of the day voicing a Benthamism, humanized by the Whig liberalism of the *Edinburgh Review*, into a philosophy for which Newman coins the term 'Broughamism'.

The range of Newman's allusions, his calculated use of rhetorical devices, his jibes at 'conventical eloquence', should be sufficient to dispel any notion of his devaluing the fruits of education: as always he is anxious only to deny any connection between reason and faith, education and morality. On the face of it the forensic skill deployed here is strangely at odds with his statement of 1870: 'I do not want to be converted by a smart syllogism; if I am asked to convert others, by it, I say plainly I do not care to overcome their reason without touching their hearts' (*An Essay in aid of a Grammar of Assent*, ed. C. F. Harrold (1947), p. 323). In the second paragraph of Letter 2, for instance, Newman operates a particularly devious sleight of hand in his use of the verb 'to know' in order to confirm his distinction between the acquisition of secular knowledge and the conscience through which alone God is revealed to man. These letters, however, were not intended to convert but to attract attention to the Tractarian warfare against liberalism. In 1870, by now a Roman Catholic, Newman acknowledged the occasional nature of their composition and, excusing the 'differences in terminology, and hardihood of assertion, befitting the circumstances of its publication', proceeded to use in the *Grammar of Assent* all but the second paragraph of Letter 6, with the explanation, 'I quote them, because, over and above their appositeness in this place, they present the doctrine which I have been insisting, from a second point of view, and with a freshness and force which I cannot now command' (pp. 69–70).

Over a century later Newman remains the freshest and most readable voice in this book, because the clarity of a style, almost devoid of technical theological vocabularly, underlines the way in which personal doctrinal convictions seem to be subsumed under the guise of a commonsensical approach to a general philosophical problem of interest to all intelligent readers. Newman, like Simeon, occasionally employs the striking homely image or metaphor as a device to ensure that abstract concepts are made clear, but in Newman's case, vividly colloquial phrasing (e.g. 'how to take care of number one', p. 159); or 'think themselves lucky', p. 160); or 'all for tinkering it', p. 168) seems part of a flexible style which can modulate easily from the tones of conversational debate (note the frequency of 'and' or 'now' to open sentences) to extreme formality. The way in which a sentence of Newman's, begun in awesome politeness, can have its initial direction and meaning undermined by a casual phrase apparently tacked on as an afterthought is reminiscent of the control with which Pope deployed the heroic couplet to ironic purpose. The intellectual force, pervasive irony and barbed wit of these letters had struck home thirty years before. Peel was much vexed by the anonymous attack and the Rev. R. W. Church, reviewing the scene from Oriel College, Oxford, in March 1841, gave this report:

> These said letters, signed 'Catholicus', with one or two others of the same sort on duelling, &c., were thought to smack strongly of Puseyism, and brought out furious attacks on the said Puseyites in the 'Globe', expostulations and remonstrances on political and theological grounds from the 'Standard', and a triumphant Macaulayism in the 'Morning Chronicle', in which the writer, with great cleverness, drew a picture of alliance between effete plausible, hollow Toryism with Puseyism, which he described as a principle which for earnestness and strength had had no parallel since the Reformers and Puritans, and rejoiced greatly

over the prospect that Puseyism must soon blow Toryism to shivers. And the 'Globe' admitted that people were most egregiously out in supposing that this same Puseyism was an affair of vestments and ceremonies: that it was, on the contrary, something far deeper and more dangerous. Such was the state of things out of doors last month (*Letters and Correspondence of John Henry Newman during his life in the English Church*, ed. A. Mozley (2 vols., 1898), vol. II, p. 293).

1. Secular Knowledge in contrast with Religion

Sir, – Sir Robert Peel's position in the country, and his high character, render it impossible that his words and deeds should be other than public property. This alone would furnish an apology for my calling the attention of your readers to the startling language, which many of them doubtless have already observed, in the Address which this most excellent and distinguished man has lately delivered upon the establishment of a Library and Reading-room at Tamworth; but he has superseded the need of apology altogether, by proceeding to present it to the public in the form of a pamphlet. His speech, then, becomes important, both from the name and the express act of its author. At the same time, I must allow that he has not published it in the fulness in which it was spoken. Still it seems to me right and fair, or rather imperative, to animadvert upon it as it has appeared in your columns, since in that shape it will have the widest circulation. A public man must not claim to harangue the whole world in newspapers, and then to offer his second thoughts to such as choose to buy them at a bookseller's.

I shall surprise no one who has carefully read Sir Robert's Address, and perhaps all who have not, by stating my conviction, that, did a person take it up without looking at the heading, he would to a certainty set it down as a production of the years 1827 and 1828 – the scene Gower Street, the speaker Mr Brougham or Dr Lushington, and the occasion, the laying the first stone, or the inauguration, of the then-called London University.[1] I profess myself quite unable to draw any satisfactory line of difference between the Gower Street and the Tamworth Exhibition, except, of course, that Sir Robert's personal religious feeling breaks out in his Address across his assumed philosophy. I say assumed, I might say affected – for I think too well of him to believe it genuine.

On the occasion in question, Sir Robert gave expression to a theory of morals and religion, which of course, in a popular speech, was not put out in a very dogmatic form, but which, when analyzed and fitted together, reads somewhat as follows:

Human nature, he seems to say, if left to itself, becomes sensual and degraded. Uneducated men live in the indulgence of their passions; or, if they are merely taught to read, they dissipate and debase their minds by trifling or vicious publications. Education is the cultivation of the intellect and heart, and Useful Knowledge is the great instrument of education. It is the parent of virtue, the nurse of religion; it exalts man to his highest perfection, and is the sufficient scope of his most earnest exertions.

Physical and moral science rouses, transports, exalts, enlarges, tranquillizes, and satisfies the mind. Its attractiveness obtains a hold over us; the excitement attending it supersedes grosser excitements; it makes us know our duty, and thereby enables us to do it; by taking the mind off itself, it destroys anxiety; and by providing objects of admiration, it soothes and subdues us.

And, in addition, it is a kind of neutral ground, on which men of every shade of politics and religion may meet together, disabuse each other of their prejudices, form intimacies, and secure co-operation.

This, it is almost needless to say, is the very theory, expressed temperately, on which Mr Brougham once expatiated in the Glasgow and London Universities.[2] Sir R. Peel, indeed, has spoken with somewhat of his characteristic moderation; but for his closeness in sentiment to the Brougham of other days, a few parallels from their respective Discourses will be a sufficient voucher.

For instance, Mr Brougham, in his Discourses upon Science, and in his Pursuit of Knowledge under Difficulties,[3] wrote about the 'pure delight' of physical knowledge, of its 'pure gratification,' of its 'tendency to purify and elevate man's nature,' of its 'elevating and refining it,' of its 'giving a dignity and *importance* to the enjoyment of life.' Sir Robert, pursuing the idea, shows us its importance even in death, observing, that physical knowledge supplied the thoughts from which 'a great experimentalist professed *in his last illness* to derive some pleasure and some consolation, when most other sources of consolation and pleasure were closed to him.'

Mr Brougham talked much and eloquently of 'the *sweetness* of knowledge,' and 'the *charms* of philosophy,' of students 'smitten with the love of knowledge,' of '*wooing* truth with the unwearied ardour of a *lover*,' of 'keen and overpowering *emotion*, of *ecstasy*,' of 'the absorbing *passion* of knowledge,' of 'the *strength* of the passion, and the exquisite pleasure of its *gratification*.' And Sir Robert, in less glowing language, but even in a more tender strain than Mr Brougham, exclaims, 'If I can only persuade you to enter upon that delightful path, I am sanguine enough to believe that there *will be opened to you gradual charms and temptations* which will induce you to persevere.'

Mr Brougham naturally went on to enlarge upon 'bold and successful adventures in the pursuit; – such, perhaps, as in the story of Paris and Helen, or Hero and Leander;' of 'daring ambition in its course to greatness,' of 'enterprising spirits,' and their 'brilliant feats,' of 'adventurers of the world of intellect,' and of 'the illustrious vanquishers of fortune.' And Sir Robert, not to be outdone, echoes back 'aspirations for knowledge and distinction,' 'simple determination of overcoming difficulties,' 'premiums on skill and intelligence,' 'mental activity,' 'steamboats and railroads,' 'producer and consumer,' 'spirit of inquiry afloat;' and at length he breaks out into almost conventical eloquence, crying, 'Every newspaper *teems with notices* of publications written upon *popular principles*, detailing all the recent discoveries of science, and their connexion with improvements in arts and manufactures. *Let me earnestly entreat you* not to neglect the *opportunity* which we are now willing to afford you! *It will not be our fault* if the ample page of knowledge, rich with the spoils of time, is not unrolled to you! *We tell you,*' etc., etc.

Mr Brougham pronounces that a man by 'learning truths wholly new to him,' and by 'satisfying himself of the grounds on which known truths rest,' 'will enjoy a *proud consciousness* of having, by his own exertions become a *wiser*, and *therefore* a more *exalted* creature.' Sir Robert runs abreast of this great sentiment. He tells us, in words which he adopts as his own, that a man 'in becoming *wiser* will become *better*:' he will 'rise *at once* in the scale of intellectual and moral existence, and by being accustomed to such contemplations, he will feel the *moral dignity* of his nature *exalted*.'

Mr Brougham, on his inauguration at Glasgow, spoke to the ingenuous youth assembled on the occasion, of 'the benefactors of mankind, when they rest from their pious labours, looking down upon the blessings with which their toils and sufferings have clothed the scene of their former existence;' and in his Discourse upon Science declared it to be 'no mean reward of our labour to become acquainted with the prodigious genius of those who have almost exalted the nature of man above his destined sphere;' and who 'hold a station apart, rising over *all* the great teachers of mankind, and spoken of reverently, as if Newton and La Place[4] were not the names of mortal men.' Sir Robert cannot, of course, equal this sublime flight; but he succeeds in calling Newton and others 'those mighty spirits which have made the *greatest* (though imperfect) advances towards the understanding of "the Divine Nature and Power".'

Mr Brougham talked at Glasgow about putting to flight the 'evil spirits of *tyranny and persecution* which haunted the long night now gone down the sky,' and about men 'no longer suffering themselves to be led *blindfold in ignorance*;' and in his Pursuit of Knowledge he speaks of Pascal having, 'under the influence of certain religious views, during a period of *depression*,' conceived scientific pursuits 'to be little better than abuse of his time and faculties.' Sir Robert, fainter in tone, but true to the key, warns his hearers, – 'Do not be deceived by the sneers that you hear against knowledge, which are uttered by men who *want to depress you*, and keep you depressed to the level of their *own contented ignorance*.'

Mr Brougham laid down at Glasgow the infidel principle, or, as he styles it, 'the great truth,' which 'has gone forth to all the ends of the earth, that man shall no more render account to man for his belief, over which he has himself no control.' And Dr Lushington applied it in Gower Street to the College then and there rising, by asking, 'Will any one argue for establishing a *monopoly* to be enjoyed by the few who are of one *denomination* of the Christian Church only?' And he went on to speak of the association and union of all *without exclusion or restriction*, of 'friendships cementing the bond of charity, and softening the asperities which *ignorance and separation* have fostered.' Long may it be before Sir Robert Peel professes the great principle itself! even though, as the following passages show, he is inconsistent enough to think highly of its application in the culture of the mind. He speaks, for instance, of 'this preliminary and fundamental rule, that no works of *controversial divinity* shall enter into the library (applause),' – of 'the institution being open to all persons of all descriptions, without reference to political opinions, or *religious creed*,' – and of 'an edifice in which men of all political opinions and *all religious feelings* may unite in the furtherance of knowledge, without the *asperities* of party feeling.' Now, that British society should consist of persons of different religions, is this a positive standing evil, to be endured at best as unavoidable, or a topic of exultation? Of exultation, answers Sir Robert; the greater differences the better, the more the merrier. So we must interpret his tone.

It is reserved for few to witness the triumph of their own opinions; much less to witness it in the instance of their own direct and personal opponents. Whether the Lord Brougham of this day feels all that satisfaction and inward peace which he attributes to success of whatever kind in intellectual efforts, it is not for me to decide; but that he has achieved, to speak in his own style, a mighty victory, and is leading in chains behind his chariot-wheels, a great captive, is a fact beyond question.

Such is the reward in 1841 for unpopularity in 1827.

What, however, is a boast to Lord Brougham, is in the same proportion a slur upon the fair fame of Sir Robert Peel, at least in the judgement of those who have hitherto thought well of him. Were there no other reason against the doctrine propounded in the Address which has been the subject of these remarks, (but I hope to be allowed an opportunity of assigning others,) its parentage would be a grave *prima facie* difficulty in receiving it. It is, indeed, most melancholy to see so sober and experienced a man practising the antics of one of the wildest performers of this wild age; and taking off the tone, manner, and gestures of the versatile ex-Chancellor, with a versatility almost equal to his own.

Yet let him be assured that the task of rivalling such a man is hopeless, as well as unprofitable. No one can equal the great sophist. Lord Brougham is inimitable in his own line.

2. *Secular Knowledge not the Principle of Moral Improvement*

A distinguished Conservative statesman tells us from the town-hall of Tamworth that 'in becoming wiser a man will become better;' meaning by wiser more conversant with the facts and theories of physical science; and that such a man will 'rise *at once* in the scale of intellectual and *moral* existence.' 'That,' he adds, 'is my belief.' He avows, also, that the fortunate individual whom he is describing, by being 'accustomed to such contemplations, will feel the *moral dignity of his nature exalted*.' He speaks also of physical knowledge as 'being the means of useful occupation and rational recreation;' of 'the pleasures of knowledge' superseding 'the indulgence of sensual appetite,' and of its 'contributing to the intellectual and *moral improvement* of the community.' Accordingly, he very consistently wishes it to be set before 'the female as well as the male portion of the population;' otherwise, as he truly observes, 'great injustice would be done to the well-educated and virtuous women' of the place. They are to 'have equal power and equal influence with others.' It will be difficult to exhaust the reflections which rise in the mind on reading avowals of this nature.

The first question which obviously suggests itself is *how* these wonderful moral effects are to be wrought under the instrumentality of the physical sciences. Can the process be analyzed and drawn out, or does it act like a dose or a charm which comes into general use empirically? Does Sir Robert Peel mean to say, that whatever be the occult reasons for the result, so it is; you have but to drench the popular mind with physics, and moral and religious advancement follows on the whole, in spite of individual failures? Yet where has the experiment been tried on so large a scale as to justify such anticipations? Or rather, does he mean, that, from the nature of the case, he who is imbued with science and literature, unless adverse influences interfere, cannot but be a better man? It is natural and becoming to seek for some clear idea of the meaning of so dark an oracle. To know is one thing, to do is another; the two things are altogether distinct. A man knows he should get up in the morning, – he lies a-bed; he knows he should not lose his temper, yet he cannot keep it. A labouring man knows he should not go to the ale-house, and his wife knows she should not filch when she goes out charing; but, nevertheless, in these cases, the consciousness of a duty is not all one with the performance of it. There are, then, large families of instances, to say the least, in which men may become wiser, without becoming better; what, then, is the meaning of this great maxim in the mouth of its promulgators?

Mr Bentham would answer, that the knowledge which carries virtue along with it, is the knowledge how to take care of number one – a clear appreciation of what is pleasurable, what painful, and what promotes the one and prevents the other. An uneducated man is ever mistaking his own interest, and standing in the way of his own true enjoyments. Useful Knowledge is that which tends to make us more useful to ourselves; – a most definite and intelligible account of the matter, and needing no explanation. But it would be a great injustice, both to Lord Brougham and to Sir Robert, to suppose, when they talk of Knowledge being Virtue, that they are Benthamizing. Bentham had not a spark of poetry in him; on the contrary, there is much of high aspiration, generous sentiment, and impassioned feeling in the tone of Lord Brougham and Sir Robert. They speak of knowledge as something 'pulchrum,' fair and glorious, exalted above the range of ordinary humanity, and so little connected with the personal interest of its votaries, that, though Sir Robert does *obiter* talk of improved modes of draining, and the chemical properties of manure, yet he must not be supposed to come short of the lofty enthusiasm of Lord Brougham, who expressly panegyrizes certain ancient philosophers who gave up riches, retired into solitude, or embraced a life of travel, smit with a sacred curiosity about physical or mathematical truth.

Here Mr Bentham, did it fall to him to offer a criticism, doubtless would take leave to inquire whether such language was anything better than a fine set of words 'signifying nothing,' – flowers of rhetoric, which bloom, smell sweet, and die. But it is impossible to suspect so grave and practical a man as Sir Robert Peel of using words literally without any meaning at all; and though I think at best they have not a very profound meaning, yet, such as it is, we ought to attempt to draw it out.

Now, without using exact theological language, we may surely take it for granted, from the experience of facts, that the human mind is at best in a very unformed or disordered state; passions and conscience, likings and reason, conflicting, – might rising against right, with the prospect of things getting worse. Under these circumstances, what is it that the School of philosophy in which Sir Robert has enrolled himself proposes to accomplish? Not a victory of the mind over itself – not the supremacy of the law – not the reduction of the rebels – not the unity of our complex nature – not an harmonizing of the chaos – but the mere lulling of the passions to rest by turning the course of thought; not a change of character, but a mere removal of temptation. This should be carefully observed. When a husband is gloomy, or an old woman peevish and fretful, those who are about them do all they can to keep dangerous topics and causes of offence out of the way, and think themselves lucky, if, by such skilful management, they get through the day without an outbreak. When a child cries, the nurserymaid dances it about, or points to the pretty black horses out of window, or shows how ashamed poll-parrot or poor puss must be of its tantarums. Such is the sort of prescription which Sir Robert Peel offers to the good people of Tamworth. He makes no pretence of subduing the giant nature, in which we were born, of smiting the loins of the domestic enemies of our peace, of overthrowing passion and fortifying reason; he does but offer to bribe the foe for the nonce with gifts which will avail for that purpose just so long as they *will* avail, and no longer.

This was mainly the philosophy of the great Tully, except when it pleased him to speak as a disciple of the Porch.[a] Cicero handed the recipe to Brougham, and Brougham has passed it on to Peel. If we

[a] i.e. as a Stoic, from *stoa*, the great hall at Athens where the philosopher Zeno lectured.

examine the old Roman's meaning in '*O philosophia, vitae dux*,'[a] it was neither more nor less than this; – that, *while* we were thinking of philosophy, we were not thinking of anything else; we did not feel grief, or anxiety, or passion, or ambition, or hatred all that time, and the only point was to keep thinking of it. How to keep thinking of it was *extra artem*.[b] If a man was in grief, he was to be amused; if disappointed, to be excited; if in a rage, to be soothed; if in love, to be roused to the pursuit of glory. No inward change was contemplated, but a change of external objects; as if we were all White Ladies or Undines,[c] our moral life being one of impulse and emotion, not subjected to laws, not consisting in habits, not capable of growth. When Cicero was outwitted by Caesar, he solaced himself with Plato; when he lost his daughter, he wrote a treatise on Consolation. Such, too, was the philosophy of that Lydian city, mentioned by the historian, who in a famine played at dice to stay their stomachs.[d]

And such is the rule of life advocated by Lord Brougham; and though, of course, he protests that knowledge 'must invigorate the mind as well as entertain it, and refine and elevate the character, while it gives listlessness and weariness their most agreeable excitement and relaxation,' yet his notions of vigour and elevation, when analyzed, will be found to resolve themselves into a mere preternatural excitement under the influence of some stimulating object, or the peace which is attained by there being nothing to quarrel with. He speaks of philosophers leaving the care of their estates, or declining public honours, from the greater desirableness of Knowledge; envies the shelter enjoyed in the University of Glasgow from the noise and bustle of the world; and, *apropos* of Pascal and Cowper, 'so mighty,' says he, 'is the power of intellectual occupation, to make the heart forget, *for the time*, its most prevailing griefs, and to change its deepest gloom to sunshine.'

Whether Sir Robert Peel meant all this, which others before him have meant, it is impossible to say; but I will be bound, if he did not mean this, he meant nothing else, and his words will certainly insinuate this meaning, wherever a reader is not content to go without any meaning at all. They will countenance, with his high authority, what in one form or other is a chief error of the day, in very distinct schools of opinion, – that our true excellence comes not from within, but from without; not wrought out through personal struggles and sufferings, but following upon a passive

[a] 'O philosophy, you who rule life', Cicero, *Tusculan Disputations* v. 2.5.
[b] Outside his theory. [c] Soulless water nymphs. [d] Herodotus, *Histories* I.94.

exposure to influences over which we have no control. They will countenance the theory that diversion is the instrument of improvement, and excitement the condition of right action; and whereas diversions cease to be diversions if they are constant, and excitements by their very nature have a crisis and run through a course, they will tend to make novelty ever in request, and will set the great teachers of morals upon the incessant search after stimulants and sedatives, by which unruly nature may, *pro re nata*,[a] be kept in order.

Hence, be it observed, Lord Brougham, in the last quoted sentence, tells us, with much accuracy of statement, that 'intellectual occupation made the heart' of Pascal or Cowper '*for the time* forget its griefs.' He frankly offers us a philosophy of expedients: he shows us how to live by medicine. Digestive pills half an hour before dinner, and a posset at bedtime at the best; and at the worst, dram-drinking and opium, – the very remedy against broken hearts, or remorse of conscience, which is in request among the many, in gin-palaces *not* intellectual.

And if these remedies be but of temporary effect at the utmost, more commonly they will have no effect at all. Strong liquors, indeed, do for a time succeed in their object; but who was ever consoled in real trouble by the small beer of literature or science? 'Sir,' said Rasselas, to the philosopher who had lost his daughter, 'mortality is an event by which a wise man can never be surprised.' 'Young man,' answered the mourner, 'you speak like one that hath never felt the pangs of separation. What comfort can truth or reason afford me? of what effect are they now but to tell me that my daughter will not be restored?' Or who was ever made more humble or more benevolent by being told, as the same practical moralist words it, 'to concur with the great and unchangeable scheme of universal felicity, and co-operate with the general dispensation and tendency of the present system of things'?[b] Or who was made to do any secret act of self-denial, or was steeled against pain, or peril, by all the lore of the infidel La Place, or those other 'mighty spirits' which Lord Brougham and Sir Robert eulogize? Or when was a choleric temperament ever brought under by a scientific King Canute planting his professor's chair before the rising waves? And as to the 'keen' and 'ecstatic' pleasures which Lord Brougham, not to say Sir Robert, ascribes to intellectual pursuit and conquest, I cannot help thinking that in that line they will find themselves

[a] As things are. [b] Samuel Johnson, *History of Rasselas*, ch. 19.

outbid in the market by gratifications much closer at hand, and on a level with the meanest capacity. Sir Robert makes it a boast that women are to be members of his institution; it is hardly necesary to remind so accomplished a classic, that Aspasia and other learned ladies in Greece[a] are not very encouraging precedents in favour of the purifying effects of science. But the strangest and most painful topic which he urges, is one which Lord Brougham has had the good taste altogether to avoid – the power, not of religion, but of scientific knowledge, on a death-bed; a subject which Sir Robert treats in language which it is far better to believe is mere oratory than is said in earnest.

Such is this new art of living, offered to the labouring classes, – we will say, for instance, in a severe winter, snow on the ground, glass falling, bread rising, coal at 20d. the cwt., and no work.

It does not require many words, then, to determine that, taking human nature as it is actually found, and assuming that there is an Art of life, to say that it consists, or in any essential manner is placed, in the cultivation of Knowledge, that the mind is changed by a discovery, or saved by a diversion, and can thus be amused into immortality, – that grief, anger, cowardice, self-conceit, pride, or passion, can be subdued by an examination of shells or grasses, or inhaling of gases, or chipping of rocks, or calculating the longitude, is the veriest of pretences which sophist or mountebank ever professed to a gaping auditory. If virtue be a mastery over the mind, if its end be action, if its perfection be inward order, harmony, and peace, we must seek it in graver and holier places than in Libraries and Reading-rooms.

3. *Secular Knowledge not a direct Means of Moral Improvement*

There are two Schools of philosophy, in high esteem, at this day, as at other times, neither of them accepting Christian principles as the guide of life, yet both of them unhappily patronized by many whom it would be the worst and most cruel uncharitableness to suspect of unbelief. Mr Bentham is the master of the one; and Sir Robert Peel is a disciple of the other.

Mr Bentham's system has nothing ideal about it; he is a stern realist, and he limits his realism to things which he can see, hear, taste, touch, and handle. He does not acknowledge the existence of

[a] Fifth-century Greek courtesan, mistress of Pericles, whose house became the meeting place for cultured Athenians.

anything which he cannot ascertain for himself. Exist it may nevertheless, but till it makes itself felt, to him it exists not; till it comes down right before him, and he is very short-sighted, it is not recognized by him as having a co-existence with himself, any more than the Emperor of China is received into the European family of Kings. With him a being out of sight is a being simply out of mind; nay, he does not allow the traces or glimpses of facts to have any claim on his regard, but with him to have a little and not much, is to have nothing at all. With him to speak truth is to be ready with a definition, and to imagine, to guess, to doubt, or to falter, is much the same as to lie. What opinion will such an iron thinker entertain of Cicero's 'glory,' or Lord Brougham's 'truth,' or Sir Robert's 'scientific consolations,' and all those other airy nothings which are my proper subject of remark, and which I have in view when, by way of contrast, I make mention of the philosophy of Bentham? And yet the doctrine of the three eminent orators, whom I have ventured to criticize, has in it much that is far nobler than Benthamism; their misfortune being, not that they look for an excellence above the beaten path of life, but that whereas Christianity has told us what the excellence is, Cicero lived before it was given to the world, and Lord Brougham and Sir Robert Peel prefer his involuntary error to their own inherited truth. Surely, there is something unearthly and superhuman in spite of Bentham; but it is not glory, or knowledge, or any abstract idea of virtue, but great and good tidings which need not here be particularly mentioned, and the pity is, that these Christian statesmen cannot be content with what is divine without as a supplement hankering after what was heathen.

Now, independent of all other considerations, the great difference, in a practical light, between the object of Christianity and of heathen belief, is this – that glory, science, knowledge, and whatever other fine names we use, never healed a wounded heart, nor changed a sinful one; but the Divine Word is with power. The ideas which Christianity brings before us are in themselves full of influence, and they are attended with a supernatural gift over and above themselves, in order to meet the special exigencies of our nature. Knowledge is not 'power,' nor is glory 'the first and only fair;' but 'Grace,' or the 'Word,' by whichever name we call it, has been from the first a quickening, renovating, organizing principle. It has now created the individual, and transferred and knit him into a social body, composed of members each similarly created. It has cleansed man of his moral diseases, raised him to hope and energy, given him to propagate a brotherhood among his fellows, and to found a family or rather a kingdom of saints all over the earth; – it introduced a new force into the world, and the impulse which it gave continues in its original vigour down to this day. Each one of us has lit his lamp from his neighbour, or received it from his fathers, and the lights thus transmitted are at this time as strong and as clear as if 1800 years had not passed since the kindling of the sacred flame. What has glory or knowledge been able to do like this? Can it raise the dead? can it create a polity? can it do more than testify man's need and typify God's remedy?

And yet, in spite of this, when we have an instrument given us, capable of changing the whole man, great orators and statesmen are busy, forsooth, with their heathen charms and nostrums, their sedatives, correctives, or restoratives; as preposterously as if we were to build our men-of-war, or conduct our iron-works, on the principles approved in Cicero's day. The utmost that Lord Brougham seems to propose to himself in the education of the mind, is to keep out bad thoughts by means of good – a great object, doubtless, but not so great in philosophical conception, as is the destruction of the bad in Christian fact. 'If it can be a pleasure,' he says, in his Discourse upon the Objects and Advantages of Science, 'if it can be a *pleasure to gratify curiosity*, to know what we were ignorant of, to have our *feelings of wonder* called forth, *how pure a delight of this very kind* does natural science hold out to its students! How wonderful are the laws that regulate the motions of fluids! Is there anything in all the idle books of tales and horrors, more truly astonishing than the fact, that a few pounds of water may, by mere pressure, without any machinery, by merely being placed in one particular way, produce very irresistible force? What can be more strange, than that an ounce weight should balance hundreds of pounds by the intervention of a few bars of thin iron? Can anything surprise us more than to find that the colour white is a mixture of all others? that water should be chiefly composed of an inflammable substance? Akin to this pleasure of contemplating new and extraordinary truths is the *gratification of a more learned curiosity*, by tracing resemblances and relations between things which to common apprehension seem widely different,' etc., etc. And in the same way Sir Robert tells us even of a *devout* curiosity. In all cases *curiosity* is the means, *diversion* of mind the highest end; and though of course I will not assert that Lord Brougham, and certainly not that Sir Robert Peel, denies any higher kind of morality, yet when the former rises above Benthamism, in which he often indulges, into what may be called *Broughamism proper*, he commonly grasps at nothing more real and substantial than these Ciceronian ethics.

In morals, as in physics, the stream cannot rise higher than its source. Christianity raises men from earth, for it comes from heaven; but human morality creeps, struts, or frets upon the earth's level, without wings to rise. The Knowledge School does not contemplate raising man above himself; it merely aims at disposing of his existing powers and tastes, as is most convenient, or is practicable under circumstances. It finds him, like the victims of the French Tyrant, doubled up in a cage in which he can neither lie, stand, sit, nor kneel, and its highest desire is to find an attitude in which his unrest may be least.[a] Or it finds him like some musical instrument, of great power and compass, but imperfect; from its very structure some keys must ever be out of tune, and its object, when ambition is highest, is to throw the *fault* of its nature where least it will be observed. It leaves man where it found him – man, and not an Angel – a sinner, not a Saint; but it tries to make him look as much like what he is not as ever it can. The poor indulge in low pleasures; they use bad language, swear loudly and recklessly, laugh at coarse jests, and are rude and boorish. Sir Robert would open on them a wider range of thought and more intellectual objects, by teaching them science; but what warrant will he give us that, if his object could be achieved, what they would gain in decency they would not lose in natural humility and faith? If so, he has exchanged a gross fault for a more subtle one. 'Temperance topics' stop drinking; let us suppose it; but will much be gained, if those who give up spirits take to opium? *Naturam expellas furcâ, tamen usque recurret*,[b] is at least a heathen truth, and universities and libraries which recur to heathenism may reclaim it from the heathen for their motto.

Nay, everywhere, so far as human nature remains hardly or partially Christianized, the heathen law remains in force; as is felt in a measure even in the most religious places and societies. Even there, where Christianity has power, the venom of the old Adam is not subdued. Those who have to do with our Colleges give us their experience, that in the case of the young committed to their care, external discipline may change the fashionable excess, but cannot allay the principle of sinning. Stop cigars, they will take to drinking parties; stop drinking, they gamble; stop gambling, and a worse license follows. You do not get rid of vice by human expedients;

[a] A torture attributed to Louis XI in nineteenth-century Gothic literature.

[b] 'If you drive nature out with a pitchfork she will soon find a way back', Horace, *Epistles* I.10.24.

you can but use them according to circumstances, and in their place, as making the best of a bad matter. You must go to a higher source for renovation of the heart and of the will. You do but play a sort of 'hunt the slipper' with the fault of our nature, till you go to Christianity.[5]

I say, you must use human methods *in their place*, and there they are useful; but they are worse than useless out of their place. I have no fanatical wish to deny to any whatever subject of thought or method of reason a place altogether, if it chooses to claim it, in the cultivation of the mind. Mr Bentham may despise verse-making, or Mr Dugald Stewart logic,[6] but the great and true maxim is to sacrifice none – to combine, and therefore to adjust, all. All cannot be first, and therefore each has its place, and the problem is to find it. It is at least not a lighter mistake to make what is secondary first, than to leave it out altogether. Here then it is that the Knowledge Society, Gower Street College, Tamworth Reading-room, Lord Brougham and Sir Robert Peel, are all so deplorably mistaken. Christianity, and nothing short of it, must be made the element and principle of all education. Where it has been laid as the first stone, and acknowledged as the governing spirit, it will take up into itself, assimilate, and give a character to literature and science. Where Revealed Truth has given the aim and direction to Knowledge, Knowledge of all kinds will minister to Revealed Truth. The evidences of Religion, natural theology, metaphysics, – or, again, poetry, history and the classics – or physics and mathematics, may all be grafted into the mind of a Christian, and give and take by the grafting. But if in education we begin with nature before grace, with evidences before faith, with science before conscience, with poetry before practice, we shall be doing much the same as if we were to indulge the appetites and passions, and turn a deaf ear to the reason. In each case we misplace what in its place is a divine gift. If we attempt to effect a moral improvement by means of poetry, we shall but mature into a mawkish, frivolous, and fastidious sentimentalism; – if by means of argument, into a dry, unamiable longheadedness; – if by good society, into a polished outside, with hollowness within, in which vice has lost its grossness, and perhaps increased its malignity; – if by experimental science, into an uppish, supercilious temper, much inclined to scepticism. But reverse the order of things: put Faith first and Knowledge second; let the University minister to the Church,[7] and then classical poetry becomes the type of Gospel truth, and physical science a comment on Genesis or Job, and Aristotle changes into Butler, and Arcesilas into Berkeley.[8]

Far from recognizing this principle, the Teachers of the Knowledge School would educate from Natural Theology[a] up to Christianity, and would amend the heart through literature and philosophy. Lord Brougham, as if faith came from science, gives out that 'henceforth nothing shall prevail over us to praise or to blame any one for' his belief, 'which he can no more change than he can the hue of his skin, or the height of his stature.' And Sir Robert, whose profession and life give the lie to his philosophy, founds a library into which 'no works of controversial divinity shall enter,' that is, no Christian doctrine at all; and he tells us that 'an increased sagacity will make men not merely believe in the cold doctrines of Natural Religion, but that it will *so prepare and temper the spirit* and understanding that they will be better *qualified to comprehend the great scheme of human redemption*.' And again, Lord Brougham considers that 'the pleasures of science tend not only to make our lives more agreeable, but better;' and Sir Robert responds, that 'he entertains the hope that there will be the means afforded of useful occupation and rational recreation, that men will prefer the pleasures of knowledge above the indulgence of sensual appetite, and that there is a prospect of contributing to the intellectual and moral improvement of the neighbourhood.'

Can the nineteenth century produce no more robust and creative philosophy than this?

4. *Secular Knowledge not the Antecedent of Moral Improvement*

Human nature wants recasting, but Lord Brougham is all for tinkering it. He does not despair of making something of it yet. He is not, indeed, of those who think that reason, passion, and whatever else is in us, are made right and tight by the principle of self-interest. He understands that something more is necessary for man's happiness than self-love; he feels that man has affections and aspirations which Bentham does not take account of, and he looks about for their legitimate objects. Christianity has provided these; but, unhappily, he passes them by. He libels them with the name of dogmatism, and conjures up instead the phantoms of Glory and Knowledge; *idola theatri*, as his famous predecessor calls them. 'There are idols,' says Lord Bacon, 'which have got into the human mind, from the different tenets of philosophers, and the perverted laws of demonstration. And these we denominate idols of the theatre; because all the philosophies that have been hitherto in-

[a] The inference of divine intelligence and goodness from the evidence of design in Creation.

vented or received, are but so many stage plays, written or acted, as having shown nothing but fictitious and theatrical worlds. Idols of the theatre, or theories, are many, and will probably grow much more numerous; for if men had not, through many ages, *been prepossessed with religion and theology*, and *if civil governments*, but particularly monarchies,' (and, I suppose, their ministers, counsellors, functionaries, inclusive,) '*had not been averse to innovations of this kind* though but intended, so as to make it dangerous and prejudicial to the private fortunes of such as take the bent of innovating, not only by depriving them of advantages, but also of exposing them to contempt and hatred, there would doubtless have been *numerous other sects* of philosophies and theories, introduced, of kin to those that in great variety formerly flourished among the Greeks. And these theatrical fables, have this in common with dramatic pieces, that the fictitious narrative is nearer, more elegant and pleasing, than the true history.'[9]

I suppose we may readily grant that the science of the day is attended by more lively interest, and issues in more entertaining knowledge, than the study of the New Testament. Accordingly, Lord Brougham fixes upon such science as the great desideratum of human nature, and puts aside faith under the nickname of opinion. I wish Sir Robert Peel had not fallen into the snare, insulting doctrine by giving it the name of 'controversial divinity.'

However, it will be said that Sir Robert, in spite of such forms of speech, differs essentially from Lord Brougham: for he goes on, in the latter part of the Address which has occasioned these remarks, to speak of Science as leading to Christianity. 'I can never think it possible,' he says, 'that a mind can be so constituted, that after being familiarized with the great truth of observing in every object of contemplation that nature presents the manifest proofs of a Divine Intelligence, if you range even from the organization of the meanest weed you trample upon, or of the insect that lives but for an hour, up to the magnificent structure of the heavens, and the still more wonderful phenomena of the soul, reason, and conscience of man; I cannot believe that any man, accustomed to such contemplations, can return from them with any other feelings than those of enlarged conceptions of the Divine Power, and greater reverence for the name of the Almighty Creator of the universe.' A long and complicated sentence, and no unfitting emblem of the demonstration it promises. It sets before us a process and deduction. Depend on it, it is not so safe a road and so expeditious a journey from premiss and conclusion as Sir Robert anticipates. The way is long, and there are not a few half-way houses and traveller's rests along it; and who is to warrant that the members of the Reading-room and Library will go steadily on to the goal he would set before them? And when at length they come to 'Christianity,' pray how do the roads lay between it and 'controversial divinity'? Or, grant the Tamworth readers to *begin* with 'Christianity' as well as science, the same question suggests itself, What *is* Christianity? Universal benevolence? Exalted morality? Supremacy of law? Conservatism? An age of light? An age of reason? – Which of them all?

Most cheerfully do I render to so religious a man as Sir Robert Peel the justice of disclaiming any insinuation on my part, that he has any intention at all to put aside Religion; yet his words either mean nothing, or they do, both on their surface, and when carried into effect, mean something very irreligious.

And now for one plain proof of this.

It is certain, then, that the multitude of men have neither time nor capacity for attending to many subjects. If they attend to one, they will not attend to the other; if they give their leisure and curiosity to this world, they will have none left for the next. We cannot be everything; as the poet says, '*non omnia possumus omnes*.'[a] We must make up our minds to be ignorant of much, if we would know anything. And we must make our choice between risking Science, and risking Religion. Sir Robert indeed says, 'Do not believe that you have not time for rational recreation. It is the idle man who wants time for everything.' However, this seems to me rhetoric; and what I have said to be the matter of fact, for the truth of which I appeal, not to argument, but to the proper judges of facts, – common sense and practical experience; and if they pronounce it to be a fact, then Sir Robert Peel, little as he means it, does unite with Lord Brougham in taking from Christianity what he gives to Science.

I will make this fair offer to both of them. Every member of the Church Established shall be eligible to the Tamworth Library on one condition – that he brings from the 'public minister of religion,' to use Sir Robert's phrase, a ticket in witness of his proficiency in Christian knowledge. We will have no 'controversial divinity' in the Library, but a little out of it. If the gentlemen of the Knowledge School will but agree to teach town and country Religion first, they shall have a *carte blanche* from me to teach anything or everything else second. Not a word has been uttered or

[a] 'We cannot all do everything', Virgil, *Eclogues* VIII.63.

intended in these Letters against Science; I would treat it, as they do *not* treat 'controversial divinity,' with respect and gratitude. They caricature doctrine under the name of controversy. I do not nickname science infidelity. I call it by their own name, 'useful and entertaining knowledge;' and I called doctrine 'Christian knowledge:' and, as thinking Christianity something more than useful and entertaining, I want faith to come first, and utility and amusement to follow.

That persons indeed are found in all classes, high and low, busy and idle, capable of proceeding from sacred to profane knowledge, is undeniable; and it is desirable they should do so. It is desirable that talent for particular departments in literature and science should be fostered and turned to account, wherever it is found. But what has this to do with this general canvass of '*all* persons of all descriptions without reference to religious creed, who shall have attained *the age of fourteen*'? Why solicit 'the working classes, without distinction of party, political opinion, or religious profession;' that is, whether they have heard of a God or no? Whence these cries rising on our ears, of 'Let me entreat you!' 'Neglect not the opportunity!' 'It will not be our fault!' 'Here is an access for you!' very like the tones of a street preacher, or the cad of an omnibus – little worthy of a great statesman and a religious philosopher?

However, the Tamworth Reading-room admits of one restriction, which is not a little curious, and has no very liberal sound. It seems that all '*virtuous* women' may be members of the Library; that 'great injustice would be done to the *well-educated and virtuous* women of the town and neighbourhood' had they been excluded. A very emphatic silence is maintained about women not virtuous. What does this mean? Does it mean to exclude them, while bad *men* are admitted? Is this accident or design, sinister and insidious, against a portion of the community? What has virtue to do with a Reading-room? It is to *make* its members virtuous; it is to 'exalt the *moral dignity* of their nature'; it is to provide 'charms and temptations' to allure them from sensuality and riot. To whom but to the vicious ought Sir Robert to discourse about 'opportunities,' and 'access,' and 'moral improvement;' and who else would prove a fitter experiment, and a more glorious triumph, of scientific influences? And yet he shuts out all but the well-educated and virtuous.

Alas, that bigotry should have left the mark of its hoof on the great 'fundamental principle of the Tamworth Institution'! Sir Robert Peel is bound in consistency to attempt its obliteration. But if that is impossible, as many will anticipate, why, O why, while he is about it, why will he not give us just a little more of it? *Cannot* we prevail on him to modify his principle, and to admit into his library none but 'well-educated and virtuous' *men*?

5. Secular Knowledge not a Principle of Social Unity

Sir Robert Peel proposes to establish a Library which 'shall be open to all persons of all descriptions, without reference to political opinions or to religious creed.' He invites those who are concerned in manufacturies, or who have many workmen, 'without distinction of party, political opinions, *or* religious profession.' He promises that 'in the selection of subjects for public lectures everything calculated to excite religious *or* political animosity shall be excluded.' Nor is any 'discussion on matters connected with religion, politics, *or* local party differences' to be permitted in the reading-room. And he congratulates himself that he has 'laid the foundation of an edifice in which men of all political opinions *and* of all religious feeling may unite in furtherance of Knowledge, without the asperities of party feeling.' In these statements religious differences are made synonymous with 'party feeling;' and, whereas the tree is 'known by its fruit,' their characteristic symptoms are felicitously described as 'asperities,' and 'animosities.' And, in order to teach us more precisely what these differences are worth, they are compared to differences between Whig and Tory – nay, even to '*local* party differences;' such, I suppose, as about a municipal election, or a hole-and-corner meeting, or a parish job, or a bill in Parliament for a railway.

But, to give him the advantage of the more honourable parallel of the two, are religious principles to be put upon a level even with political? Is it as bad to be a republican as an unbeliever? Is it as magnanimous to humour a scoffer as to spare an opponent in the House? Is a difference about the Reform Bill all one with a difference about the Creed? Is it as polluting to hear arguments for Lord Melbourne[a] as to hear a scoff against the Apostles? To a statesman, indeed, like Sir Robert, to abandon one's party is a far greater sacrifice than to unparliamentary men; and it would be uncandid to doubt that he is rather magnifying politics than degrading Religion in throwing them together; but still, when he advocates concessions in theology *and* politics, he must be plainly told to make presents of things that belong to him, nor seek to be

[a] The Whig Prime Minister whose government was brought down by the Tory Peel later in 1841.

generous with other people's substance. There are entails[a] in more matters than parks and old places. He made his politics for himself, but Another made theology.

Christianity is faith, faith implies a doctrine, a doctrine propositions, propositions yes or no, yes or no differences. Differences, then, are the natural attendants on Christianity, and you cannot have Christianity, and not have differences. When, then, Sir Robert Peel calls such differences points of 'party feeling,' what is this but to insult Christianity? Yet so cautious, so correct a man, cannot have made such a sacrifice for nothing; nor does he long leave us in doubt what is his inducement. He tells us that this great aim is the peace and good order of the community, and the easy working of the national machine. With this in view, any price is cheap, everything is marketable; all impediments are a nuisance. He does not undo for undoing's sake; he gains more than an equivalent. It is a mistake, too, to say that he considers all differences of opinion as equal in importance; no, they are only equally in the way. He only compares them together where they *are* comparable, – in their common inconvenience to a minister of State. They may be as little homogeneous as chalk is to cheese, or Macedon to Monmouth, but they agree in interfering with social harmony; and, since that harmony is the first of goods and the end of life, what is left us but to discard all that disunites us, and to cultivate all that may amalgamate?

Could Sir Robert have set a more remarkable example of self-sacrifice than in thus becoming the disciple of his political foe, accepting from Lord Brougham his new principle of combination, rejecting Faith for the fulcrum of Society, and proceeding to rest it upon Knowledge?

'I cannot help thinking,' he exclaims at Tamworth, 'that *by bringing together in an institution of this kind* intelligent men of all classes and conditions of life, by uniting together, in the committee of this institution, the gentleman of ancient family and great landed possessions with the skilful mechanic and artificer of good character, I cannot help believing that we are *harmonizing* the gradations of society, and binding men together by a *new* bond, which will have *more than ordinary* strength on account of the object which unites us.' The old bond, he seems to say, was Religion; Lord Brougham's is Knowledge. Faith, once the soul of social union, is now but the spirit of division. Not a single doctrine but is

[a] Settlement of property so that no one subsequent possessor can behave as absolute owner. See Miall Endnote 7.

'controversial divinity;' not an abstraction can be imagined (could abstractions constrain), not a comprehension projected (could comprehensions connect), but will leave out one or other portion or element of the social fabric. We must abandon Religion, if we aspire to be statesmen. Once, indeed, it was a living power, kindling hearts, leavening them with one idea, moulding them on one model, developing them into one polity. Ere now it has been the life of morality: it has given birth to heroes; it has wielded empire. But another age has come in, and Faith is effete; let us submit to what we cannot change; let us not hang over our dead, but bury it out of sight. Seek we out some young and vigorous principle, rich in sap, and fierce in life, to give form to elements which are fast resolving into their inorganic chaos; and where shall we find such a principle but in Knowledge?

Accordingly, though Sir Robert somewhat chivalrously battles for the appointment upon the Book Committee of what he calls two 'public ministers of religion, holding prominent and responsible offices, endowed by the State,' and that *ex officio*, yet he is untrue to his new principle only in appearance: for he couples his concession with explanations, restrictions, and safeguards quite sufficient to prevent old Faith becoming insurgent against young Knowledge. First he takes his Vicar and Curate as 'conversant with literary subjects and with literary works', and then as having duties 'immediately connected with the moral condition and improvement' of the place. Further he admits 'it is perfectly right to be *jealous* of all power held by such a tenure:' and he insists on the 'fundamental' condition that these sacred functionaries shall permit no doctrinal works to be introduced or lectures to be delivered. Lastly, he reserves in the general body the power of withdrawing this indulgence 'if the existing checks be not sufficient, and the power be *abused*,' – abused, that is, by the vicar and curate; also he desires to secure Knowledge from being *perverted* to '*evil* or *immoral* purposes' – such perversion of course, if attempted, being the natural antithesis, or *pendant*, to the vicar's contraband introduction of the doctrines of Faith.

Lord Brougham will make all this clearer to us. A work of high interest and varied information, to which I have already referred, is attributed to him, and at least is of his school, and in which the ingenious author, whoever he is, shows how Knowledge can do for Society what has hitherto been supposed the prerogative of Faith. As to Faith and its preachers, he had already complimented them at Glasgow, as 'the evil spirits of tyranny and persecution,' and had bid them good morning as the scared and dazzled creatures of the 'long night now gone down the sky.'

'The great truth,' he proclaimed in language borrowed from the records of faith (for after parsons no men quote Scripture more familiarly than Liberals and Whigs), has finally *gone forth to all the ends of the earth*, that man shall no more render account to man for his belief, over which he has himself no control. Henceforth nothing shall prevail on us to *praise or to blame* any one for that which he can no more change than he can the hue of his skin or the height of his stature.' And then he or his scholar proceeds to his new *Vitae Sanctorum*, or, as he calls it, 'Illustrations of the Pursuit of Knowledge;' and, whereas the badge of Christian saintliness is conflict, he writes of the 'Pursuit of Knowledge *under difficulties*;' and, whereas this Knowledge is to stand in the place of Religion, he assumes a hortatory tone, a species of eloquence in which decidedly he has no rival but Sir Robert. 'Knowledge,' he says, 'is happiness, as well as power and virtue;' and he demands 'the dedication of our faculties' to it. 'The *struggle*,' he gravely observes, which its disciple 'has to wage may be a protracted, but it ought not to be a *cheerless* one: for, if he do not *relax his exertions*, every movement he makes is necessarily a *step forward*, if not towards that distinction which intellectual attainments sometimes confer, at least to that *inward satisfaction and enjoyment* which is always their reward. No one stands in the way of another, or can deprive him of any part of his chance, we should rather say of his certainty, of success; on the contrary, they are all *fellow-workers*, and may materially *help each other* forward.' And he enumerates in various places the virtues which adorn the children of Knowledge – ardour united to humility, childlike alacrity, teachableness, truthfulness, patience, concentration of attention, husbandry of time, self-denial, self-command, and heroism.

Faith, viewed in its history through past ages, presents us with the fulfilment of one great idea in particular – that, namely, of an aristocracy of exalted spirits, drawn together out of all countries, ranks, and ages, raised above the condition of humanity, specimens of the capabilities of our race, incentives to rivalry and patterns for imitation. This Christian idea Lord Brougham has borrowed for his new Pantheon, which is equally various in all attributes and appendages of mind, with this one characteristic in all its specimens, – the pursuit of Knowledge. Some of his worthies are low born, others of high degree; some are in Europe, others in the Antipodes; some in the dark ages, others in the ages of light; some exercise a voluntary, others an involuntary toil; some give up riches, and others gain them; some are fixtures, and others adventure much; some are profligate, and others ascetic; and some are believers, and others are infidels.

Alfred, severely good and Christian, takes his place in this new hagiology beside the gay and graceful Lorenzo de Medicis; for did not the one 'import civilization into England,' and was not the other 'the wealthy and munificient patron of all the liberal arts'? Edward VI. and Haroun al Raschid, Dr Johnson and Dr Franklin, Newton and Protagoras, Pascal and Julian the Apostate, Joseph Milner and Lord Byron, Cromwell and Ovid, Bayle and Boyle, Adrian pope and Adrian emperor, Lady Jane Grey and Madame Roland, – human beings who agreed in nothing but in their humanity and in their love of Knowledge, are all admitted by this writer to one beatification, in proof of the Catholic character of his substitute for Faith.[10]

The persecuting Marcus is a 'good and enlightened emperor,' and a 'delightful' spectacle, when 'mixing in the religious processions and ceremonies' of Athens, 're-building and re-endowing the schools,' whence St. Paul was driven in derision. The royal Alphery, on the contrary, 'preferred his humble parsonage' to the throne of the Czars. West was 'nurtured among the quiet and gentle affections of a Quaker family.' Kirke White's 'feelings became ardently devotional, and he determined to give up his life to the preaching of Christianity.' Roger Bacon was 'a brother of the Franciscan Order, at that time the great support and ornament of both Universities.' Belzoni seized 'the opportunity' of Bonaparte's arrival in Italy to 'throw off his monastic habit,' 'its idleness and obscurity,' and to engage himself as a performer at Astley's. Duval, 'a very able antiquarian of the last century,' began his studies as a peasant boy, and finished them in a Jesuits' College. Mr Davy, 'having written a system of divinity,' effected the printing of it in thirteen years 'with a press of his own construction,' and the assistance of his female servant, working off page by page for twenty-six volumes 8vo, of nearly 500 pages each. Raleigh, in spite of 'immoderate ambition,' was 'one of the very chief glories of an age crowded with towering spirits.'

Nothing comes amiss to this author; saints and sinners, the precious and the vile, are torn from their proper homes and recklessly thrown together under the category of Knowledge. 'Tis a pity he did not extend his view, as Christianity has done, to beings out of sight of man. Milton could have helped him to some angelic personages, as patrons and guardians of his intellectual temple, who of old time, before faith had birth,

> Apart sat on a hill retired
> In thoughts more elevate, and reasoned high
> Of providence, foreknowledge, will, and fate,
> Passion and apathy, and glory, and shame –
> Vain wisdom all, and false philosophy.

And, indeed, he does make some guesses that way, speaking most catholically of being 'admitted to a fellowship with those loftier minds' who 'by universal consent *held a station apart*,' and are 'spoken of *reverently*,' as if their names were not those 'of mortal men;' and he speaks of these 'benefactors of mankind, when they *rest* from their *pious* labours, looking down' upon the blessings with which their '*toils and sufferings* have clothed the scene of their former existence.'

Such is the oratory which has fascinated Sir Robert; yet we must recollect that in the year 1832, even the venerable Society for Promoting Christian Knowledge herself, catching its sound, and hearing something about sublimity, and universality, and brotherhood, and effort, and felicity, was beguiled into an admission of this singularly irreligious work into the list of publications which she had delegated to a Committee to select *in usum laicorum*.[a]

That a Venerable Society should be caught by the vision of a Church Catholic is not wonderful; but what could possess philosophers and statesmen to dazzle her with it, but man's need of some such support, and the divine excellence and sovereign virtue of that which Faith once created?

6. Secular Knowledge not a Principle of Action

People say to me, that it is but a dream to suppose that Christianity should regain the organic power in human society which once it possessed. I cannot help that; I never said it could. I am not a politician; I am proposing no measures, but exposing a fallacy, and resisting a pretence. Let Benthamism reign, if men have no aspirations; but do not tell them to be romantic, and then solace them with glory; do not attempt by philosophy what once was done by religion. The ascendency of Faith may be impracticable, but the reign of Knowledge is incomprehensible. The problem for statesmen of this age is how to educate the masses, and literature and science cannot give the solution.

[a] For the benefit of the laity.

Not so deems Sir Robert Peel; his firm belief and hope is, 'that an increased sagacity will administer to an exalted faith; that it will make men not merely believe in the cold doctrines of Natural Religion, but that it will so prepare and temper the spirit and understanding, that they will be better qualified to comprehend the great scheme of human redemption.' He certainly thinks that scientific pursuits have some considerable power of impressing religion upon the mind of the multitude. I think not, and will now say why.

Science gives us the grounds or premisses from which religious truths are to be inferred; but it does not set about inferring them, much less does it reach the inference – that is not its province. It brings before us phenomena, and it leaves us, if we will, to call them works of design, wisdom, or benevolence; and further still, if we will, to proceed to confess an Intelligent Creator. We have to take its facts, and to give them a meaning, and to draw our own conclusions from them. First comes Knowledge, then a view, then reasoning, and then belief. This is why Science has so little of a religious tendency; deductions have no power of persuasion. The heart is commonly reached, not through the reason, but through the imagination, by means of direct impressions, by the testimony of facts and events, by history, by description. Persons influence us, voices melt us, looks subdue us, deeds inflame us. Many a man will live and die upon a dogma: no man will be a martyr for a conclusion. A conclusion is but an opinion; it is not a thing which *is*, but which *we are* '*certain about*;' and it has often been observed, that we never say we are certain without implying that we doubt. To say that a thing *must* be, is to admit that it *may not* be. No one, I say, will die for his own calculations; he dies for realities. This is why a literary religion is so little to be depended upon; it looks well in fair weather, but its doctrines are opinions, and, when called to suffer for them, it slips them between its folios, or burns them at its hearth. And this again is the secret of the distrust and raillery with which moralists have been so commonly visited. They say and do not. Why? Because they are contemplating the fitness of things, and they live by the square, when they should be realizing their high maxims in the concrete. Now Sir Robert thinks better of natural history, chemistry, and astronomy, than of such ethics; but they too, what are they more than divinity *in posse*? He protests against 'controversial divinity:' is *inferential* much better?

I have no confidence, then, in philosophers who cannot help being religious, and are Christians by implication. They sit at home, and reach forward to distances which astonish us; but they hit without grasping, and are sometimes as confident about shadows as about realities. They have worked out by a calculation the lie of a country which they never saw, and mapped it by means of a gazetteer; and like blind men, though they can put a stranger on his way, they cannot walk straight themselves, and do not feel it quite their business to walk at all.

Logic makes but a sorry rhetoric with the multitude; first shoot round corners, and you may not despair of converting by a syllogism. Tell men to gain notions of a Creator from His works, and, if they were to set about it (which nobody does), they would be jaded and wearied by the labyrinth they were tracing. Their minds would be gorged and surfeited by the logical operation. Logicians are more set upon concluding rightly, than on right conclusions. They cannot see the end for the process. Few men have that power of mind which may hold fast and firmly a variety of thoughts. We ridicule 'men of one idea;' but a great many of us are born to be such, and we should be happier if we knew it. To most men argument makes the point in hand only more doubtful, and considerably less impressive. After all, man is *not* a reasoning animal; he is a seeing, feeling, contemplating, acting animal. He is influenced by what is direct and precise. It is very well to freshen our impressions and convictions from physics, but to create them we must go elsewhere. Sir Robert Peel 'never can think it possible that a mind can be so constituted, that, after being familiarized with the wonderful discoveries which have been made in every part of experimental science, it can retire from such contemplations without more enlarged conceptions of God's providence, and a higher reverence for His name.' If he speaks of religious minds, he perpetrates a truism; if of irreligious, he insinuates a paradox.

Life is not long enough for a religion of inferences; we shall never have done beginning, if we determine to begin with proof. We shall ever be laying our foundations; we shall turn theology into evidences, and divines into textuaries. We shall never get at our first principles. Resolve to believe nothing, and you must prove your proofs and analyze your elements, sinking further and further, and finding 'in the lowest depth a lower deep,' till you come to the broad bosom of scepticism. I would rather be bound to defend the reasonableness of assuming that Christianity is true, than to demonstrate a moral governance from the physical world. Life is for action. If we insist on proofs for everything, we shall never come to action: to act you must assume, and that assumption is faith.

Let no one suppose that in saying this I am maintaining that all proofs are equally difficult, and all propositions equally debatable. Some assumptions are greater than others, and some doctrines involve postulates larger than others, and more numerous. I only say that impressions lead to action, and that reasonings lead from it. Knowledge of premisses, and inferences upon them – this is not to *live*. It is very well as a matter of liberal curiosity and of philosophy to analyze our modes of thought; but let this come second, and when there is leisure for it, and then our examinations will in many ways even be subservient to action. But if we commence with scientific knowledge and argumentative proof, or lay any great stress upon it as the basis of personal Christianity, or attempt to make man moral and religious by Libraries and Museums, let us in consistency take chemists for our cooks, and mineralogists for our masons.

Now I wish to state all this as matter of fact, to be judged by the candid testimony of any persons whatever. Why we are so constituted that Faith, not Knowledge or Argument, is our principle of action, is a question with which I have nothing to do; but I think it is a fact, and if it be such, we must resign ourselves to it as best we may, unless we take refuge in the intolerable paradox, that the mass of men are created for nothing, and are meant to leave life as they entered it. So well has this practically been understood in all ages of the world, that no Religion has yet been a Religion of physics or of philosophy. It has ever been synonymous with Revelation. It never has been a deduction from what we know: it has ever been an assertion of what we are to believe. It has never lived in a conclusion; it has never been a message, or a history, or a vision. No legislator or priest ever dreamed of educating our moral nature by science or by argument. There is no difference here between true Religions and pretended. Moses was instructed, not to reason from the creation, but to work miracles. Christianity is a history supernatural, and almost scenic: it tells us what its Author is, by telling us what He has done. I have no wish at all to speak otherwise than respectfully of conscientious Dissenters, but I have heard it said by those who were not their enemies, and who had known much of their preaching, that they had often heard narrow-minded and bigoted clergymen, and often Dissenting ministers of a far more intellectual cast; but that Dissenting teaching came to nothing – that it was dissipated in thoughts which had no point, and inquiries which converged to no centre, that it ended as it began, and sent away its hearers as it found them – whereas the instruction in the Church, with all its defects and mistakes, comes to some end, for it started from some beginning. Such is the difference between the dogmatism of faith and the speculations of logic.

Lord Brougham himself, as we have already seen, has recognized the force of this principle. He has not left his philosophical religion to argument; he has committed it to the keeping of the imagination. Why should he depict a great republic of letters, and an intellectual Pantheon, but that he feels that instances and patterns, not logical reasonings, are the living conclusions which alone have a hold over the affections, or can form the character?

7. *Secular Knowledge without Personal Religion tends to Unbelief*

When Sir Robert Peel assures us from the Town-hall at Tamworth that physical science must lead to religion, it is no bad compliment to him to say that he is unreal. He speaks of what he knows nothing about. To a religious man like him, Science has ever suggested religious thoughts; he colours the phenomena of physics with the hues of his own mind, and mistakes an interpretation for a deduction. 'I am sanguine enough to believe,' he says, 'that that superior sagacity which is most conversant with the course and constitution of Nature will be first to turn a deaf ear to objections and presumptions against Revealed Religion, and to acknowledge the complete harmony of the Christian Dispensation with all that Reason, assisted by Revelation, tells us of the course and constitution of Nature.' Now, considering that we are all of us educated as Christians from infancy, it is not easy to decide at this day whether Science creates Faith, or only confirms it; but we have this remarkable fact in the history of heathen Greece against the former supposition, that her most eminent empirical philosophers were atheists, and that it was their atheism which was the cause of their eminence. 'The natural philosophies of Democritus[a] and others,' says Lord Bacon, '*who allow no God or mind* in the frame of things, but attribute the structure of the universe to infinite essays and trials of nature, or what they call fate or fortune, and assigned the causes of particular things to the necessity of matter, *without any intermixture of final causes*, seem, as far as we can judge from the remains of their philosophy, *much more solid*, and to have *gone deeper into nature*, with regard to physical causes, than the philosophies of Aristotle or Plato: and this only because they *never meddled with final causes*, which the others were perpetually inculcating.'

Lord Bacon gives us both the fact and the reason for it. Physical philosophers are ever inquiring *whence* things are, not *why*; referring them to nature, not to mind; and thus they tend to make a system a

[a] Democritus (460–361 BC) held the universe to be formed by an infinite number of atoms capable of an infinite variety of combinations dictated by chance.

substitute for a God. Each pursuit or calling has its own dangers, and each numbers among its professors men who rise superior to them. As the soldier is tempted to dissipation, and the merchant to acquisitiveness, and the lawyer to the sophistical, and the statesman to the expedient, and the country clergyman to ease and comfort, yet there are good clergymen, statesmen, lawyers, merchants, and soldiers, notwithstanding; so there are religious experimentalists, though physics, taken by themselves, tend to infidelity; but to have recourse to physics to *make* men religious is like recommending a canonry as a cure for the gout, or giving a youngster a commission as a penance for irregularities.

The whole framework of Nature is confessedly a tissue of antecedents and consequents; we may refer all things forwards to design, or backwards on a physical cause. La Place is said to have considered he had a formula which solved all the motions of the solar system; shall we say that those motions came from this formula or from a Divine Fiat? Shall we have recourse for our theory to physics or to theology? Shall we assume Matter and its necessary properties to be eternal, or Mind with its divine attributes? Does the sun shine to warm the earth, or is the earth warmed because the sun shines? The one hypothesis will solve the phenomena as well as the other. Say not it is but a puzzle in argument, and that no one ever felt it in fact. So far from it, I believe that the study of Nature, when religious feeling is away, leads the mind, rightly or wrongly, to acquiesce in the atheistic theory, as the simplest and easiest. It is but parallel to that tendency in anatomical studies, which no one will deny, to solve all the phenomena of the human frame into material elements and powers, and to dispense with the soul. To those who are conscious of matter, but not conscious of mind, it seems more rational to refer all things to one origin, such as they know, than to assume the existence of a second origin such as they know not.[11] It is Religion, then, which suggests to Science its true conclusions; the facts come from Knowledge, but the principles come of Faith.[12]

There are two ways, then, of reading Nature – as a machine and as a work.[13] If we come to it with the assumption that it is a creation, we shall study it with awe; if assuming it to be a system, with mere curiosity. Sir Robert does not make this distinction. He subscribes to the belief that the man 'accustomed to such contemplations, *struck with awe* by the manifold proofs of infinite power and infinite wisdom, will yield more ready and hearty assent – yes, the assent of the heart, and not only of the understanding, to the pious exclamation, "O Lord, how glorious are Thy works!"' He considers that greater insight into Nature will lead a man to say, 'How great and wise is the Creator, who has done this!' True: but it is possible that his thoughts may take the form of 'How clever is the creature who has discovered it!' and self-conceit may stand proxy for adoration. This is no idle apprehension. Sir Robert himself, religious as he is, gives cause for it; for the first reflection that rises in his mind, as expressed in the above passage, *before* his notice of Divine Power and Wisdom, is, that 'the man accustomed to such contemplations will feel the *moral dignity of his nature exalted*.' But Lord Brougham speaks out. 'The delight,' he says, 'is inexpressible of *being able to follow*, as it were, with our eyes, the marvellous works of the Great Architect of Nature.' And more clearly still: 'One of the most *gratifying treats* which science affords us is *the knowledge of the extraordinary powers* with which the human mind is endowed. No man, until he has studied philosophy, can have a just idea of the great things for which Providence has fitted his understanding, the extraordinary disproportion which there is between his natural strength and the powers of his mind, and the force which he derives from these powers. When we survey the marvellous truths of astronomy, we are first of all lost in the feeling of immense space, and of the comparative insignificance of this globe and its inhabitants. But there soon arises a *sense of gratification and of new wonder* at perceiving how so insignificant a creature has been *able to reach such a knowledge* of the unbounded system of the universe.' So, this is the religion we are to gain from the study of Nature; how miserable! The god we attain is our own mind; our veneration is even professedly the worship of self.

The truth is that the system of Nature is just as much connected with Religion, where minds are not religious, as a watch or a steam-carriage. The material world, indeed, is infinitely more wonderful than any human contrivance; but wonder is not religion, or we should be worshipping our railroads. What the physical creation presents to us in itself is a piece of machinery, and when men speak of a Divine Intelligence as its Author, this god of theirs is not the Living and True, unless the spring is the god of a watch, or steam the creator of the engine. Their idol, taken at advantage (though it is *not* an idol, for they do not worship it), is the animating principle of a vast and complicated system; it is subjected to laws, and it is connatural and co-extensive with matter. Well does Lord Brougham call it 'the great architect of nature'; it is an instinct, or a soul of the world, or a vital power; it is not the Almighty God.

It is observable that Lord Brougham does not allude to any *relation* as existing between his *god* and ourselves. He is filled with awe, it seems, at the powers of the human mind, as displayed in their analysis of the vast creation. Is not this a fitting time to say a word about gratitude towards Him who gave them? Not a syllable. What we gain from his contemplation of Nature is 'a gratifying treat,' the knowledge of the 'great things for which Providence has fitted man's understanding;' our admiration terminates in man; it passes on to no prototype. I am not quarrelling with his result as illogical or unfair; it is but consistent with the principles with which he started. Take the system of Nature by itself, detached from the axioms of Religion, and I am willing to confess – nay, I have been expressly urging – that it does not force us to take it for *more* than a system; but why, then, persist in calling the study of it religious, when it can be treated, and is treated, thus atheistically? Say that Religion hallows the study, not that the study is a true ground of Religion. The essence of Religion is the idea of a Moral Governor, and a particular Providence; now let me ask, is the doctrine of moral governance and a particular providence conveyed to us through the physical sciences at all? Would they be physical sciences if they treated of morals? Can physics teach moral matters without ceasing to be physics? But are not virtue and vice, and responsibility, and reward and punishment, anything else than moral matters, and are *they* not of the essence of Religion? In what department, then, of physics are they to be found? Can the problems and principles they involve be expressed in the differential calculus? Is the galvanic battery a whit more akin to conscience and will than the mechanical powers? What we seek is what concerns us, the traces of a Moral Governor; even religious minds cannot discern these in the physical sciences; astronomy witnesses divine power, and physics divine skill; and all of them divine beneficence; but which teaches of divine holiness, truth, justice, or mercy? Is that much of a Religion which is silent about duty, sin, and its remedies? Was there ever a Religion which was without the idea of an expiation?

Sir Robert Peel tells us, that physical science imparts 'pleasure and *consolation*' on a death-bed. Lord Brougham confines himself to the 'gratifying treat;' but Sir Robert ventures to speak of 'consolation.' Now, if we are on trial in this life, and if death be the time when our account is gathered in, is it at all serious or real to be talking of 'consoling' ourselves at such a time with scientific subjects? Are these topics to suggest to us the thought of the Creator or not? If not, are they better than story books, to beguile the mind from what lies before it? But, if they are to speak of Him, can a dying man find rest in the mere notion of his Creator, when he knows Him also so awfully as His Moral Governor and his Judge? Meditate indeed on the wonders of Nature on a death-bed! Rather stay your hunger with corn grown in Jupiter, and warm yourself by the Moon.

But enough on this most painful portion of Sir Robert's Address. As I am coming to an end, I suppose I ought to sum up in a few words what I have been saying. I consider, then, that intrinsically excellent and noble as are scientific pursuits, and worthy of a place in a liberal education, and fruitful in temporal benefits to the community, still they are not, and cannot be, *the instrument* of an ethical training; that physics do not supply a basis, but only materials for religious sentiment; that knowledge does but occupy, does not form the mind; that apprehension of the unseen is the only known principle capable of subduing moral evil, educating the multitude, and organizing society; and that, whereas man is born for action, action flows not from inferences, but from impressions – not from reasonings, but from Faith.

That Sir Robert would deny these propositions I am far from contending; I do not even contend that he has asserted the contrary at Tamworth. It matters little to me whether he spoke boldly and intelligibly, as the newspapers represent, or guarded his strong sayings with the contradictory matter with which they are intercalated in his own report. In either case the drift and the effect of his Address are the same. He has given his respected name to a sophistical School, and condescended to mimic the gestures and tones of Lord Brougham. How melancholy is it that a man of such exemplary life, such cultivated tastes, such political distinction, such Parliamentary tact, and such varied experience, should have so little confidence in himself, so little faith in his own principles, so little hope of sympathy in others, so little heart for a great venture, so little of romantic aspiration, and of firm resolve, and stern dutifulness to the Unseen! How sad that he who might have had the affections of many, should have thought, in a day like this, that a Statesman's praise lay in preserving the mean, not in aiming at the high; that to be safe was his first merit, and to kindle enthusiasm his most disgraceful blunder! How pitiable that such a man should not have understood that a body without a soul has no life, and a political party without an idea, no unity!

February, 1841.

Edward Bouverie Pusey

(1800–1882)

13. *The Holy Eucharist, a Comfort to the Penitent* (Oxford, 1843), pp. 1–12, 14–15, 18–32

In 1825, by then a fellow of Oriel College, Pusey embarked upon two years study in Germany where he was to acquaint himself with the new school of Biblical exegesis. The so-called Higher Criticism emanating from Germany treated the Bible as a form of comparative literature, applying to it the techniques of classical and historical scholarship and perceiving in it man's myth-making capacities. Pusey swiftly realized how unprepared the Anglican Church was, both scholastically and spiritually, to counteract the onslaught of Rationalism upon Revealed religion. In 'High and Dry' religious orthodoxy he saw a ready prey for Rationalism's arid spirit. He returned from Germany convinced that philosophy was an inappropriate tool to use in theological matters, that the only firm stand upon which to resist Rationalism was provided by the authority found in Scripture and in the Tradition of the Primitive Church, and with a greater degree of tolerance for the spiritual vitality displayed by the German Pietists or English Evangelicals than many of his fellow Tractarians. Pusey had been brought up in his mother's High Church Anglicanism but he learnt to love 'those who are called "Evangelicals". I loved them', he wrote in 1865, 'because they loved our Lord. I loved them for their zeal for souls' (H. P. Liddon, *The Life of Edward Bouverie Pusey* (4 vols., 1893–7), vol. II, p. 8).

Despite his hermit-like existence preaching was for Pusey, as for the Evangelicals, a primary duty. Concerned by the distress his teaching on the awfulness of post-baptismal sin (awful because it involved the deliberate abuse of the purity conferred by baptismal regeneration) had caused, Pusey 'was led to preach a course of sermons on Comforts to the Penitent. Of these the sermon on the Holy Eucharist was one. It was a singular case of mistaking what people's feelings would be. For I chose the Holy Eucharist as the subject at which they would be less likely to take offence than at Absolution' (*ibid.*, vol. II, p. 307). Controversial theology was remote from Pusey's mind as he preached the sermon, *The Holy Eucharist, a Comfort to the Penitent* (1843), from which this extract is taken: it was not to remain so. Dr Fausset, Lady Margaret Professor of Divinity and declared opponent of the Tractarians, delated the sermon to the Vice-Chancellor, who selected a court to judge whether Pusey's sermon had been heterodox. No precise charge was ever formulated. After the court had condemned the undefended sermon Pusey was asked, under a vow of secrecy, to retract certain statements, refused, and was then suspended from preaching before the University for two years. Non-Tractarians were critical of the mode of procedure whilst Tractarians felt that an act akin to sacrilege had taken place. Isaac Williams wrote, 'Nothing has occurred in our time so pregnant with great consequences as the late conspiracy in Oxford. A barrier has given way, as in the march of revolutionary measures, when the divinity that hedges round the person of a king has been broken through' (*Autobiography of Isaac Williams*, ed. Prevost, p. 156).

Before submitting the sermon Pusey spent two or three days annotating his references to the Fathers. In the interests of economy I have deleted these lengthy additions, but they are worth remembering as an example of the scholarship with which Pusey transformed the Tracts from stirring pamplets to learned treatises.

The sermon was considered suspect because it contained high sacramental language concerning Christ's Presence at the Eucharist. That the Eucharist, meaning 'thanksgiving', either because at its institution Christ 'gave thanks', or because the service is the supreme act of Christian thanksgiving, conveyed to the believer the Body and Blood of Christ was universally accepted, but precisely how and whether the elements themselves changed had been the subject of much debate. At least three doctrines concerning the Eucharist had co-existed in the Anglican Church: the lowest view being that it was a commemorative service where Christ was present only as He was in any other form of worship; the second, or Receptionist view, that Christ, although not present in the elements of bread and wine, was present and received by faithful communicants; the third, or Virtualist view, was that whilst Christ was not actually present yet the elements were more than mere symbols in that they conveyed true virtue or grace. The doctrine of the Real Presence, as implied by Pusey, held that Christ was really and objectively present, spiritually not carnally, in the eucharistic sacrifice. I have used the endnotes to draw attention more precisely to the doctrinal implications of Pusey's sermon but the animus of the work was devotional rather than theological. By the 1830s some Evangelical parishes had instituted monthly Communions but most parishes still celebrated quarterly only. In 1837 Newman had introduced weekly Communion to Oxford's University Church and Pusey still sees as a remote ideal, lost sight of by the Anglican Church, the practice of communicating daily.

Pusey's whole cast of thought inclined him to see the Eucharist as central to the Church's worship because it was the means by which we become 'very members incorporate in the mystical body of thy Son'. Characteristically in this sermon Pusey's sense of man's unworthiness led him to contemplate with amazed rapture the wonder of Christ's Incarnation and to underline the need for man to observe this lesson in humility and prepare himself penitentially to receive the sacraments. This emphasis upon the Incarnation as a central truth is fundamental to the Tractarians' sacramental view of the universe.

The Romantic spirit of Wordsworth's warning to dry philosophers, 'We murder to dissect', reverberates in Pusey's remark to the Rationalists, 'and we, if we are wise, shall never ask how' (below, p. 193). The way in which Pusey culls his evidence – overwhelming torrents of prophetic manifestations of the Eucharist taken from the Bible as a whole rather than minutely examined isolated incidents – typifies the methodology he offered as an alternative to rationalism, which 'in becoming clear . . . became also shallow. Men wished to grasp the whole evidence of prophecy and to collect it into one focus, and so narrowed their conceptions of it. They were content with nothing but the mid-day Sun and so lost all sympathy for the refreshing hues of its rising or setting light, or those glimpses into a far distant land, which indistinct though they may be, open a wider range of vision' (quoted from Pusey's unpublished 'Lectures on Types and Prophecies' (1836) in J. Coulson and A. M. Allchin, *The Rediscovery of Newman* (1967), p. 57).

Pusey's sermon provides ample evidence for the influence of conviction upon style. The belief that 'our highest knowledge must be our indistinctest' (*ibid.*, p. 57) fosters the notion that it is irreverent to introduce logical analysis where God has left a mystery. The most one can do is 'to trace out the analogies, which are actually impressed upon the creation' (*ibid*., p. 64). Pusey's prose seeks to provide a series of images to corroborate or deny a given proposition. Readers and listeners alike may find difficulty in tracing the intellectual lines of the argument; instead they have to submit themselves to the tenor of thought and feeling which is established as parallel clauses and phrase are piled one upon another to offer different pictures of one truth. Pusey's 'judges' must have been further hampered in their task of finding out exactly what Pusey had said by the curious way in which his own words merge with his quotations. In the archaism of his grammar, syntax and, to a lesser extent, vocabulary, Pusey seems to inhabit the world of Biblical and liturgical translation with which his own work had familiarized him. He intermittently employs the 'eth' ending of the third-person singular present indicative of verbs, standard when the Book of Common Prayer was composed in the sixteenth century but already old-fashioned and considered as a suitable choice for religious diction when the Authorized Version was written. Pusey's use of the subjunctive (e.g. 'Picture we', below, p. 193) is another device characteristic of artificial archaism. The fact that much liturgical translation was from Latin may help to explain the appearance of archaic Latinate constructions such as 'this His body being perfected' (below, p. 194) an absolute participial construction based upon the Latin ablative absolute, or 'As blind, He is our Wisdom' (below, p. 189), an elliptical form of an archaic construction to convey equal proportion (*even as* we are blind, *so* He is our Wisdom), modelled on the Latin *Cum* . . . *tum* . . . construction. Archaic vocabulary is sometimes a reflection of archaic grammar or syntax (e.g. 'whereof' where normal nineteenth-century usage would be 'of which') sometimes a matter of obsolete words (e.g. 'engraffs' below, p. 190) and sometimes of the use of an older word where another equivalent would be more usual (e.g. 'disputings' rather than 'disputations' below, p. 190).

Also reminiscent of liturgical language is Pusey's use of the word 'we' as an impersonal universalizing plural, containing none of that note of intimacy which it might achieve in an Evangelical sermon. The choice of a style so wholly remote from contemporary speech or prose as a channel for a personally ecstatic vision of God's mysteries undoubtedly went far to create the sense of timeless spirituality attested to by this listener:

> He is certainly, to my feelings, more impressive than any one else in the pulpit, though he has not one of the graces of oratory. His discourse is generally a rhapsody, describing, with infinite repetition and accumulativeness, the wickedness of sin, the worthlessness of earth, and the blessedness of heaven. He is as still as a statue all the time he is uttering it, looks as white as a sheet, and is as monotonous in delivery as possible. While listening to him you do not seem to see and hear a *preacher*, but to have visible before you a most earnest and devout spirit, striving to carry out in this world a high religious theory (*Memoir and Letters of Sara Coleridge*, ed. E. Coleridge (2 vols., 1873), vol. 1, pp. 332–3).

Matt. xxvi. 28. This is My blood of the New Testament, which is shed for many for the remission of sins

It is part of the manifold wisdom of God, that His gifts, in nature and in grace, minister to distinct, and, as it often seems, unconnected ends; manifesting thereby the more His own Unity, as the secret cause and power of all things, putting Itself forward in varied forms and divers manners, yet Itself the one Cause of all that is. The element which is the image of our Baptism, cleanses alike and refreshes, enlighteneth the fainting eye, wakens to life, as it falls, a world in seeming exhaustion and death, changes the barren land into a garden of the Lord, gives health and nourishment and growth. And if in nature, much more in the Gifts of Grace. For therein God, not by Will or by Power only, but by Himself and the Effluence of His Spirit, is the Life of all which lives through Him. Our One Lord is to us, in varied forms, all, yea more than all, His disciples dare ask or think. All are His Life, flowing through all His members, and in all, as it is admitted, effacing death, enlarging life. As blind, He is our Wisdom; as sinful, our Righteousness; as hallowed, our Sanctification; as recovered from Satan, our Redemption; as sick, our Physician; as weak, our Strength; as unclean, our Fountain; as darkness, our Light; as daily fainting, our daily Bread; as dying, Life Eternal; as asleep in Him, our Resurrection.

It is, then, according to the analogy of His other gifts, that His two great Sacraments have in themselves manifold gifts. Baptism containeth not only remission of sin, actual or original, but maketh members of Christ, children of God, heirs of Heaven, hath the seal and earnest of the Spirit, the germ of spiritual life; the Holy Eucharist imparteth not life only, spiritual strength, and oneness with Christ, and His Indwelling, and participation of Him, but, in its degree, remission of sins also. As the manna is said to have 'contented every man's delight and agreed to every taste,'[a] so He, the Heavenly Manna, becometh to every man what he needeth, and what he can receive; to the penitent perhaps chiefly remission of sins and continued life, to those who have 'loved Him and kept His word,' His own transporting, irradiating Presence, full of His own grace and life and love; yet to each full contentment, because to each His own overflowing, undeserved, goodness.

Having then, on former occasions, spoken of the Fountain of all comfort, our Redeeming Lord, His Life for us and Intercession with the Father, as the penitent's stay amid the overwhelming consciousness of his sins, it may well suit, in this our season of deepest joy, to speak of that, which, flowing from the throne of the Lamb which was slain, is to the penitent, the deepest river of his joy, the Holy Mysteries; from which, as from Paradise, he feels that he

[a] Wisdom 16:20.

deserves to be shut out, from which perhaps, in the holier discipline of the Ancient Church, he would have been for a time removed, but which to his soul must be the more exceeding precious, because they are the Body and Blood of His Redeemer. While others joy with a more Angelic joy, as feeding on Him, Who is the Angels' food, and 'sit,' as St. Chrysostom says, 'with Angels and Archangels and heavenly powers, clad with the kingly robe of Christ itself, yea clad with the King Himself, and having spiritual armoury,' he may be the object of the joy of Angels; and while as a penitent he approaches as to the Redeemer's Side, he may hope that having so been brought, he, with the penitent, shall not be parted from It, but be with Him and near Him in Paradise. 'To the holier,' says another, 'He is more precious as God; to the sinner more precious is the Redeemer. Of higher value and avail is He to him, who hath more grace; yet to him also to whom much is forgiven, doth He the more avail, because 'to whom much is forgiven, he loveth much.'

Would that in the deep joy of this our Easter festival, the pledge of our sealed forgiveness, and the earnest of endless life in God, we could, for His sake by Whom we have been redeemed, lay aside our wearisome strifes, and that to speak of the mysteries of Divine love might not become the occasion of unloving and irreverent disputings. Would that, at least in this sacred place, we could dwell in thought, together, on His endless condescension and loving-kindness, without weighing in our own measures, words which must feebly convey Divine mysteries; rather intent (as so many in this day seem) on detecting that others have spoken too strongly on that which is unfathomable, than on ourselves adoring that Love, which is past finding out. 'When we speak of spiritual things,' is S. Chrysostom's warning, on approaching this same subject, 'be there nothing of this life, nothing earthly in our thoughts; let all such things depart and be cast out, and be we wholly given to the hearing of the Divine word. When the Spirit discourseth to us, we should listen with much stillness, yea with much awe. For the things this day read are worthy of awe. "Except ye eat the Flesh of the Son of man and drink His Blood, ye have no life in you."'

The penitent's joy, then, in the Holy Eucharist is not the less deep, because the pardon of sins is not, as in Baptism, its direct provision. The two great Sacraments, as their very signs shew, have not the same end. Baptism gives, the Holy Eucharist preserves and enlarges life. Baptism engraffs into the true Vine; the Holy Eucharist derives the richness and fulness of His life into the branches thus engraffed. Baptism buries in Christ's tomb, and through it He quickens with His life; the Holy Eucharist is given not to the dead, but to the living. It augments life, or – death; gives immortality to the living; to the dead it gives not life, but death; it is a savour of life or death, is received to salvation or damnation. Whence the ancient Church so anxiously withheld from it such as sinned grievously, not as an example only to others, but in tenderness to themselves, lest they break through and perish; 'profane,' says S. Cyprian, 'the Holy Body of the Lord,' not themselves be sanctified; fall deeper, not be restored; be wounded more grievously, not be healed; since it is said, he adds, 'Whoso eateth the Bread and drinketh the Cup of the Lord unworthily, is guilty of the Body and Blood of the Lord.'[1]

The chief object, then, of the Holy Eucharist, as conveyed by type or prophecy, by the very elements chosen, or by the words of our Lord, is the support and enlargement of life, and that in Him. In type, the tree of life was within the Paradise of God, given as a nourishment of immortality, withheld from Adam when he sinned; the bread and wine, wherewith Melchizedek met Abraham, were to refresh the father of the faithful, the weary warrior of God; the Paschal Lamb was a commemorative sacrifice; the saving blood had been shed; it was to be eaten with the unleavened bread of sincerity and truth, and with bitter herbs, the type of mortification, and by those only who were undefiled. The Manna was given to them after they had passed the Red Sea, the image of cleansing Baptism, and, as He Himself interprets it, represented Him as coming down from heaven, to give life unto the world, the food of Angels and the holy hosts of heaven; the Shew-bread[2] was eaten only by those hallowed to the Priesthood, (as the whole Christian people has in this sense been made kings and priests,) and, when once given to David and those that were with him, still on the ground that the 'vessels of the young men were holy.' The Angel brought the cake to Elijah, that in the strength of that food, he might go forty days and forty nights unto the Mount of God. In verbal prophecy, it is foretold under the images of the very elements, and so of strengthening and overflowing joy. 'Wisdom,' that is, He Who is the Wisdom of God, in a parable corresponding to that of the marriage feast, crieth, 'Come eat of My bread and drink of the wine I have mingled.' Or, in the very Psalm of His Passion and atoning Sacrifice, it is foretold, that 'the poor shall eat and be satisfied;' or that He, the good Shepherd, shall prepare a Table for those whom He leadeth by the still waters of the Church, and giveth them the Cup of overflowing joy; or as the source of gladness, 'Thou hast put gladness into my heart, since the time that their corn and wine and oil (the emblem of the Spirit of which the faithful drink) increased,' and 'the wine which gladdeneth man's heart, and the oil which maketh his face to shine, and bread which strengtheneth man's heart;' or of spiritual growth, 'corn and wine shall make the young men and maidens of Zion to grow;' or as that which alone is satisfying, 'buy wine without money and without price,' for that 'which is not bread;' or as the special Gift to the faithful, 'He hath given meat unto them that fear Him;' or that which, after His Passion, He drinketh anew with His disciples in His Father's kingdom, 'I have gathered my myrrh, I have drunk my wine with my milk; eat, O friends; drink, yea, drink abundantly, O beloved.'[3]

In all these varied symbols, strength, renewed life, growth, refreshment, gladness, likeness to the Angels, immortality, are the gifts set forth; they are gifts as to the Redeemed of the Lord placed anew in the Paradise of His Church, admitted to His Sanctuary, joying in His Presence, growing before Him, filled with the river of His joy, feasting with Him, yea Himself feasting in them, as in them He hungereth. Hitherto, there is no allusion to sin; it is what the Church should be, walking in the brightness of His light, and itself reflecting that brightness.

And when our Lord most largely and directly is setting forth the fruits of eating His Flesh and drinking His Blood, He speaks throughout of one Gift, life; freedom from death, life through Him, through His indwelling, and therefore resurrection from the dead, and life eternal. 'This is the Bread, which cometh down from heaven, that a man may eat thereof and not die. If any man eat of this Bread, he shall live for ever; and the Bread that I will give is My Flesh, which I will give for the life of the world.' 'Except ye eat the Flesh of the Son of man and drink His blood, ye have no life in you.' 'Whose eateth My Flesh and drinketh My Blood hath eternal life, and I will raise him up at the last Day.' 'He that eateth My Flesh and drinketh My Blood dwelleth in Me and I in Him.' 'As the Living Father hath sent Me and I live by The Father, so he that eateth Me, he also shall live by Me.' 'He that eateth of this Bread shall live for ever.'[4] No one can observe how this whole discourse circleth round this gift of life, and how our Lord, with unwearied patience, bringeth this one truth before us in so many different forms, without feeling that He means to inculcate, that life in Him is His chief gift in His Sacrament, and to make a reverent longing for it an incentive to our faith. Yet although life in Him is the substance of His whole teaching, the teaching itself is manifold. Our Lord inculcates not one truth only in varied forms, but in its different bearings. He answers not the strivings of the Jews, 'how can this man give us His Flesh to eat?' Such an 'how can these things be?' He never answereth; and we, if we are wise, shall never ask how they can be elements of this world and yet His very Body and Blood. But how they give life to us, He does answer; and amid this apparent uniformity of His teaching, each separate sentence gives us a portion of that answer. And the teaching of the whole, as far as such as we may grasp it, is this. That He is the Living Bread, because He came down from Heaven, and as being One God with the Father, hath life in Himself, even as the Father hath life in Himself; the life then which He is, He imparted to that Flesh which He took into Himself, yea, which He took so wholly, that Holy Scripture says, He became it, 'the Word became flesh,' and since it is thus a part of Himself, 'Whoso eateth My Flesh, and drinketh My Blood,' (He Himself says the amazing words,) 'eateth Me,' and so receiveth into Himself, in an ineffable manner, his Lord Himself, 'dwelleth' (our Lord says) 'in Me and I in Him,' and having Christ within him, not only *shall* he *have*, but he '*hath*' already 'eternal Life,' because he hath Him Who is 'the Only True God and Eternal Life;' and so Christ 'will raise him up at the last Day,' because he hath His life in him. Receiving Him into this very body, they who are His, receive life, which shall pass over to our very decaying flesh; they have within them Him Who is Life and Immortality and Incorruption, to cast out or absorb into itself our natural mortality and death and corruption, and 'shall live for ever,' because made one with Him Who Alone 'liveth for evermore.' It is not then life only as an outward gift, to be possessed by us, as His gift; it is no *mere* strengthening and refreshing of our souls, by the renewal and confirming our wills, and invigorating of our moral nature, giving us more fixedness of purpose, or implanting in us Christian graces; it is no gift, such as we might imagine given to the most perfect of God's created beings in himself. Picture we the most perfect wisdom, knowledge, strength, harmony, proportion, brightness, beauty, fitness, completeness of created being; fair as was that angel 'in the garden of God' before he fell, 'the seal of comeliness, full of wisdom, and complete in beauty – perfect in his ways from the day he was created.'[5] Yet let this be a perfection, upheld indeed of God, yet external to Him, as a mere creation, and it would fall unutterably short of the depth of the mystery of the Sacraments of Christ, and the gift, the germ whereof is therein contained for us; although such as we actually are, we know that, for strength we have weakness, for knowledge ignorance, our nature jarring still, disharmonized, obscured, deformed, both by the remains of original corruption and our own superadded sins. For the life therein bestowed is greater than any gift, since it is life in Christ, life through His indwelling, Himself Who is Life. And Holy Scripture hints, that the blessed Angels, who never fell, shall in some way to us unknown, gain by the mystery of the Incarnation, being with us gathered together under One Head, our Incarnate Lord, into His One Body, the fulness of Him Who filleth all in all. Certainly, Scripture seems to imply, that, although He 'took not the nature of angels' but 'of man,' yet all created beings, 'thrones and dominions and principalities and powers,' shall, if one may reverently say it, be more filled with God, when, this His body being perfected, there shall be no check or hindrance to the full effluence of His Divine Nature, circulating through the whole Body, into which He shall have 'knit things in heaven and things in earth,' 'the innumerable company of the Angels,' and 'the just made perfect;' and the whole glorified Church shall be clothed and radiant with Him, the Sun of Righteousness.

And of this we have the germs and first beginnings now. This is (if we may reverently so speak) the order of the mystery of the Incarnation, that the Eternal Word so took our flesh into Himself, as to impart to it His own inherent life; so then we, partaking of It, that life is transmitted on to us also, and not to our souls only, but our bodies also, since we become flesh of His flesh, and bone of His bone, and He Who is wholly life is imparted to us wholly. The Life which He is, spreads around, first giving Its own vitality to that sinless Flesh which He united indissolubly with Himself and in It encircling and vivifying our whole nature, and then, through that bread which is His Flesh, finding an entrance to us individually, penetrating us, soul and body, and spirit, and irradiating and transforming into His own light and life. . . .

Would that, instead of vain and profane disputings, we could but catch the echoes of these hallowed sounds, and forgetting the jarrings of our earthly discords, live in this harmony and unity of Heaven, where, through and in our Lord, we are all one in God. Would that, borne above ourselves, we could be caught up within the influence of the mystery of that ineffable love whereby the Father would draw us to that oneness with Him in His Son, which is the perfection of eternal bliss, where will, thought, affections shall be one, because we shall be, by communication of His Divine Nature, one. Yet such is undoubted Catholic teaching, and the most literal import of Holy Scripture, and the mystery of the Sacrament, that the Eternal Word, Who is God, having taken to Him our flesh and joined it indissolubly with Himself, and so, where His Flesh is, there He is and we receiving it, receive Him, and receiving Him are joined on to Him through His flesh to the Father, and He dwelling in us, dwell in Him, and with Him in God. 'I,' He saith, 'in the Father, and ye in Me, and I in you.'[a] This is the perfection after which all the rational creation groans, this for which the Church, which hath the first fruits of the Spirit, groaneth within herself, yea this for which our Lord Himself tarrieth, that His yet imperfect members advancing onwards in Him, and the whole multitude of the Redeemed being gathered into the One Body, His whole Body should, in Him, be perfected in the Unity of the Father. And so is He also, as Man, truly the Mediator between God and Man, in that being as God, One with the Father, as man, one with us, we truly are in Him who is truly in the Father. He, by the truth of the Sacrament, dwelleth in us, in Whom, by Nature, all the fulness of the Godhead dwelleth; and lowest is joined on with highest, earth with heaven, corruption with incorruption, man with God.

But where, one may feel, is there here any place for the sinner? Here all breathes of holy life, life in God, the life of God imparted to man, the indwelling of the All Holy and Incarnate Word, the Presence of God in the soul and body, incorruption and eternal life, through His Holy Presence and union with Him, Who, being God, is Life. Where seems there room for one, the mansion of whose soul has been broken down, and he to have no place where Christ may lay His head; the vessel has been broken, if not defiled, and now seems unfit to contain God's Holy Presence; the tenement has been narrowed by self-love, and seems incapable of expanding to receive the love of God, or God Who is love; or choked and thronged with evil or foul imaginations; or luxury and self indulgence have dissolved it, or evil thoughts and desires have made room for evil spirits in that which was the dwelling-place of the Trinity?

Doubtless, God's highest and 'holy' gift, is as the Ancient Church proclaimed, chiefly 'for the holy.' 'Ye cannot be partakers of the Table of the Lord, and the table of devils.'[b] And as Holy Scripture, so also the Ancient Church, when alluding to the fruits of this ineffable gift, speak of them mostly as they would be to those, who, on earth, already live in Heaven, and on Him Who is its life and bliss. . . .

Yet although most which is spoken belongs to Christians as belonging already to the household of saints and the family of Heaven and the Communion of Angels and unity with God, still, here as

[a] John 14:20. [b] I Corinthians 10:21.

elsewhere in the New Testament, there is a subordinate and subdued notion of sin; and what wraps the Saint already in the third Heaven, may yet uphold us sinners, that the pit shut not her mouth upon us. The same reality of the Divine Gift makes It Angels' food to the Saint, the ransom to the sinner. And both because It is the Body and Blood of Christ. Were it *only* a thankful commemoration of His redeeming love, or *only* a shewing forth of His Death, or a strengthening *only* and refreshing of the soul, it were indeed a reasonable service, but it would have no direct healing for the sinner. To him its special joy is that it is His Redeemer's very broken Body, It is His Blood, which was shed for the remission of his sins. In the words of the ancient Church,[6] 'drinks his ransom,' he eateth that, 'the very Body and Blood of the Lord, the only Sacrifice for sin,' God 'poureth out' for him yet 'the most precious Blood of His Only-Begotten,' they 'are fed from the Cross of the Lord, because they eat His Body and Blood;' and as of the Jews of old, even those who had been the betrayers and murderers of their Lord, it was said, 'the Blood, which in their phrenzy they shed, believing they drank,' so of the true penitent it may be said, whatever may have been his sins, so he could repent, awful as it is to say, – the Blood he in deed despised, and profaned, and trampled under foot, may he, when himself humbled in the dust, drink, and therein drink his salvation. 'He Who refused not to shed His Blood for us, and again gave us of His Flesh and His very Blood, what will He refuse for our salvation?' 'He,' says S. Ambrose, 'is the Bread of life. Whoso then eateth life cannot die. How should he die, whose food is life? How perish, who hath a living substance? Approach to Him and be filled, because He is Bread; approach to Him and drink, because He is a Fountain; approach to Him and be enlightened, because He is Light; approach to Him and be freed, because, where the Spirit of the Lord is, there is liberty; approach to Him and be absolved, because He is Remission of sins.'

In each place in Holy Scripture, where the doctrine of the Holy Eucharist is taught, there is, at least, some indication of the remission of sins. Our Blessed Lord, while chiefly speaking of Himself, as the Bread of life, the true meat, the true drink, His Indwelling, Resurrection from the dead, and Life everlasting, still says also, 'the Bread that I will give is My Flesh, which I will give for the life of the world.' As amid the apparent identity of this teaching, each separate oracle enounces some fresh portion of the whole truth, so also does this; that His Flesh and Blood in the Sacrament shall give life, not only because they are the Flesh and

Blood of the Incarnate Word, Who is Life, but also because they are the very Flesh and Blood which were given and shed for the life of the world, and are given *to* those, *for* whom they had been given. This is said yet more distinctly in the awful words, whereby He consecrated for ever elements of this world to be His Body and Blood. It has been remarked, as that which cannot be incidental, (as how should any words of the Eternal Word be incidental?) how amid lesser variations in the order or fulness of those solemn words, they still, wherever recorded, speak of the act as a present act.[7] 'This is My Body which *is* given for you;' 'This is My Body which *is* broken for you;' 'This is My Blood of the New Testament which *is* shed for many for the remission of sins;' 'This Cup is the New Testament in My Blood, which is shed for you.' He saith not, 'which shall be given,' 'shall be broken,' 'shall be shed,' but 'is being given,' 'being broken,' 'being shed,' (*διδόμενον, κλώμενον, ἐκχυνόμενον,*) and this in remarkable contrast with His own words, when speaking of that same Gift, as yet future, 'The Bread which I will give is My Flesh, which I will give (*ὃν ἐγὼ δώσω*) for the life of the world.' And of one of the words used, S. Chrysostome remarks how it could not be said of the Cross, but is true of the Holy Eucharist.[8] 'For "a bone of Him," it saith, "shall not be broken." *But that which He suffered not on the Cross, this He suffers in the oblation for thy sake, and submits to be broken that He may fill all men.*' Hereby He seems as well to teach us that the great Act of His Passion then began; then, as a Priest, did He through the Eternal Spirit offer Himself without spot to God; then did He 'consecrate' Himself, before He was by wicked hands crucified and slain; and all which followed, until He commended His Blessed Spirit to the Hands of His Heavenly Father, was One protracted, willing, Suffering. Then did He begin His lonely journey, where there was none to help or uphold, but He 'travelled in the greatness of His strength;' then did He begin to 'tread the wine-press alone,' and to 'stain all His raiment;' then to 'wash the garments' of His Humanity 'with' the 'Wine' of His Blood; and therefore does the Blood bedew us too; it cleanses us, because it is the Blood shed for the remission of our sins. And this may have been another truth, which our Lord intended to convey to us, when He pronounced the words as the form which consecrates the sacramental elements into His Body and Blood, that *that Precious Blood is still, in continuance and application of His One Oblation once made upon the Cross, poured out for us now, conveying to our souls, as being His Blood, with the other benefits of His Passion, the remission of our sins also*. And so, when St. Paul says,

'The cup of blessing which we bless, is it not the participation of the Blood of Christ?' remission of sins is implied by the very words. For, if we be indeed partakers of His atoning Blood, how should we not be partakers of its fruits? '*That which is in the Cup*,' S. Chrysostome paraphrases, '*is that which flowed from His side, and of that do we partake.' How should we approach His Sacred Side, and remain leprous still? Touching with our very lips that cleansing Blood, how may we not, with the Ancient Church, confess, 'Lo, this hath touched my lips, and shall take away mine iniquities and cleanse my sins?'*

There is, accordingly, an entire agreement in the Eucharistic Liturgies of the universal Church, in prayer, in benediction, in declaration, confessing that in the Holy Eucharist there is forgiveness of sins also. Those of S. James and S. Mark so paraphrase the words of Consecration as to develope the sense that they relate not only to the past act of His Precious Bloodshedding on the Cross, but to the communication of that Blood to us now. 'This is My Body which for you is broken and given for the remission of sins.' 'This is My Blood of the New Testament, which for you and for many is poured out and given for the remission of sins.' Again, the Liturgies join together manifoldly, remission of sins and life eternal, as the two great fruits of this Sacrament. Thus in the prayer for the descent of the Holy Ghost on the sacred elements, 'that they may be to all who partake of them to the remission of sins, and to life eternal,' or in intercession, 'that we may become meet to be partakers of Thy holy mysteries to the remission of sins and life eternal,' or in the words of communicating, 'I give thee the precious and holy and undefiled Body of our Lord and God and Saviour Jesus Christ for the remission of sins and life eternal.' And the prayer in our own liturgy is almost in the very words of an Eastern and in the character of a Western Liturgy, 'that our sinful bodies may be made clean by His Body and our souls washed by His most precious Blood.' Even the Roman Liturgy, though less full on this point, has prayers, 'that the Communion may cleanse us from sin,' 'may be the washing away of guilt, the remission of all offences.'

It will then seem probably too refined and narrowing a distinction, when some Divines of that Communion, countenanced by the language of the Council of Trent,[a] maintain, in opposition to other error, that venial sins only are remitted by the Holy Eucharist, since to approach it in mortal sin were itself mortal sin. For although our

[a] See Extract 6, p. 67, note c.

own Church also requires at least confession to God, and pronounces His absolution over us before we dare approach those holy Mysteries, yet because we are so far freed from our sins, that we may approach, to our salvation not to condemnation, yet can we say that we are so freed, that nothing remains to be washed away? that the absolution, which admits to that cleansing Blood, is every thing, that cleansing Blood Itself, in this respect also, addeth nothing? Rather, the penitent's comfort is, that, as, in S. Basil's words on frequent communion, 'continual participation of life is nothing else than manifold life,' so, often communion of that Body which was broken and that Blood which was shed for the remission of sins, is manifold remission of those sins over which he mourns, that as the loving-kindness of God admits him again and again to that Body and that Blood, the stains which his soul had contracted are more and more effaced, the guilt more and more purged, the wounds more and more healed, that atoning Blood more and more interposed between him and his sins, himself more united with his Lord, Who Alone is Righteousness and Sanctification and Redemption.

Since then, this Divine Sacrament has, as its immediate and proper end, union with Him Who hath taken our manhood into God, and the infusion into us of His Spirit and life and immortality, making us one with His glorified Humanity, as He is One in the Godhead with the Father, and, besides this, it is ulteriorly, the cleansing of our sins, the refining our corruptions, the repairing of our decays, what must be the loss of the Church of the latter days, in which Communions are so infrequent! How can we wonder that love should have waxed cold, corruptions so abound, grievous falls have been, among our youth, almost the rule, to stand upright the exception, Heathen strictness reproach Christian laxity, the Divine life become so rare, all higher instances of it so few and faint, when 'the stay and the staff,' the strength of that life is willingly forfeited? How should there be the fulness of the Divine life, amid all but a month-long fast from our 'daily Bread?' while in the largest portion of the Church, the people mostly gaze at the threshold of the Heaven where they do not enter,[9] what do we? We seem alas! even to have forgotten, in our very thoughts, that daily Communion, which once was the common privilege of the whole Church, which, when the Eastern Church relaxed in her first love, the Western continued, and which they from whom we have our Communion Service in its present form, at first hoped to restore.[10] It implies a life, so different from this our common-place ordinary tenor, a life so above this world as knit with Him Who hath overcome the world; so Angelic as living on Him Who is Angels' Food; an union with God so close; that we cannot mostly, I suppose, imagine to ourselves, how we could daily thus be in Heaven, and in our daily business here below, how sanctify our daily duties, thoughts, refreshment, so that they should be tinged with the hues reflected by our daily Heaven, not that heavenly Gift be dimmed with our earthliness; how our souls should through the day shine with the glory of that ineffable Presence to which we had approached, not we approach to it with earth-dimmed souls. It must ever be so; we cannot know the Gift of God, if we forfeit it; we must cease mostly even to long for what we forego. We lose the very sense to understand it.

It is not in blame of others, my brethren, God forbid! it is as the confession of a common fault, to which others have contributed least who have been least unworthy, and which, if we confess, God may the rather teach us how to amend, that I dare not but notice, how, even in this privileged and protected place, we still mostly forego even what remains, and what our Liturgy still enjoins. We have learned even, as people needs must, to justify the omission. As those, who know not our privileges of daily service, think set daily prayers must become a lifeless form, so right-minded persons speak, (and perhaps until they know it, must needs speak,) as though not we needed more reverence to partake worthily of the Communion weekly, but as though weekly Communions must needs decrease, not increase, reverence. And thus in this abode, which God has encompassed and blessed with privileges above all others, where so many have been brought into an especial nearness to Him, and a sacredness of office, so many look to be so brought, and yet on that account need the more watchfulness and Divine strength that they fall not, – where, if we will, we may retire into ourselves, as much as we will, and have daily prayers to prepare our souls, – we have, in very many cases, not even the privileges which are becoming common in village-Churches; we all, to whom it is expressly, as by name, enjoined, to 'receive the Holy Communion with the Priest every Sunday *at the least*,' have it perhaps scarcely monthly; and the thanksgiving for the Ascension of our Lord stands in our Prayer Book year by year unuttered, because when He ascended up on high to receive gifts for men, there are none here below to receive the Gift He won for us, or Himself Who is the Giver and the Gift. Nor has this been ever thus; even a century and a half ago, this Cathedral was remarked as one of those, where, after the desolation of the Great Rebellion, weekly Communions were still celebrated.

But, however we may see that our present decay and negligence should not continue, restoration must not be rashly compassed. It is not a matter of obeying rubrics, but of life or death, of health or decay, of coming together for the better or for the worse, to salvation or to condemnation. Healthful restoration is a work of humility, not to be essayed as though we had the disposal of things, and could at our will replace, what by our forefathers' negligence was lost, and by our sins bound up with theirs is yet forfeited. Sound restoration must be the gift of God, to be sought of Him in humiliation, in prayer, in mutual forbearance and charity, with increased strictness of life and more diligent use of what we have. We must consult one for the other. There is, in our fallen state, a reverent abstaining from more frequent Communion, founded on real though undue fears; there is and ought to be a real consciousness that more frequent Communion should involve a change of life, more collectedness in God, more retirement, at times, from society, deeper consciousness of His Presence, more sacredness in our ordinary actions whom He so vouchsafeth to hallow, greater love for His Passion which we celebrate, and carrying it about, in strictness of self-rule and self-discipline, and self-denying love. And these graces, we know too well, come slowly. Better, then, for a time forego what any would long for, or obtain it, where by God's bounty and Providence that Gift may be had, than by premature urgency, 'walk not charitably,' or risk injury to a brother's soul. He Who alone can make more frequent Communion a blessing, and Who gave such strength to that one heavenly meal, whereby through forty days and forty nights of pilgrimage He carried Elijah to His Presence at the Mount of God, can, if we be faithful and keep His Gift which we receive, give such abundant strength to our rarer Communions, that they shall carry us through our forty years of trial unto His own Holy Hill, and the Vision of Himself in bliss. Rather should those who long for it, fear that if It were given them, they might not be fitted for it, or, if we have it, that we come short of the fulness of its blessing, than use inconsiderate eagerness in its restoration. Ask we it of God, so will He teach us, how to obtain it of those whom He has made its dispensers to us. They too have their responsibilities, not to bestow it prematurely, though they be involved in the common loss. Let us each suspect ourselves, not others; the backward their own backwardness, the forward their own eagerness; each habitually interpret well the other's actions and motives; they who seek to partake more often of the heavenly Food, honour the reverence and humility which abstains, and they who think it reverent to abstain, censure not as innovation, the return to ancient devotion and love; restore it, if we may, at such an hour of the day, when to be absent need not cause pain or perplexity, and may make least distinction; so, while we each think all good of the other, may we all together, strengthened by the Same Bread, washed by the Same Blood, be led, in the unity of the Spirit and the bond of peace and holiness of life, to that ineffable Feast, where not, as now, in Mysteries, but, face to face, we shall ever see God, and be ever filled with His Goodness and His Love.

Meantime such of us, as long to be penitents, may well feel that we are less than the least of God's mercies; that we have already far more than we deserve; (for whereas we deserved Hell, we have the antepast of Heaven;) that the children's bread is indeed taken and given unto dogs; that He, Who is undefiled, spotless, separate from sinners, cometh to be a guest with us sinners; and therein may we indeed find our comfort and our stay. For where He is, how should there not be forgiveness and life and peace and joy? What other hope need we, if we may indeed hope that we thereby dwell in Him and He in us; He in us, if not by the fulness of His graces, yet with such at least as are fitted to our state, cleansing our iniquities and healing our infirmities, Himself the forgiveness we long for; we in Him, in Whom if we be found in that Day, our pardon is for ever sealed, ourselves for ever cleansed, our iniquity forgiven, and our sin covered.

Notes

CHARLES SIMEON (1759–1836)

1. In 1801 Simeon republished a translation of the seventeenth-century Frenchman, Jean Claude's *Essay on the Composition of a Sermon*, subsequently binding it with the *Horae Homileticae*. In his Preface to the *Essay* Simeon advanced many of the doctrinal views here advanced for the benefit of undergraduates. It is interesting to note Simeon's approval of Edward Copleston's *An Inquiry into the Doctrines of Necessity and Predestination* (1821), a work by the founder of Oriel's Noetic School – characterized by intellectual liberalism.
2. Thomas Scott (1747–1821), the Calvinist Biblical commentator whose venture Simeon helped financially. The man 'to whom (humanly speaking) I almost owe my soul', Newman claimed (*Apologia pro Vita Sua*, ed. M. J. Svaglic (Oxford, 1967), p. 18).
3. James Hervey (1714–58), a very popular Evangelical author and contributor, on the Calvinist side, to the 'Calvinistic controversy', in such works as *Dialogues between Theron and Aspasio* (3 vols., 1755) where Aspasio tries to convince Theron of the doctrine of imputed righteousness. See also below, p. 29.
4. Matthew Henry (1662–1714), a Nonconformist, whose Biblical commentary, begun in 1704, was admired by Anglicans.
5. Melanchthon (1497–1560), the humanist and Protestant Reformer, made Justification by Faith the keystone of his theology in his *Loci Communes* (1521). Although he never relinquished his belief in this, the events of the Reformation caused him to stress the place of such guides for living as the Ten Commandments in his later work. Calvin's views changed very little between the 1536 and 1559 version of the *Institutes* but, as controversies arose, he amplified his arguments. The ecclesiological and parochial aspects of this necessary doctrine became clearer as Calvin increasingly stressed the promise of a final reward as an encouragement to the faithful.
6. It is worth observing Simeon's balanced appraisal of the Reformers in the light of their subsequent elevation by Evangelicals to near-sainthood in reaction to the Oxford Movement's appeal to the authority of the Fathers. Cf. Simeon on the Fathers: 'We must call no man master, but must judge for ourselves out of the Bible. The early Christians are good authorities as to the readings of the text, and we bow to them; but their interpretations are not of more *a priori* worth than ours, not perhaps of so much, because we have the accumulated ideas of eighteen centuries to compare with each other, and to try by Scripture' (Brown, *Recollections*, p. 298).
7. Joseph Milner (1744–97). An Evangelical who, perhaps as a reaction to Gibbon's *Decline and Fall* (1776–88), determined to publish *The History of the Church of Christ*, which was to be more than a record of heresy and dispute. Three volumes appeared between 1794 and 1797. This Evangelical best-seller, which first

introduced Newman to the Fathers, was continued, first by Isaac, Joseph's brother, and subsequently by John Scott, son of Thomas Scott, the commentator.

8. *An Essay on Human Liberty* (1824), the posthumous publication of Isaac Milner (1750–1820), President of Queens' College, Cambridge, Dean of Carlisle and brother of the above.
9. 'So then this foreknowledge is no other, but that Eternal love of God, or decree of Election by which some are appointed unto life, and being foreknown or elected to that end, they are predestinate to the way to it', *A Practical Commentary upon the first Chapters of the first Epistle General of St. Peter* (1693), pp. 23–4, by Robert Leighton (1611–84).
10. A favourite Evangelical analogy, originating with John Newton (1725–1807), the regenerate slave trader and parson of Olney, who had been an early Calvinist mentor of Simeon's.
11. Thomas Erskine (1788–1870), a Scottish theologian, believed that ultimately all men would be saved. Life was thus an education, not a period of probation, for the Christian. The three works referred to are his *Remarks on the Internal Evidence for the truth of Revealed Religion* (Edinburgh, 1820), *An Essay on Faith* (Edinburgh, 1822) and *The Unconditional Freeness of the Gospel* (Edinburgh, 1828).
12. Cesar Henri Malan (1787–1864), a popular Swiss preacher, whose unorthodox opinions led to his being banned from preaching in Calvinist Geneva on original sin, election and related doctrines.
13. The Samarian sorcerer, converted by Philip, referred to in Acts 8:9–24. The word 'simony' derives from his attempt to attain miraculous powers by offering money to the Apostles.
14. Daniel Whitby (1638–1726), *A Discourse concerning Election and Reprobation* (1710). This work, which aimed to demonstrate that Arminianism had always formed the backbone of Anglican doctrine, had been republished as recently as 1819.
15. John William Fletcher (1729–85), often spoken of as 'the saintly Mr. Fletcher of Madeley', was educated in Calvinist Geneva. His best-known work, *Checks to Antinomianism* (1771), was a contribution, on the Arminian side, to the Calvinistic controversy.
16. *For Missionaries after the Apostolic School: A Series of Orations in Four Parts* (1825). The text of a three-hour sermon Irving delivered to the London Missionary Society in 1824. Irving's avid preaching of apostolic simplicity roused Simeon to remark 'Irving would have missionaries go forth literally "without staff or scrip"; he ought himself to set the example' (Brown, *Recollections*, p. 205).
17. *The Coming of Messiah in Glory and Majesty by Juan Josafat Ben-Ezra, a converted Jew* (1827). Irving's growing sense of persecution in the Lord's service and Simeon's revulsion at the note it produced in Irving's writing can be appreciated in this brief extract from Irving's Preface, written from 'this lonely watch tower where the Lord hath stationed me in his wonderful providence; – mine appointed post, from which, by the grace of God, I shall make known unto the Church whatever I hear and see; fearing not, Oh my Lord, these Pharisaical and Sadducean enemies, with whom I am surrounded, nor caring that I have not communion of the brethren for which my soul longeth'.
18. Robert Story, *Peace in Believing: a Memoir of Isabella Campbell of Fernicarry by her minister* (Greenock, 1829; new ed. 1854). In this record of ecstatic faith, Story, a millenarian friend of Irving's, notes that his parishioner was 'deeply impressed with the low state of true piety among the people, notwithstanding the ostentatious bustle and activity of what is called the evangelical world of this

country' (p. 75). He is anxious to confirm that Isabella always took the medicines provided, but Simeon's allegation of suicide was doubtless prompted by remarks such as 'We had often conversation regarding the jealousy with which believers ought to watch their longings to depart' (p. 176).

19. Thomas Hartwell Horne (1780–1862), *Romanism Contradictory to the Bible* (1827). John Jewel (1522–71), author of *Apologia pro Ecclesia Anglicana* (1562), a systematic defence of the Elizabethan compromise. When Tractarians seemed to be elevating the Fathers above the Reformers a positive flurry of reprints and new translations of Jewel's *Apologia* appeared: three such appeared in 1839 alone.
20. Richard Baxter (1615–91). The passage to which Simeon refers reads: 'They are those whom he embraceth with a peculiar Love, and do again love him above all', but the full title of the book best indicates his position: *The Saint's Everlasting Rest: or a Treatise of the Blessed State of the Saints in their enjoyment of God in Glory. Wherein is shewed its excellency and certainty; the misery of those that lose it, the way to Attain it, and Assurance of it; and how to live in the continual delightful Foretastes of it, by the help of Meditation* (1650).
21. Walter Marshall (1628–80). His posthumously published *The Gospel Mystery of Sanctification* (1692) was republished with a commendatory letter by James Hervey in 1756.
22. William Romaine (1714–95), in his day the most renowned Evangelical exponent of Calvinist views within the Anglican Church.
23. Upon his conversion as an undergraduate Simeon held prayers in his room on Sunday nights for friends and servants. At home, despite the indifference of most of his relatives, he was permitted to hold prayers for the servants. For those diffident at leading prayers Simeon adapted a Calvinist model, Benjamin Jenks, *Prayers and Offices for families* (1697), publishing an 'altered and improved' version in 1808.

FRANCIS CLOSE (1797–1882)

1. Close's theory of mind is derived from those portions of seventeenth- and eighteenth-century thought compatible with his Calvinist position. Newton's mechanistic universe presupposed a Great Spirit or Mechanic who had formed it. The Lockean idea (John Locke, 1632–1704) of the mind as a blank sheet receiving impressions is here manipulated so as to denigrate mental powers rather than to express admiration for the mind's subsequent creativity in combining, comparing and selecting. Calvinist belief in total depravity, a fall which had tainted every part of man, including his reason, is wholly at odds with Locke's contention that reason is one of God's modes of Revelation.
2. G. Townsend, *The New Testament arranged in Chronological and Historical Order* (2 vols., 1825), vol. II, pp. 7–8.
3. It seems unlikely that Close took the trouble to read William Ellery Channing's *Self-Culture* (1838), since he lifts this precise quotation from Dowling's book (see below, note 4), whilst inserting his own italics and punctuation.
4. J. G. Dowling, *The Effects of Literature upon the Moral Character* (1840), p. 46.
5. As corroborative evidence Close offers the following note: '"What Socrates said of the Deity, what Plato writ, and the rest of the heathen philosophers of several nations, is all no more than the twilight of revelation, after the sun of it was set in the race of Noah." – *Dryden's Preface to Religio Laici.*'
6. Olinthus Gilbert Gregory (1774–1841), a mathematician and founder member of University College, wrote *Letters . . . on the Evidences, Doctrines, and Duties of the Christian Religion* (2 vols., 1811) for the religious instruction of his children.

Close refers to the sixth edition and by 1857 it merited a ninth edition. The work's anti-Deist tone was sympathetic to an Evangelical: it argued that the ancients suffered from the lack of the one source of Revelation, the Word as given by the Holy Spirit, and had therefore been unable to make use of the evidence of God as seen in His universe.

7. Although Socrates himself taught the immortality of the soul.
8. Gregory brackets these three as evidence for his assertion that disbelief in a future state predominated amongst Roman philosophers.
9. Expurgated and annotated classical texts for use in schools began to make a regular appearance in the 1860s, although schools like Eton and Westminster often had their own special editions of authors in previous centuries.
10. Robert Owen (1771–1858) believed religion to be the great obstacle to progress. His experimental community in New Lanarkshire was founded on the conviction that men are moulded by circumstances and can therefore be moulded into goodness. Close was a vociferous opponent of Owen's radical views, although he had become interested in his educational experiments at the infant-school level.
11. Once again Close shows himself prepared to use any evidence in favour of his argument, despite its provenance. Rousseau, arguing from an assumption of natural goodness, claims that each man may, by the use of God-given reason, effect his own salvation.
12. *Émile, ou De l'éducation* (1762).
13. Close's phraseology is here loosely derived from the one poet whose doctrinal purity invited unstinting Evangelical approval. Milton's *Paradise Lost*, v, lines 150–208 provides the account of morning worship in Eden lurking behind this passage.
14. Gilbert Scott, the doyen of Victorian Gothic architecture, told how his Evangelical family hunted assiduously not for a successful, but for a religious architect to whom he might be apprenticed (*Personal and Professional Recollections* (1879), p. 53).
15. Nathaniel Lardner (1684–1768), *The Credibility of Gospel History* (12 vols., 1727–55). This conservative but scholarly Nonconformist critic of patristic literature planned his apologetic work so that those without scholarship would be enabled to form an opinion for themselves.
16. From the time of Sir Christopher Wren English church-building had tended to diminish the size of the chancel. The importance attributed to preaching was attested by the pulpit or reading-desk placed near the congregation becoming the focal point of the church. In campaigning for the reinstatement of the chancel and praising rood screens which divided chancel from nave, the ecclesiologists perhaps forgot that the medieval form on which they based their designs had reflected a form of worship where priests said the offices and the congregation, scarcely able to see, took no part. Hook (see below, note 18) used the chancel of his new church at Leeds for seating the choir and this practice won Camdenian approval.
17. The nineteenth century re-enacted the sixteenth- and seventeenth-century debate over the name, significance and material of the Communion table. An immoveable stone altar was felt by Evangelicals to indicate the concept of a repeated sacrifice celebrated by a priest, whereas they favoured a moveable wooden Holy Table at which all might communicate. Close's attention had been drawn to the Camden Society's affairs when the society had attempted to place a stone altar in the medieval Cambridge church of St Sepulchre's and the non-resident incum-

bent had appealed for funds to help him fight this restoration in the courts. As one critic of Close was swift to point out his instantly assumed partisanship seemed all the more fictitious when it was known that his recently built Christ Church, Cheltenham, incorporated an altar with stone panels.

18. Close here refers the reader to a work by the High Church ally of the Tractarians, Walter Farquhar Hook (1798–1875). In alluding to Hook's *Church Dictionary* (1842), intended 'to explain things relating to the Church to his poorer parishioners', Close suppresses Hook's assertion that consecration almost certainly took place without being recorded before the fourth century.
19. The orientation of the church so as to secure the altar in an eastward position was expressive of an attitude to worship. Tractarians preferred the priest to celebrate the Eucharist facing the altar, as opposed to Protestants who turned westwards and manwards. (See Isaac Williams, *Tract No. 86* (1839), p. 76.)
20. The exclamatory upper-case letters are used in a sarcastic echo of the Camdenian claim: 'The Decorated or Edwardian style, that employed, we mean, between the years 1260 and 1360, is that to which only, except for some very peculiar circumstances, we ought to return. The reason of this is plain. During the so-called Norman era, the Catholick Church was forming her architectural language: in the Tudor period she was unlearning it' (*Few Words to Church Builders*, 3rd ed. (Cambridge, 1844), pp. 5–6).
21. The entry under *Church* in Hook's *Church Dictionary* reads: 'some persons have been found, who acting on the principles of Judas Iscariot think all expense a waste which is bestowed on the decoration of churches'.
22. Close's social assumption prompted the *Ecclesiologist* to rejoin. 'We really think there ought to be a Cheltenham central committee to allot the comparative amounts of comfort and ceremonial to the different classes of society; to the operatives deal benches, stucco and Irish; to the *elite* of Cheltenham, cushioned pues, stoves, silk dress gowns and cambrick' (3 (1844), 179).

WILLIAM GOODE (1801–1868)

1. Richard Hurrell Froude (1803–36). Four volumes of his *Remains* were posthumously published with a preface by J. H. Newman between 1838 and 1839. Newman felt that the revelations in the private journal of Froude's self-imposed penances, together with his reverence for the Catholic Church of Antiquity would serve as a practical illustration of the aims of the Tractarian movement. Evangelical and many orthodox High Churchmen were shocked by the openly declared hatred for the Reformed Protestant element of Anglicanism.
2. Goode's choice of Archbishop Whitgift (1530?–1604) as a representative of the Reformed English Church is singularly apt since Whitgift was renowned as much for opposing Puritanism, where it conflicted with the Prayer Book, as Roman Catholicism.
3. *A Letter on Catholic Unity* (1841), by Nicholas Wiseman (1802–65), elevated to a Roman Catholic bishopric in June 1840. He had concerned himself, in his new English appointment, with demonstrating the illogicalities of the Tractarian position. The outcry against his elevation in 1850 to the archbishopric of the recreated Papal hierarchy in England forms the substance of the next extract.
4. The 'General Answer to Mr Kingsley' and the 'Appendix' of Newman's *Apologia* (1864) form the best account and rebuttal of Victorian prejudice concerning the Roman Catholic Church's alleged sanctioning of lying and equivocation.
5. In the summer of 1841 Frederick Oakley and William George Ward, two

extremist Tractarians, who later seceded to Rome, began a series of pamphlets defending *Tract No. XC*. In the July issue of the *British Critic* (59), which had been edited by Newman between 1838 and 1841, they began the attack on the Reformers, in which this remark occurs.

6. Thomas Brett (1667–1744), George Hickes (1642–1715) and John Johnson (1662–1725). The Nonjurors were those beneficed Anglican clergy who refused to take the oath of allegiance to William and Mary in 1689, or again to George I in 1714. In their high estimate of the historical episcopate, the ministry and the liturgy, they were united in their opposition to Erastianism, but divided on much else. In *Lectures on certain difficulties felt by Anglicans in submitting to the Catholic Church* (1850) Newman warned against the Nonjuring Church as an alternative home for those right-minded Tractarians who felt it their duty to secede.
7. E. B. Pusey, *A Letter to the Bishop of Oxford* (Oxford, 1839), p. 53.
8. *British Critic*, 59 (July 1841), 28.
9. The Wesleyan Methodist Conference, maintaining an apolitical stance and preferring to see itself as a society rather than a Dissenting sect, dissociated itself from other discontented Dissenters who banded together in 1833 in the hope that they might win disestablishment from a Whig government, supposedly on the side of religious tolerance and reform.
10. As a royal chaplain Hook preached a sermon entitled 'Hear the Church' in 1838, in which he claimed that the Church of England was reformed, not founded, in the sixteenth century, that the Roman Catholics were the seceders and the English bishops the true successors of the Apostles. Hook had preached these views for some ten years before the Oxford Movement started, but was inevitably tarred with the same brush. (See also Close Endnote 20.)
11. The correspondent of the *British Magazine* (May 1839, 518), signing himself S.T.R., complained in scathing tones of the Tractarians' lack of scholarship and, like Goode, attacked their interpretation of the Fathers as based upon mistranslations.
12. III John 1:9–10: 'I wrote unto the church: but Diotrephes, who loveth to have the pre-eminence among them, receiveth us not. / Wherefore, if I come, I will remember his deed which he doeth, prating against us with malicious words: and not content therewith, neither doth he receive the brethren, and forbiddeth them that would, and casteth them out of the church.'
13. Possibly an allusion to Pusey's refusal, in the days after the Gorham Judgement, to endorse any declaration, on the subject of the Royal Supremacy or allegiance to the Church of England, which took its stand on declared anti-Romanism.

EDWARD MIALL (1809–1881)

1. (See also below, p. 94.) Nonconformist radicals continued to deploy the arguments and illustrations used by abolitionists of the slave trade when they made war at home against State tyranny.
2. The Ragged School Union, founded in 1844, had as its president Lord Ashley, later Earl of Shaftesbury. It recruited its pupils from the very poor of all ages who would otherwise have been prevented from attending because of their destitute appearance. Free food and clothes were provided as an inducement to elementary education. By 1849 there were eighty-two Ragged Schools with 8,000 pupils, 124 paid, and 929 voluntary teachers.
3. The Religious Tract Society, founded in 1799 as an interdenominational society to distribute Bibles, tracts and moral literature, was the largest of its kind.

4. The Crown claims especial prerogative rights and grants sole privilege of printing the 1611 Authorized Version of the Bible. The University Presses of Oxford and Cambridge share this right with the Queen's printers by virtue of a charter empowering them to print 'all manner of books'. After the Queen's Scottish printer's patent had lapsed in 1839 Scottish publishers were free to print the Bible subject only to the supervision of the text by a licensing board. The 'individual zeal' of one such publisher, William Collins, was evident when, knowing that the English patent was to lapse in 1859, he set up an office in London from where he issued Bibles. The competition he offered halved the price of Bibles but, despite a House of Commons inquiry, the English patent was renewed in 1860.
5. The repeal of the so-called 'taxes on knowledge' was an integral part of the Radical programme. In 1851 a select parliamentary committee was set up, in 1855 the newspaper tax was abolished and in 1861 the paper duty removed.
6. Miall's editorial in the opening number of the *Nonconformist* had declared the paper in favour of Free Trade and against state interference in the form of the Corn Laws.
7. Topical investigations of the Court of Chancery had brought these two long-standing grievances to the fore. Feudal tenure was finally abolished in 1925 so that the rules of primogeniture henceforth applied only to the titles. In practice entail had been the more important issue since the eighteenth century. After 1925 the current holder of the land gained greater freedom of administration.
8. Not until 1854–56 were non-Anglicans permitted to enter Oxford or take degrees at Cambridge.
9. Responding as a Dissenter to the cry of 'the Church in danger' in a speech made on 16 October 1833, the Rev. T. Binney had made a notorious attack upon the institution of the Established Church as a national evil. Miall gives us his actual words rather than his generally reported claim that 'the Church of England damns more souls than it saves'.

ISAAC WILLIAMS (1802–1865)

1. Three names chosen by Williams to stress the high moral content of Christian doctrine and practice. St. Chrysostom (AD 347–407) excited the admiration of the people and the enmity of the higher classes of Constantinople by his own ascetic life style, and the rebukes he offered to the immorality of the wealthy and his severity to worldly-minded monks and clergy. Thomas Wilson (1663–1775), Bishop of Sodor and Man, was renowned for his efforts to restore the moral discipline of the Anglican Church. His collected works were published in *The Library of Anglo-Catholic Theology* (7 vols., Oxford, 1847–63), by Keble, who laboured for sixteen years on the accompanying biography.
2. A footnote by Williams amplified this: 'St. Augustine (vol. vi. p. 994) supposes the case of a person who hears Christ preached by an heretical preacher, and is in doubt what to do: to which Augustine answers, That Christ is preached openly, and on the housetops; that he has made His pavilion in the sun, that is to say, that the true doctrine of Christ is in the Church, which is a light to all nations; the question is whether his doctrine is that of the Catholic Church. This is precisely a case in point; and it is in this sense that the Church is "clothed with the sun," that Christ is as the lightning seen from the East to the West; and that with respect to those who say, "Lo He is here! or Lo He is there!" command is given, "Go not after them."'
3. Williams is here referring to the welter of Evangelical books and pamphlets published in response to *Tract No. 80*. Whilst not denying the value of Tradition as a witness to the practices of the Primitive Church, Evangelical writers refused to

recognize Tradition as having authority in any way comparable with the sole Rule of Faith contained in the Scriptures.

4. In a note Williams considers the bearing of a text much quoted by Evangelicals upon his claim: 'One instance in Scripture has been applied otherwise, "Make the tree good and his fruit good; or else make the tree corrupt and his fruit corrupt;" but this passage bears quite a different meaning; the obvious purport being, that hypocritical, bad actions, like those of the Pharisees, flowed from a bad principle in the heart, that the whole heart needed to be amended. It is not a very overstrained interpretation to apply this to the doctrine of the Atonement, on the supposition that the infinite and incomprehensible love of God manifested therein will, on being published, powerfully affect men's minds, and, on being heard, regenerate their souls? Is there any sanction whatever for this in Holy Scripture?'
5. By way of a footnote Williams adds: 'This is simply founded on the account which Bishop Butler gives of the formation of moral habits. See *The Analogy. Of a State of Moral Discipline.* It is, moreover, curious to observe how entirely Aristotle's system in this respect coincides with Holy Scripture, which makes our salvation to depend both on our mode of life, and also on our accepting certain articles of faith. For according to Aristotle, the perception of any moral truth depends on the life which a person leads. He says, that it depends not on intellect itself, as in pure science; but that the understanding must have combined with it a certain desire, love, or motive (*ὄρεξις* or *ἕνεκα τοῦ*); but this desire or motive depends on the mode of life (*ἠθικὴ ἕξις*), and is given by it. (B. vii.) In another place he says, that which is truly good does not appear but to him who leads a good life; and at another time, that a man be brought up well to understand morals; and that the faculty of discerning truth, vice destroys. From which it would follow, that if any article of the Creed is less received than another, it is owing to some peculiarity in the life and conduct, either of an individual or an age, that rejects it.' In reading the works of Tractarian thinkers a recurrent tendency to allude to Aristotle's *Ethics* alongside Butler's *Analogy* swiftly becomes apparent. Newman, Williams and Keble alike had read and taught the Oxford Greats course on which both were compulsory texts. For their influence and the reverence in which they were held by Oxford men, see D. Newsome, *Two Classes of Men* (1974), ch. 5.
6. Williams adds an illustrative footnote: 'An instance of this may be mentioned in the solemn injunction of St Paul to Timothy, 'Preach the word; be instant in season, out of season:' in the meaning which is often attached to this passage, it might readily be quoted against us, and is often made use of to hold the opposite opinions. But when the true sense of the expression is considered, and it is taken together with the context, it would serve to set forth all we say of the right teaching of the doctrine of the Atonement, in contradistinction from that which we condemn. 'Preach the word; be instant in season, out of season; reprove, rebuke, exhort, with all long-suffering and doctrine. For the time will come when they will not endure sound doctrine.' Here there is nothing at all respecting a display of the doctrine of the Atonement; but, on the contrary, it is enjoined that with long-suffering, reproof, rebuke, and exhortation are to be instantly urged. It is a testimony to the truth, which requires patience and courage.'
7. The *Gorgias* is a dialogue by Plato in which Socrates discusses with his celebrated contemporary rhetorician, Gorgias, the nature of his art. Socrates claims that rhetoric is an art of flattery, directed to pleasure. Unlike the other sophists of his time Socrates never opened a school nor delivered public lectures. His method of

dialectic inquiry, as reported by Plato, was to develop inborn moral consciousness rather than communicate his own maxims. Pythagoras admitted 300 aristocratic disciples to a select brotherhood. This élite band, amongst whom there were further gradations, practised reserve concerning their beliefs and practices and were renowned for their asceticism.

8. In their endeavour to dispense with the dead forms of 'nominal' Christianity many Evangelicals had sought to replace the daily reading of services and other devotions prescribed by the Church with weekday evening lectures in the vestry or schoolroom.
9. Williams still sees the Methodists as seceders from the Anglican Church, although they had, by this stage, recruited from those never previously attached to the Church of England. He is presumably alluding, not only to their particular religious argot, but also to the introduction of 'love-feasts' and their emphasis on 'the new birth' which Tractarians felt detracted from the centrality of the Sacraments of the Eucharist and Baptism respectively.

JOHN KEBLE (1792–1866)

1. Francois de Salignac de la Mothe Fénelon (1651–1715), a French Roman Catholic theologian who produced an apologia for mystical spirituality.
2. William Law (1686–1761), a nonjuring theologian. Law's *A Serious Call* was read and esteemed by Evangelicals and High Churchmen alike. Wesley was an early admirer, though he later learned to distrust Law's mysticism. Law attacked the Lockean view of reason as a mode of Revelation. (See the Introductory Essay.)
3. Conyers Middleton (1683–1750). Middleton's sceptical rationalism can best be seen in the title of his work from which Keble quotes below, p. 136: *A Free Inquiry into the Miraculous Powers which are supposed to have subsisted in the Christian Church from the Earliest Ages through several successive centuries. By which it is shewn that we have no sufficient reason to believe, upon the authority of the Primitive Fathers, that any such powers were continued to the Church, after the days of the Apostles* (1749). The Fathers' account of miracles, he reasons, are part and parcel of the credulity of those primitive times.
4. Edward Gibbon (1737–94). From his ironic treatment of the rise of Christianity in *The History of the Decline and Fall of the Roman Empire* (1776–81) Gibbon's name had become a by-word for scepticism. He did not believe in the supernatural and sought to explain the growth of Christianity naturalistically.
5. William Warburton (1698–1779), Bishop of Gloucester. His *Julian* (1750) attempted to answer Middleton's *A Free Inquiry*. Whilst apparently arguing against Deist rationalism it was felt that he conceded too much of the case in allowing that some of the circumstances reported in the Father's account of miracles were natural, not supernatural as claimed.
6. A quotation from Bishop Law which Keble found in Middleton's *A Free Inquiry*. Edmund Law (1703–87), Bishop of Carlisle, was a disciple of Locke's. Although he never disputed the evidence of miracles, he argued that religion, both natural and revealed, was, like every other form of human knowledge, progressive.
7. Robert Boyle (1627–91), natural philosopher. The tenor of Boyle's work in reconciling science and religion can best be captured in the title of a later work: *The Christian Virtuoso: Shewing that by Being Addicted to Experimental Philosophy a Man is Rather Assisted than Indisposed to be a Good Christian.*

8. William Laud (1573–1645), Charles I's Archbishop, beheaded for his alleged Roman Catholic sympathies.
9. *Verba visibilia*: visible signs. Keble carefully distinguished the Tractarian sacramental view of the universe from any pantheistic view of God and His Creation as identical. For Keble God remains transcendental and natural objects carry no spiritual potency.

JOHN HENRY NEWMAN (1801–1890)

1. Stephen Lushington, M.P., and Henry Brougham (made Whig Lord Chancellor in 1830) were both founder members of the Society for the Diffusion of Useful Knowledge and active in obtaining a charter for University College. Not until 1836, when it was incorporated in the examining body of the University of London, was opposition overcome to a university, founded by utilitarians and Dissenters, which offered no religious education.
2. In the *Inagural Discourse of Henry Brougham on being installed Lord Rector of the University of Glasgow* (1825) Brougham recommended 'study of the Rhetorical Art, by which useful truths are promulgated with effect, and the Purposes to which a Proficiency in this art should be made subservient'.
3. Newman later noted: 'This latter work is wrongly ascribed to Lord Brougham in this passage. It is, however, of the Brougham school.' Brougham wrote *The Objects, Advantages and Pleasures of Science* (1827), for the Society for the Diffusion of Useful Knowledge; it went through nineteen editions in its first year of publication. For the Library of Entertaining Knowledge George Lillie Craik wrote *The Pursuit of Knowledge under Difficulties: illustrated by anecdotes* which was still being reprinted in 1906. It is from these anecdotes that Newman, clearly working with the text before him, quotes the otherwise obscure examples on pp. 161, 175–6.
4. Pierre-Simon, marquis de La Place (1749–1827), mathematician, astronomer and physicist. See also below, pp. 162, 182. Unlike Newton, who assumed the need for the Great Artificer to return to rectify irregularities in the planetary system, La Place reputedly told Napoleon that his stable solar system needed no creator, since age-long planetary changes were eventually exactly symmetrical.
5. This insistence upon the absolute and awful reality of human sinfulness was a characteristic feature of Newman's thought. See, for example, 'Moral Consequences of Single Sins', *Parochial and Plain Sermons* (1868).
6. A taunt at the empiricism of this Scottish philosopher whose liberal opinions made him the 'patron saint' of the early *Edinburgh Review* men.
7. 'Let the University minister to the Church', is no casually chosen phrase, but an exact rebuttal of Dr Hampden's call, in 1834, for the abolition of tests preventing Dissenters from attending Oxford and Cambridge, which Newman saw as 'the commencement of the assault of Liberalism upon the old orthodoxy of Oxford and England' (*Apologia pro Vita Sua*, ed. M. J. Svaglic (Oxford, 1967), p. 62).
8. From reading the Fathers Newman had learnt that 'pagan literature, philosophy, and mythology, properly understood were but a preparation for the Gospel' (*Apologia*, p. 36). As a moral philosopher Aristotle was a forerunner of Butler in pointing to virtue as a state of the will and not of the reason. Bishop Butler, whose work had been a formative influence on Newman (see Williams Endnote 5), affirmed an intuitional theory of virtue. In the *Grammar of Assent* Newman developed his notion of the 'Illative Sense' which recognized the personal

workings and impulses of the mind not as distorting but as a means to the knowledge of truth. If conscience rather than rational judgement becomes the great rule for determining moral choice and action then Arcesilas and Berkeley become two further progenitors of this idea. The Greek philosopher Arcesilas reputedly believed intellectual certainty impossible and claimed that a wise man need know only that his reactions are reasonable. Of Berkeley Newman wrote, 'As to Berkeley I do not know enough to talk, but it seems to me, while a man holds the moral governance of God as *existing in and through his conscience*, it matters not whether he believes his senses or not. For, at least he will hold the external world as a *divine* intimation, a scene of trial whether a reality or not – just as a child's game may be a trial . . . I conceive Hume denied conscience, Berkeley confessed it' (*Letters*, ed. Mozley, vol. II, p. 36).

9. Newman appeals to the writings of Francis Bacon (p. 168, *Novum Organum*; p. 181, *The Advancement of Learning*), because Bacon insisted on separating Revelation from scientific truth. 'Sacred theology must be drawn from the word and oracles of God, not from the light of nature, or the dictates of reason' (*De Augmentis*).

10. Some of the references in this and the ensuing paragraph are self-explanatory, or well-known. For the rest: Haroun Al Raschid (766–809), fifth caliph of Baghdad and a connoisseur of music and poetry. The legendary wealth and colour of his court is represented in *The Arabian Nights*. Blaise Pascal (1623–62), French mathematician and moralist, whose posthumously published *Pensées* (1670) were fragments of a projected defence of Christianity. Julian the Apostate, a fourth-century Roman emperor, brought up as a Christian and educated alongside the Christian Fathers, Gregory and Basil. On becoming emperor he avowed himself a pagan, although proclaiming toleration of Christian subjects. Joseph Milner – see Simeon Endnote 7. Pierre Bayle (1647–1706), sceptical philosopher suspected of atheism, whose *Dictionnaire historique et critique* (1697) has been seen as the seminal work of the French Enlightenment. Robert Boyle – see Keble Endnote 7. Madame Roland (1754–93), influential member of the Girondist party (the moderate Republican party of the French Revolution) who, in her five months imprisonment before being guillotined, wrote her *Mémoires*, which revealed her to be an intelligent and talented woman. Alphery – Nikephor Alphery (*fl.* 1618–60), a member of the Russian imperial family who was sent to England for education in safety. Although ejected from his Anglican living in 1643, he twice refused invitations to resume his position in Russia. Benjamin West (1738–1820) American painter of historical and Biblical scenes, patronized by George III. Henry Kirke White (1785–1806), a self-taught, minor poet, helped by Simeon and Wilberforce to obtain a place at Cambridge, where he died before taking a degree. Giovanni Baptista Belzoni (1778–1823), an Italian of six foot seven inches, who, on arrival in England, earned his living by exhibiting himself at Astley's, a theatre renowned for spectacular extravaganzas. He subsequently achieved fame as an engineer and excavator of Egyptian pyramids.

11. Newman himself inclined more to the immaterialist school of Berkeley. 'To what extent Berkeley denied the existence of the external world I am not aware; nor do I mean to go so far myself (far from it) as to deny the existence of matter, though I should deny that *what we saw* was more than accidents of it, and say that space perhaps is but a condition of the objects of sense, not a reality' (*Letters*, ed. Mozley, vol. II, p. 36). The clear connections between 'Berkeleyism' and the sacramental system Newman learnt from Butler and Keble, 'that is the doctrine

that material phenomena are both the types and the instruments of real things unseen', is acknowledged in the *Apologia*, p. 29.

12. Newman later wrote: 'This is too absolute, if it is taken to mean that the legitimate, and what may be called the objective, conclusion from the fact of Nature viewed in the concrete is not in favour of the being and providence of God.'
13. Newman's rejection of the Lockean concept of mind as a *tabula rasa* filled by experience of two kinds – sensation and the operation of the mind in contemplating the ideas it has received – leads him to embrace a Romantic theory of the imagination. 'According as the apprehension is notional or imaginative so may the assent be called one or the other, the notional assent being languid, and the imaginative energetic. . . . If abstract truths, (or what nominalists call 'generalizations' from experience) are objective, (as realists would hold,) therefore they are objects – what *is* the *object?* Beautifulness, for instance, – *what* does the mind see when it contemplates this abstraction? – is it God? If not, is it one of the Platonic everlasting ideas external to God? if not, can it be anything at all, and are we not driven to agreement with the school of Locke and of sensible experiences? (*The Theological Papers of John Henry Newman on Faith and Certainty*, ed. H. M. de Achaval and J. D. Holmes (Oxford, 1976), p. 135). The Romantic inheritance behind Tractarian emphasis upon the necessity of first cultivating 'right feeling' for a true perception of God's universe can be seen in these lines by Wordsworth:

> I remember well
> That in life's everyday appearances
> I seemed about this time to gain clear sight
> Of a new world – a world, too, that was fit
> To be transmitted, and to other eyes
> Made visible; as ruled by those fixed laws
> Whence spiritual dignity originates,
> Which do both give it being and maintain
> A balance, an ennobling interchange
> Of action from without and from within;
> The excellence, pure function, and best power
> Both of the object seen, and eye that sees.
>
> *The Prelude* (1850), XIII, lines 367–78

EDWARD BOUVERIE PUSEY (1800–1882)

1. *manducatio indignorum*: the question whether the impenitent receive the Body and Blood of Christ in the Eucharist is bound up with belief in the Real Presence. If Christ is really and objectively present in the elements (and this is in no way dependent upon the receiver's state of mind) the sin of blasphemy can be committed by an impenitent partaker, whereas this additional sin cannot be committed in a purely commemorative service.
2. The twelve loaves placed 'before the Lord' every Sabbath by Jewish priests who were alone entitled to consume them at the end of the week. Pusey here refers to the occasion when the fugitive David requisitioned the shewbread to feed his starving followers, having first assured the priests that his band were ritually 'clean' (I Samuel 21:1–7). The sense in which this incident foresha-

dowed Christ's provision for His needy followers can be found in Matthew 12:1–4.

3. Pusey's references in the last paragraph are respectively to Genesis 14:8; Exodus 12:1–28; John 6:31–3; I Samuel 21:5; I Kings 19:5–8; Proverbs 9:5; Psalms 22:26; 23; 4:7; 104:15; Zechariah 9:17; Isaiah 55:1; Psalms 111:5; Song of Solomon 5:1.
4. Pusey quotes extensively from John 6:50–8 before proceeding to exposition.
5. This quotation and those in the remainder of the paragraph are drawn respectively from Ezekiel 28:12, 15; Hebrews 2:16; Colossians 1:16; Philippians 2:10; Hebrews 12:22–3.
6. In the published version Pusey meticulously footnoted each phrase culled from the Fathers.
7. In quoting the words of consecration Pusey drew respectively upon I Corinthians 11:24; Matthew 26:28; I Corinthians 11:25; and John 6.51.
8. In the remainder of this paragraph occur the phrases which attracted the most odium in Pusey's sermon. I have italicized the three phrases applying to St Chrysostom's teaching, which seemed to careful readers, rather than the initial hearers, possibly to imply the suffering of Christ anew in every Eucharist and therefore to diminish the once-and-for-all sacrifice made upon the Cross.
9. Pusey's notes explained this allusion: '"*Hearing* Mass" in the Roman Communion. This is, of course, said of the general declension of Communions; at early Masses, even on week-days, the writer is informed that there are Communicants, but not to what extent.'
10. Pusey regarded the Edward VI Prayerbook of 1549 as 'our genuine English Liturgy' (*Tract No. 81* (1837), p. 15) connecting the Anglican Church with the Primitive Church. The alterations in subsequent Prayer Books he attributed to the undue influence of exiled foreign Reformers.

Select Booklist

The intention is to offer a guide to further reading rather than to provide a comprehensive bibliography of either movement.

PRIMARY SOURCES

Full bibliographical details of the texts in the main body of the book can be found in the headnotes.

Close, F. *Occasional Sermons* (1844)
National Education (1852)
The Stage; Ancient and Modern; its tendencies on Morals and Religion (1877) (first delivered as a lecture in 1851)

Froude, R. H. *Remains* (2 vols., 1838)

Goode, W. *Altars prohibited by the Church of England* (1844)
Tract XC historically refuted (1845)
The Doctrine of the Church of England as to the effects of Baptism in the Case of Infants (1849)

Keble, J. *The Christian Year: Thoughts in verse for the Sundays and Holy Days throughout the year* (1827)
Sermons, Academic and Occasional (Oxford, 1847)
On Eucharistical Adoration (Oxford, 1857)
Occasional Papers and Reviews (Oxford, 1877)

Miall, E. *The Ethics of Nonconformity* (1848)
The Politics of Christianity (1863) (reprinted from the *Nonconformist* 1847–8)

Newman, J. H. (The works listed below are relevant to his life as an Anglican.)
The Prophetical Office of the Church (1837)
Lectures on the Doctrine of Justification (1838)
Parochial and Plain Sermons (8 vols., 1834–43)
Loss and Gain (1848)
Apologia pro Vita Sua (1864), ed. M. J. Svaglic (Oxford, 1967)
Letters and Correspondence of John Henry Newman during his life in the English Church, ed. A. Mozley (2 vols., 1898)
The Letters and Diaries of John Henry Newman, 1801–34, ed. I. Ker and T. Gornall (4 vols., Oxford, 1978–80)

Plain Sermons, by contributors to the *Tracts for the Times* (10 vols., 1839–48)

Pusey, E. B. *A Course of Sermons on Solemn Subjects preached in St. Saviour's Leeds* (1845)
Nine Sermons preached before the University of Oxford 1843–55 (Oxford, 1865)

Simeon, C., W. Carus, *Memoirs of the Life of Charles Simeon* (1847) (contains many excerpts from his writing)

Tracts for the Times, by Members of the University of Oxford (6 vols., 1834–41)

Williams, I. *The Cathedral, or the Catholic and Apostolic Church in England* (1838)
Devotional Commentaries on the Gospel Narrative (10 vols., 1839–48)
The Autobiography of Isaac Williams, ed. Sir G. Prevost (1892)

Select booklist

MODERN ANTHOLOGIES

O. Chadwick (ed.), *The Mind of the Oxford Movement* (1960) contains an excellent introduction and numerous short extracts. E. Fairweather (ed.), *The Oxford Movement* (New York, 1964), gives longer extracts and less measured editorial judgements.

D. M. Thompson (ed.), *Nonconformity in the Nineteenth Century* (1972), starts with a useful essay summarizing varieties of class and attitude embraced by the term 'Dissent'; taken together with J. H. Y. Briggs and I. Sellers (eds.), *Victorian Nonconformity* (1973) Nonconformist writing is well represented.

SECONDARY MATERIAL

Biographical Studies

Religious hagiography was a major literary activity in the first half of the nineteenth century and such biographies still provide one of the best sources of information for Evangelical beliefs and practices. Many twentieth-century biographies have been little more than limp précis of these fuller predecessors. Brief biographical sketches of leading Evangelicals may be found in J. Stephen, *Essays in Ecclesiastical Biography* (2 vols., 1849) and M. Hennell, *Sons of the Prophets: Evangelical Leaders of the Victorian Church* (1979). Various aspects of Simeon's career have been treated in C. Smyth, *Simeon and Church Order* (Cambridge, 1940) and A. Pollard and M. Hennell (eds.), *Charles Simeon: Essays written in commemoration of his Bi-Centenary* (1959), whilst H. E. Hopkins, *Charles Simeon of Cambridge* (1977) provides a readable compilation of nineteenth-century sources. An interpretation of Close's life may be found in G. Berwick, 'Close of Cheltenham: Parish Pope; a study in the Evangelical background to the Oxford Movement', *Theology*, 39 (1939), which is challenged in Hennell's *Sons of the Prophets*. Goode remains without a biography. A. Miall, *The Life of Edward Miall* (1884) is the fullest account of Miall, though he also merits a highly allusive chapter in C. Binfield, *So Down to Prayers: Studies in English Nonconformity 1780–1920* (1977).

Biographies of Newman abound. Most useful for an account of his religious thought is C. S. Dessain, *John Henry Newman* (1966). G. Battiscombe's *John Keble: A Study in Limitations* (1963) concentrates on the earlier Tractarian phase, though not as critically as the title might suggest. His writings receive more attention in W. J. A. M. Beek, *John Keble's Literary and Religious Contribution to the Oxford Movement* (Nijmegen, 1959), and B. Martin, *John Keble: Priest, Professor and Poet* (1976). Keble's work as a revered country parson is charmingly captured in C. M. Yonge, *Musings over the 'Christian Year' . . . together with a few Gleanings of Recollections of the Rev. J. Keble* (Oxford, 1871). Although Pusey himself remains hidden in H. P. Liddon's massive *Life of Edward Bouverie Pusey* (4 vols., 1893–7), this is an invaluable reference work; the third volume has an appendix listing the authors of each *Tract*. The central figure emerges no more clearly from O. W. Jones, *Isaac Williams and His Circle* (1971), but this does provide a useful account of Tractarianism outside Oxford.

Critical Works

Nineteenth-century essayists and historians supply some of the liveliest impressions. As a witty and concise survey of mid-century Anglicanism W. J. Conybeare, 'Church Parties', *Edinburgh Review*, 98 (1853), 273–342, remains unsurpassed. Works by two High Churchmen – W. E. Gladstone, 'The Evangelical Movement: Its Parentage, Progress and Issue', *Gleanings of Past Years 1875–8* (1879), vol. VII; and W. H. B. Proby, *Annals of the 'Low Church' Party in England down to the death of*

Archbishop Tait (2 vols., 1888) – read against the Evangelical E. Stock, *The History of the Church Missionary Society* (3 vols., and supplement, 1899–1916); supplemented by G. R. Balleine, *A history of the Evangelical Party in The Church of England* (new ed., 1951) still form the best guide to nineteenth-centry Evangelicalism. Personal knowledge of the leaders of the Oxford Movement informs the accounts by T. Arnold, 'The Oxford Malignants', *Edinburgh Review*, 63 (1836); R. W. Church, *The Oxford Movement: Twelve Years, 1833–1845* (1891); J. A. Froude, 'The Oxford Counter Reformation', *Short Studies on Great Subjects* (1893), vol. IV; T. Mozley, *Reminiscences chiefly of Oriel College and the Oxford Movement* (2 vols., 1882); and M. Pattison, *Memoirs* (1885).

For the eighteenth-century background L. Stephen, *History of English Thought in the Eighteenth Century* (2 vols., 1876) still provides a useful reference book, to be supplemented by N. Sykes, *Church and State in the Eighteenth Century* (Cambridge, 1934); and the lighter S. S. Carpenter, *Eighteenth Century Church and People* (1959). Basil Willey writes of Locke and Butler in *The Seventeenth Century Background* (1934); and *The Eighteenth Century Background* (1940); respectively. A concise guide to the by-ways of Dissent is provided by M. R. Watts, *The Dissenters from the Reformation to the French Revolution* (Oxford, 1978). An introduction to Anglican Evangelicalism may be found in L. E. Elliott-Binns, *The Early Evangelicals* (1953) and G. C. B. Davies, *The Early Cornish Evangelicals, 1735–60* (1951). The turn-of-the-century activities of the Clapham Sect are covered in E. M. Howse, *Saints in Politics* (1952) and a heavily documented book, weakened by its anti-Calvinist bias, F. K. Brown, *Fathers of the Victorians* (Cambridge, 1961).

O. Chadwick, *The Victorian Church* (1966) is the major standard work for the period covered by this book. Methodist history is covered by J. Kent, *The Age of Disunity* (1966); W. R. Ward, *Religion and Society in England, 1790–1850* (1972); and *A History of The Methodist Church II*, ed. R. Davies and G. Rupp (1978). R. T. Jones, *Congregationalism in England, 1662–1962* (1962) is the most comprehensive history of this denomination. H. H. Rowdon, *The Origins of the Brethren, 1825–1850* (1967), gives an interesting picture of Evangelical seceders. I. Bradley, *The Call to Seriousness* (New York, 1976) is a popular, but not lightweight account of Evangelical attitudes. The following four works study the relation of the Evangelical and Tractarian Movements, the first three with a bias of interest toward the latter : Y. Brilioth, *The Anglican Revival* (1925) and *Three Lectures on Evangelicalism and the Oxford Movement* (1934); D. Newsome, *The Parting of Friends* (1966); and P. Toon, *Evangelical Theology 1833–1856: A Response to Tractarianism* (1979).

The following are more specialized studies:

Coulson, J. and Allchin, A. M. (eds.), *The Rediscovery of Newman* (1967)

Davies, H. *Worship and Theology in England,* vols. III and IV (Princeton and London, 1961, 1962)

Hardelin, A. *The Tractarian Understanding of the Eucharist* (Uppsala, 1965) (an excellent account of the growth of Tractarian thought)

Heasman, K. *Evangelicals in Action: An Appraisal of their Social Work in the Victorian Era* (1962)

Machin, G. I. T. *Politics and the Churches in Great Britain 1832–1868* (Oxford, 1977)

McDonald, H. D. *Ideas of a Revelation: An Historical Study A.D. 1700–1860* (1959)

Norman, E. R. *Anti-Catholicism in Victorian England* (1968)

Church and Society in England 1770–1970 (Oxford, 1976)

Sandeen, E. R. *The roots of fundamentalism: British and American fundamentalism 1800–1930* (Chicago and London, 1970)

Vargish, T. *Newman: the Contemplation of Mind* (Oxford, 1970)

White, J. *The Cambridge Movement: the Ecclesiologists and the Gothic Revival* (Cambridge, 1962)

Discussion of the relation between these movements and the imaginative literature of the period can be found in the following books. The first three are useful mainly as works of reference:

Chapman, R. *Faith and Revolt: Studies in the literary influence of the Oxford Movement* (1970)

Maison, M. *Search Your Soul, Eustace: A survey of the religious novel in the Victorian Age* (1961)

Wolff, R. L. *Gains and Losses: Novels of Faith and Doubt in Victorian England* (New York, 1977)

Baker, J. E. *The Novel and the Oxford Movement* (Princeton, 1932)

Cunningham, V. *Everywhere Spoken Against: Dissent in the Victorian Novel* (Oxford, 1975)

Davie, D. *A gathered church, the literature of the English dissenting interest, 1700–1930* (1976)

De Laura, D. J. *Hebrew and Hellene in Victorian England: Newman, Arnold and Pater* (Austin, 1969)

Fairchild, H. N. *Religious Trends in English Poetry*, vols. II and IV (New York, 1942, 1957)

Holloway, J. *The Victorian Sage: Studies in Argument* (1962)

Jay, E. *The Religion of the Heart: Anglican Evangelicalism and the Nineteenth Century Novel* (Oxford, 1979)

Prickett, S. *Romanticism and Religion: The Tradition of Coleridge and Wordsworth in the Victorian Church* (Cambridge, 1976)

Tennyson, G. B. *Victorian Devotional Poetry: the Tractarian Mode* (Cambridge, Mass., 1981)

Willey, B. *Nineteenth Century Studies* (1949)

The Evangelical and Oxford Movements

CAMBRIDGE ENGLISH PROSE TEXTS

General editor: GRAHAM STOREY

OTHER BOOKS IN THE SERIES
Revolutionary Prose of the English Civil War,
edited by Howard Erskine-Hill & Graham Storey

FORTHCOMING
Science and Religion in the Nineteenth Century,
edited by Tess Cosslett
Romantic Critical Essays, edited by David Bromwich
Burke, Godwin, Paine and the Revolution Controversy,
edited by Marilyn Butler
American Colonial Prose: John Smith to Thomas Jefferson,
edited by Mary Radzinowicz

S. Matt. 26, 28

This is My Blood, of the New Testament, which is shed for many for the remission of sins.

This is the first page of the manuscript of Edward Pusey's *The Holy Eucharist, a Comfort to the Penitent* and is reproduced by permission of the governors of Pusey House